VINTAGE
WALKING WITH NANAK

Haroon Khalid has an academic background in anthropology. He got his undergraduate degree from Lahore University of Management Sciences (LUMS) in social sciences with a focus on anthropology and history, and his graduate degree in anthropology from the University of Toronto. He has been a freelance journalist since 2008 and has written over 350 articles for numerous publications, including *Al Jazeera*, *CBC*, *MacLean's*, Scroll.in, Wire.in, TRT World, *Himal*, *Dawn*, the *News* and *Express Tribune*. He has travelled extensively around Pakistan and has written about minority rights, folk traditions, the politicization of history and heritage, nationalism and identity, and several other topics.

Haroon is the author of four books—*A White Trail* (2013), *In Search of Shiva* (2015), *Walking with Nanak* (2016) and *Imagining Lahore* (2018). He has also written a non-fiction short book called *The Enigma of Pakistani Identity* (2017) and *Beyond the Other* (2016). In his work, Haroon explores fluid identities, traditions and religious practices that challenge the notion of exclusivist identities, which defines communities in South Asia today. His writings have been translated into many languages, including Punjabi, Urdu, Hindi, Bengali, Gujarati and Italian. He is based in Toronto, Canada.

WALKING
WITH
NANAK

HAROON KHALID

VINTAGE
An imprint of Penguin Random House

VINTAGE

USA | Canada | UK | Ireland | Australia
New Zealand | India | South Africa | China

Vintage is part of the Penguin Random House group of companies
whose addresses can be found at global.penguinrandomhouse.com

Published by Penguin Random House India Pvt. Ltd
4th Floor, Capital Tower 1, MG Road,
Gurugram 122 002, Haryana, India

Penguin
Random House
India

First published in hardback in Tranquebar Press by Westland Limited 2016
First published in paperback in Tranquebar Press by Westland Publications
Private Limited 2018
This edition published in Vintage by Penguin Random House India 2023

ISBN 9780143460787

Typeset in Adobe Caslon Pro by SÜRYA, New Delhi

www.penguin.co.in

To Iqbal Qaiser, my mentor

CONTENTS

Contents

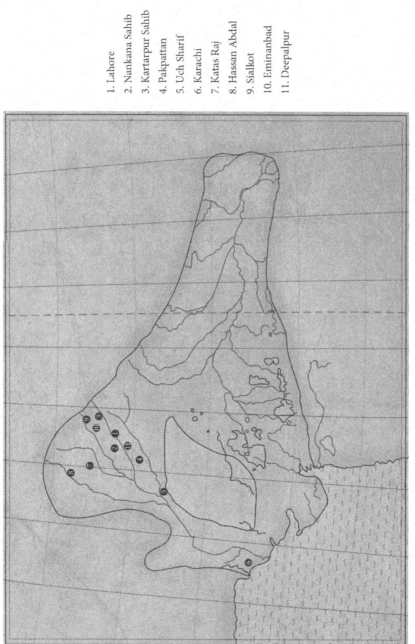

1. Lahore
2. Nankana Sahib
3. Kartarpur Sahib
4. Pakpattan
5. Uch Sharif
6. Karachi
7. Katas Raj
8. Hassan Abdal
9. Sialkot
10. Eminanbad
11. Deepalpur

Introduction

I had always been fascinated with Guru Nanak, before I had even read a single word written by him or about him. Guru Nanak was someone who was so near and yet so elusive. Having been born and brought up in Pakistani Punjab, I had heard of Guru Nanak—about him being the founder of Sikhism, about him being a poet and about him being a spiritual leader. Yet given the Muslim-dominant culture of Pakistani Punjab, there were no avenues available for me within the culture to explore his personality. He was on the one hand someone who was my own, being a Punjabi, and yet on the other hand, he was an alien, since he was a non-Muslim. When I did eventually read books about him I was disappointed. I was disappointed because even after reading several books I did not feel I had the slightest clue as to who Guru Nanak was as a person or what his life was like. This was particularly disheartening because he had lived only five centuries before the present day and there have been better records of people who had lived even before that time.

I truly discovered Guru Nanak for the first time through my mentor, Iqbal Qaiser. We spent several hours talking about him, his poetry, and this gave me a much better idea about Guru Nanak as a person, compared to any book that I had read. Iqbal Qaiser recited Nanak's *Babur Bani* to me, a long poem that Nanak wrote at the time the Mughal marauder Babur attacked Punjab, destroying the cities of Eminabad and Lahore on the way. The poem was riveting. It had a huge impact on me and I saw for the first time glimpses of the man I had been trying to discover. Here was a man who is considered a religious figure, the founder of Sikhism and a believer in God and then there was this poem of his which lays the blame of Babur's wrath at God's feet. Through his poem Nanak challenges the divinity of the Divine and asks if this bloodshed is the blessing that God had promised. This man might as well have been the prophet of those who questioned the existence of God. I realized that one way of getting to know Nanak better was through his poetry.

My fascination with Guru Nanak increased further when I learned on my travels with Iqbal Qaiser that he had spent a major portion of his life in present-day Pakistan. He was born here. He initially preached his new religion here by travelling around this region and eventually settled in a small village which is now on the Pakistani side of the border.

Wherever I went to see gurdwaras raised in the memory of Guru Nanak, I felt his presence around me. I could see him sitting with Bhai Mardana, his Muslim companion, oblivious to our presence and detached from the world around him. In my imagination, I began visualising Iqbal Qaiser and my journey as an extension of Guru Nanak and Bhai Mardana's journey. We too travelled like vagabonds, learning the ways of the different people we met on the way. We too engaged in philosophical and religious discussions and despite our intellectual differences, adored each other's company. It was through this understanding of our interactions, struggles and experiences that I was able to make sense of the experiences of Guru Nanak. For me then the second way of discovering Nanak was by walking with him. I wasn't interested in Nanak the saint but in Nanak the son, Nanak the father, Nanak the philosopher, Nanak the poet and Nanak the wanderer.

Discovering Nanak should have satisfied my curiosity; however, it only exacerbated the situation. I began seeing the contradictions between Nanak the man and Nanak the saint. Nanak vehemently spoke against organised religion and yet today, the religion that is attributed to him is one of the most prominent organised religions in the world. He abhorred the concept of associating miracles with religious personalities, but today, his biography is nothing but a story of his miracles. On his deathbed, he appointed not his son but his most loyal student as his spiritual successor. This was a clear indication that Nanak did not want his legacy to become a legacy based on kinship, but on intellectual and philosophical heritage. However, only a couple of successors down the line, the institution of

'Guruhood' became a family affair, with all the Gurus hailing from the same family and drawing their legitimacy from Guru Nanak, calling themselves reincarnations of the first Guru.

ੴ

The *Janamsakhis* are Sikh texts on Nanak's life, written by his devotees after his death. These are the primary sources we have on Nanak's life. These Janamsakhis, however, don't give us a clear picture of Nanak's life story. What they give us is a collection of Nanak's encounters with various people throughout his travels, recording the stories of his miracles. There are also different versions of Janamsakhis, which make it difficult to sift the truth about Nanak's life.

By drawing from his Janamsakhis, his poetry and my travels along Nanak's path, I have attempted to create a brief picture of Nanak's story, his beliefs, his strengths, his insecurities and his resilience. This part of the book is fictionalised. It was not possible to incorporate all the stories associated with Nanak into this book as I wanted to experience all the tales first-hand through travel to write about them and with my limited resources it was not possible to go everywhere Nanak had been on his travels. My research was limited to a few areas in Pakistan and therefore only a few tales from the Janamsakhis have been included in this book. My aim was not to dissect each and every tale associated with Nanak but rather to understand, holistically, the religious and philosophical ideas of Nanak.

Within this fictional part of the book that attempts to narrate Nanak's journey, I have attempted to interweave the story of my own travels. In the spaces that appeared to be empty as a result of these two worlds coming together, I have put in the stories of the miracles and magic that were attributed to Guru Nanak, to see Nanak through the eyes of his devotees.

The second section of the book looks at the history of Sikhism after the death of Guru Nanak. It traces the history of the institutionalisation of this religion through the stories of the Sikh Gurus and their devotees. In doing so, the book juxtaposes the philosophy of Guru Nanak and the politicisation of the religious philosophy of Sikhism as the institution of Guruhood rose in prominence and influence.

Towards the end of the book the various open threads of the book come together, similar to Nanak's concept of Oneness through Monism. The story of Nanak, the Gurus and us, converges at Kartarpur Sahib, where Guru Nanak lay on his deathbed, breathing life into a new religion.

HAROON KHALID

1
The Prophecy

Decades of poverty, vulnerability and rejection were tucked away neatly under the folds of the old man's skin. His hand trembled as he extended it. His shirt was slashed. It too had aged along with its wearer. He had folded his legs under his body, seated on this ancient staircase.

Of all the other beggars sitting on the way it was this old man who had captured the attention of Tripta. Maybe it was his age, in complete contrast to her youthful vigour. She felt as if his staring eyes sucked the youth out of her skin. She ran the back of her hand over her cheek to make sure it was still young. It was sweaty.

A breeze blew across the mound, taking away her perspiration and her anxiety. It was not the old man's stare that had mesmerised her, but her own vivid imagination and emotional state. As if waking up suddenly from a nightmare, she untied the tiny knot at the edge of her *dupatta* and placed two silver coins on the beggar's palm, who gripped it strongly, feeling the weight of the coins. After making sure they actually existed, he thanked her.

To her surprise, he looked sadder compared to before she had handed him the coins. It was as if the realisation of his poverty had just dawned upon him. A little offended by what she perceived to be the insolence of the beggar, she turned away from him and headed further up, to the summit of the mound. She never learned anything more about the beggar, not even the fact that he had once been a rich merchant from Lahore who had been reduced to penury after his son had betrayed him in business.

Chanting 'Hare Ram, Hare Krishna', a group of *jogis*[1] were descending while Tripta was struggling upwards. She had taken off her shoes at the base of the stairs to make her journey more difficult and hence more spiritually rewarding.

Even though it was still the month of *Chet* (March–April), the sun was particularly strong in the afternoons. Tiny blisters had developed under her feet after coming into contact with the burning surface of the black stone. Her pain increased with every single step. 'Hare Ram, Hare Krishna', she chanted and joined the chorus, trying to divert her thoughts away from the pain in her feet.

The leader of the jogis was a lean man with long grey locks running down to his waist. His beard too was thick and untamed. His torso was covered in a saffron cloth. In one hand he carried a short wooden stick which he used to support his hand during meditation, while in the other he carried a small golden flask. His followers' bodies were smeared with ash. They wore only saffron loin cloths.

The strong smell of burning cannabis reached Tripta before the jogis did. From the rear of the group, an ash smeared jogi placed a mud pipe on the lips of the leader. Tripta bowed reverentially as he passed by, a gesture that was acknowledged and the supplicant blessed in reciprocation. 'May all your wishes come true. Your spirit tells me that you are a true devotee of Vishnu; Vishnu who is the preserver of this world and beyond. Remember that the world is balanced by evil and good, pain and ecstasy, deprivation and bounty. Know that whatever has been taken from you was needed to maintain the divine equilibrium and whatever will be given to you will be by Him to fill a void. *Bolo* Hare Ram, Hare Krishna.'

Thoughts that Tripta had repressed for a long time began to resurface. Maybe she was not meant to be a mother. Her friends, married around

---

[1]Jogis are religious ascetics who travel in groups and rely upon the generosity of devotees for food. They hold unorthodox religious views and do not always observe the strict divisions between religious groups. Historically, their adherents have come from both Hindu and Muslim backgrounds.

the same time as her had been blessed with several children, but she was still childless. A fire burned within her that could only be quenched by the love of her own child. She longed to see tiny feet running around in the mud of the courtyard. She would often imagine what it would feel like to have a baby. In the winters she would knit woollen sweaters and caps for the baby. Walking towards the family well, she would imagine a little baby walking alongside, gripping the edge of her *kameez*. At night she would sing lullabies, while during the day, in front of her family, she would pretend that nothing was wrong.

She felt worse for her husband, Mehta Kalu, who she knew was distressed, even though he never said anything. Of late, the couple had grown distant and Tripta blamed her barrenness for it. A couple of times when she had suggested to her husband that he should marry another woman to bear him a child, he had ridiculed the suggestion. She was touched that the thought of another woman repulsed him, but the sight of her husband's sad eyes tore at her heart.

In these desperate times, she paid heed to all sorts of suggestions. She would present herself to any *sadhu* or *fakir* who would stop temporarily in the forest around Rai Bhoi di Talwindi. Every morning, at sunrise she would visit the Laxmi temple and present offerings of a coconut, sweetmeats and flowers to the *pandit*. When someone suggested to her that she should also offer a *chadar* (sheet) at the shrine of Ali Hajveri in Lahore, she did so. On another occasion, she accompanied her husband to Tilla Jogian, the most important pilgrimage site for jogis in the Punjab. There the couple paid for the jogis' food for one day, as a result of which the jogis prayed all night to bless this young couple. On the way back they stopped at Katas Raj, where both of them took a dip in the holy pond, considered to have been filled up by a tear drop of Lord Shiva.

When one of her neighbours, a Brahmin woman, suggested that the couple should visit an ancient Hindu temple located at the top of a mound three *kos* (about eleven kilometres) from their city, Mehta Kalu turned down the advice. He had been to too many temples and shrines to continue believing in miracles. In fact, he had accepted his fate and given up hope of having a child. In order to fill the void, he had started spending more time at work, maintaining meticulously the accounts of the ruler of Talwindi, Rai Bular Bhatti. Worried for Mehta Kalu's wife, Rai Bular had suggested to him several times that he should spend more time at home, keeping his wife company. Despite their friendship, Mehta Kalu could not explain to his employer that the sight of an empty and silent courtyard haunted him.

Tripta wanted to hold on to any sign of hope. For her this would be a pilgrimage, a holy act even if her wish was not granted. Social mores dictated that women should remain confined within the boundaries of their homes. However, religious pilgrimages provided them with the opportunity to explore a world otherwise closed to them. Despite being a woman, Tripta liked to travel, observe different religious practices, and see different cultures.

'Why won't you take the palanquin?' argued Mehta Kalu with his young wife. 'The sun, after the first quarter of the day is particularly harsh this year. You will be uncomfortable on the way.' This was the first argument between the couple in a long time. On any other day she would have complied immediately with what her husband suggested, even if it went against her wishes, but not today. Cocooned within this disagreement, however, was love. Her husband's protectiveness melted her heart. She wanted to tell him that she would do whatever he wanted if he would love her like this all his life, but she constructed a wall around her emotions.

'Whoever goes to a pilgrimage like a princess?' she countered. She was surprised at her audacity. If her mother ever heard her refusing her husband's wishes, she would have been disappointed in her daughter. But pain is an effective teacher. It can mature someone in a short period of time. Tripta also took advantage of the fact that Mehta Kalu was a genteel man who listened to and cared for the opinions of others, even if the other was of the gentler sex. 'Only if I go as a mendicant will the goddess be convinced of my devotion,' said Tripta, putting an end to the conversation.

Had this been a long journey Mehta would have ensured that guards travelled with his wife. The jungles of Punjab were infested with thugs and dacoits who attacked innocent travellers. But since this was a short journey, he allowed the expedition to go ahead without sentries.

Accompanying Tripta was a retinue of half a dozen attendants including male and female servants.

It was a short walk to the temple. From afar one could see a tall mound rising from the middle of the trees. A steep staircase led to the top, which was packed with ascending and descending pilgrims. At the top was a small temple constructed of thick black stone. All over the mound there were small rooms made of mud and stone for jogis and fakirs to mediate. At the base of the mound was a small city of tents. These belonged to traders who had been attracted by the lure of the pilgrims.

Walking through the streets of this makeshift settlement, rubbing shoulders with other pilgrims, Tripta stopped in front of a stall selling wooden carts and other toys for children. She picked up a small cart and inspected it closely. 'Do you want this for your son?' asked the vendor, a plump woman sitting on a wooden platform. Her son was sitting next to her and was busy counting the money they had made since morning. Tripta caught a glimpse of the child and said, 'Yes.'

'Stay here at the base and buy everyone else something to eat,' said Tripta to the head servant, Kanwal, a middle-aged man, handing him a few coins. Carrying a few rose petals and a wooden cart she prepared to climb this set of around one thousand steps.

At the top, the first thing that captured her attention was the panoramic view. A gentle wind blew across the plain. She looked in vain towards the direction of Talwindi trying to locate the silhouette of distant homes. Eagles overhead glided gently in the wind. Cut off from civilization, this was a magical place, truly spiritual.

Tripta, who was fond of losing herself in her imagination, used these moments to take a break from her daily chores. She was brought back to reality by the tolling of a bell. The female devotee ahead of her in line had returned following her *darshan* of the goddess and now it was her turn. She entered by ringing the bell thrice. The priest wearing a white *chola* (gown) with a saffron scarf around his neck was squatting on the floor, collecting the offerings presented to him by devotees. She handed him the rose petals. He took it and then presented one back to Tripta, saying, 'Eat this.' She wanted to ask him why but the priest's hurried manner intimidated her. In front of her was a rock, the object of veneration of this temple. It had a red paw at its centre. 'That's the feet of Kali *mata*,' said the priest in a tone that made it clear that he did not welcome questions. 'Here, take this *prasad* (offerings to and from divinity),' he said, placing some *halwa* (a sweet dish) on her palm and asked, 'Do you have a special prayer?'

'My husband and I have been deprived of the blessing of a child,' she said. 'I have been told that Mata pays particular attention to unfortunate women like me at this temple.'

'You have come to the right place. What is that you hold in your hand? Is that a cart? Present that to Mata and within a year there will be a child in your house,' said the priest as he took the cart and placed it next to the other offerings, which included fruit, coconuts, clothes and rose petals. 'Go out in the courtyard,' he continued. 'There is an acacia tree there. Take this thread and with it tie seven knots around it. Then recite *Kai Maha Kali, Jai Ma Kalika, Jai Maha Kali, Jai Ma Kalika, Kali Mate, Namo Nama, Kali Mate, Namo Nama*, a hundred times sitting under that tree without stopping. If at any point you are distracted or you stop, start from the beginning again.' Later in the night when the priest returned home to a village not far from the temple, he took the cart with him for his four-year-old son.

Despite the popularity of the temple, the courtyard outside did not contain many people. Most of the devotees left immediately after paying tribute to the goddess. Sitting inside a small nook amidst the rocks that were found in large numbers across the mound was an ascetic wearing nothing but a loin cloth. With his eyes shut and his entire body covered in dust, he sat in a yogic position. Tying the sacred thread around the tree, Tripta sat under it facing the trunk. She shut her eyes and started to recite the prescribed mantra.

'Do you have anything to eat?' she heard the high-pitched voice of a man say. She opened her eyes, still reciting the mantra to find a middle-aged mendicant, wearing a green chola with a skull cap on his head, as worn by Muslims, looking at her curiously, as if witnessing an interesting scene unfold.

He had a long black beard streaked with grey. She shook her head without stopping the recitation of the mantra, making sure that the instructions of the pandit were followed. 'You at least must have some money that could buy me food,' said the mendicant, looking at her and then the tree as if trying to figure out the conversation between the two. She nodded and still reciting, unfolded her dupatta to take out a silver coin and handed it over to the mendicant. He took it and without thanking her, put it in a pocket of his chola. The confident manner with which he took the money gave the impression that this was his hard-earned income.

'Why are you reciting this mantra?' He continued talking to her, despite her reluctance to engage in a conversation. She managed to finish the mantra a hundred times and in an exasperated tone told him about her problem.

'Your wish has been granted,' said the enigmatic fakir and then asked, 'Do you know the history of the temple?'

'How do you know that my wish has been granted?' she asked him, surprised at the casual manner of the mendicant.

'I have a special relationship with the goddess. We sort of have a deal. I do things for her and as a reward she gives me special knowledge. Tell me, do you know how this mound was created?' he asked.

'What sort of things do you do for her?' Tripta asked.

'Nothing much. You may think of me as her deputy. I reinforce people's faith in her and also sometimes make them unbelievers. So once Devi Mata was sitting here engaged in meditation when a *rakshasa* (demon) approached her...'

'I don't understand,' said Tripta, cutting in. 'How can you reinforce the faith of the believers as well as make them unbelievers?'

'It's easy, you see. Faith and the lack of it are different sides of the same coin. When you toss a coin up there are equal chances of it landing heads or tails. It is the same in the case of faith. For someone, a certain event might reinforce their faith, while for others it might push them out of the boundaries of belief. So I was telling you about the rakshasa. He, who was a bloodthirsty carnivorous animal, thought that the Devi was an ordinary devotee. Had he known she was a goddess he would never have attempted to distract her. He didn't like the fact that she was lost in worshipping Brahma. He wanted her to worship him instead.'

Once again Tripta cut him off and asked, 'But why would Devi Mata allow you to make unbelievers out of her believers?'

The fakir answered patiently. He was eager to narrate the story but also wanted to answer her questions. 'Well, you see the goddess doesn't care about rituals and recitation of mantras if they lack conviction and truth. Several of her "believers" are those who lack this characteristic. She would rather not have them as her devotees. So I was telling you about the rakshasa. He wanted to distract the goddess whom he had mistaken for an ordinary devotee. He would have never done so if he had known that she was a goddess. But what the rakshasa also did not understand was the power of a true believer; a true believer, a true *bhagat*, is stronger than a devi or rakshasa. With the power of their conviction they too become divine, defying all sorts of limitations. So when the rakshasa attempted to devour this lonely woman sitting under this very acacia tree praying to Brahma, she took her actual form and rose several kos in height, much higher than the rakshasa himself. She trampled him under her feet, leaving a mark on the rock with her feet. The sacred rock you saw inside the temple is her footprint.'

'But it is so small,' said Tripta.

'Yes, it has shrunk with age. This is a very old story. Many millennia ago. Slowly that rock will become so small that it will become invisible to the eye, and then one day it will disappear. When that happens, the world will cease to be and the Day of Judgement will come when God will separate the good ones from the evil ones. Those who have been kind to orphans and have looked out for their neighbours will be sent to heaven, where there will be streams of honey and milk and everlasting youth and beauty, while those who have eaten the flesh of other human beings will burn in the eternal fire of hell.'

Tripta listened with rapt attention.

'After destroying the rakshasa, the goddess started to dance. She danced so furiously that it triggered the process of destroying the world. With her whirling she sucked in everything—buildings, temples, mosques, humans, animals, trees, mountains, rivers. All these things piled up under her feet as she slowly rose towards heaven, her final abode. Since it was still not the prescribed time for the world to end, Lord

Brahma was left with no other option but to interfere. He sent down lightning from the sky, which hit the goddess and she fell. The world had been saved but a giant mound had been created, with thriving cities and villages buried beneath it and on top of it, placed like a crown was the rock with the mark of her feet. Then as a reward for her devotion to him, Brahma told her that the mound she had created would forever serve as a warning to humans of what would happen to them if they didn't follow the path of truth; while as a reminder of the ferociousness of gods and goddesses, the rock with the mark of her feet would become sacred. Pilgrims and devotees would come here till the end of the world and would be granted their wishes. The rock, which was gigantic at that time, would shrink with age, and the day it ceases to be, the world would also come to an end.'

'The end is not very far then,' said Tripta. 'The rock is already so small. How much longer do you think it will last?'

'I don't know.'

'Tell me something, fakir. How do you know that my wish will come true?'

'Because you are a true devotee with conviction. Had you stopped the recitation of the mantra to cast me away, the goddess would have been upset with you. Had you stopped the recitation to give me some money she would still not have been pleased. You continued the recitation while also responding to me, which is the perfect state of being—a delicate balance between spirituality and worldliness. A true believer walks this middle path. That is the message of my Prophet, peace be upon him (PBUH), and also of this temple. You have the traits of a true devotee and a true devotee never returns empty-handed from the house of God.'

A year after her trip to the shrine, Tripta prepared to undertake another journey. This time she agreed to be taken in a palanquin while a group of servants and guards travelled with her. Five months after her meeting with the fakir she had become pregnant. She believed that it was due to the intercession of the fakir that Kali Mata had bestowed her with this blessing. After her first visit to the shrine she visited it twice but never found the fakir again. When she asked the pandit about him, he snobbishly ignored the question and made offensive remarks about low-caste, meat-eating Muslims. However, the vendors around the temple were aware of the fakir, whom they called Naulakha Hazari. She was told that he was a Muslim fakir who visited the temple regularly. A few times when the pandit tried to send him away, he refused, saying that the entire world belonged to Allah and no one had any right to banish him from anywhere.

The fakir spoke kindly to the pilgrims and vendors and so over the years he had become a much-liked figure. Seeing his growing popularity the pandit decided against chasing him away, fearing that it might have a negative impact on his reputation as a man of religion. In reality though, he hated the Muslim fakir whom he considered an untouchable and wished that he would disappear forever.

Naulakha Hazari would often be sighted sitting inside one of the stone rooms, lost in mediation like other yogis and jogis. Sometimes, he would sit like a beggar on the temple stairs, counting on the generosity of pilgrims. But his favourite spot was the acacia tree on the summit of the mound, next to the temple. Here, he would sometimes spend days lost in his inner world without a care for food or water. Often, wandering goats would gather around, eating up the food that devotees would place next to him while he was in a meditative state. Tripta was told that he was particularly fond of goats and often served them food and water. 'Love animals even before you love your neighbours,' people had heard him say more than once. Sometimes the fakir would disappear for months. No one knew where he went or when he would be back. When he returned, he would tell no one about his journeys and spend most of his time in mediation.

Upon returning from the temple, Tripta had told her husband about the interaction with the fakir. Mehta Kalu could see that she was inspired by the discussion. There was a visible change in her. The worries which had accumulated on her visage over the past few years now vanished. Even though he did not pay much attention to the fakir's prediction, he was glad to see his wife in a positive frame of mind. He started coming back early from work to spend more time with her. This added to Tripta's happiness. She started regarding this too as a miracle wrought by the fakir. The fakir's prediction had bridged the distance between the young couple.

Mehta Kalu was a religious person but not as much as his wife. Being a *kshatriya* (warrior caste) Hindu he respected the rites and rituals of the Hindu religion. He respected mystics and often offered them food when they resided in the forest around Rai Bhoi di Talwindi but he preferred consulting conventional religious authorities like the pandits of temples for his religious and spiritual requirements. He found the unconventional lifestyles of mendicants hard to reconcile with his own beliefs. There were rumours that they engaged in unrestricted sex, consumed drugs and defied societal codes. Mehta Kalu was particularly bothered by their itinerant lifestyle. He worshipped work and looked down upon anyone he perceived to be shirking their duty of working for a living. He valued the mystics' philosophical depth and spiritual prowess but above all he valued the duty of a man to earn his living.

Tripta on the other hand was much more sympathetic towards mystics and fakirs. Religious rites and rituals were more of a social convention for her as opposed to evoking religious devotion. She found the discourse of the mystics more in tune with her spiritual leanings.

Five months into her pregnancy, Tripta was planning to travel to her maternal home, a village called Dera Chahal at a little distance from Lahore. Even though Mehta Kalu wanted her to stay at Rai Bhoi di Talwindi he knew this was a tradition and he did not want to take any risks around the birth of his first child by breaking societal codes. God knows what hell would break loose if he defied tradition.

So about six years after their wedding, the couple was blessed with a beautiful daughter. When it came to naming the child, it was suggested by Tripta's mother that since the child was born in her maternal house, *Nanaka* in Punjabi, she should be called Nanaki. Thus, Tripta's and Mehta Kalu's first child came to be called Nanaki.

ੴ

A gentle breeze blew against the plain, auguring a howling silence. The city was far from here, silent in the distance. Here on the mound, sitting under an acacia tree was an old man lost in his thoughts. On the other side of the mound there were construction cranes slowly digging into the ancient mound, not to unearth its archaeological secrets but to flatten the mound to make way for a new suburban locality.

'That is why the mound has diminished in size,' said Iqbal Qaiser. 'I came here a few years ago. The mound was spread over this entire region,' he said, indicating with his arm the network of roads that had been laid for this new township, called Rehman Gardenia Society.

We climbed the final portion of the mound; a set of staircases, the only one there, to get to the top of the mound, where the shrine was located. Here, a man who must have been in his late sixties, sat on a mat laid out on the floor, showing a group of pilgrims who stood before him, the sacred rocks. We waited for our turn.

He removed the green cloth covering the rocks and pointed out hurriedly with a stick—a niche within the rock, and told us that this is where Naulakha's pets, a lion and a lamb drank water. 'He was sitting alone on top of this mound,' he said. 'When he felt thirsty, he prayed to Allah and miraculously, water appeared in this bowl.' Ten rupee notes were placed within it. Next to it he pointed to other marks on the rocks which he claimed were the footprints of the lamb and the lion. Then without letting us dwell on the sight any longer, he covered the rock with the green cloth and pointed towards another set of rocks placed next to them, which he claimed read 'Allah' and 'Muhammad'. There was a tear shaped mark on one rock which he said was the lamp of the saint and next to it was the forest that existed there, sketched in the shape of coniferous trees on a small rock which was around two feet by two feet in size.

'Give your offerings to the rock,' he told me and I was forced to place a ten rupee note on the rock. He then picked up a rose petal and placed it in my mouth. 'Eat it,' he said. He then smeared oil on his finger from a lamp nearby and put it on my hair. My ritualistic offering at the shrine was complete. There was another pilgrim waiting behind me.

Next to the shrine was a small room made of rocks. 'There were structures like these all over the mound,' Iqbal Qaiser told me. It was a small room where only one person could sit. 'They must have been for ascetics who wanted to meditate.'

In the book called *The First Sikh Spiritual Master* by Harish Dhillon it is stated that Mata Triptaji, the mother of Guru Nanak, did not have a child for a long time after her marriage and she would regularly visit an ancient Hindu temple situated on top of a mound not very far from Rai Bhoi di Talwindi to pray for a child. The name of Rai Bhoi di Talwindi has been changed to Nankana Sahib in honour of the first Sikh Guru who was born there. This mound, the only one in this area, is next to a city called Shahkot, which is only a few kilometres from the holy city of Nankana Sahib.

'Could that temple on top of a mound be *the* mound next to the shrine of Baba Naulakha Hazari?' I asked Iqbal Qaiser as we walked down. Prior to our visit to the mound, we had visited the main shrine where the saint is said to have been buried. Here the officials of the Auqaf (Wakf in India) Department, a government organisation responsible for managing the affairs of this Muslim shrine, had handed us a booklet describing the history of this Muslim saint. In that booklet, the period of existence of the saint is recorded to be a few years before the birth of Guru Nanak and it was also stated that Guru Nanak was born after Baba Naulakha Hazari prayed for his mother.

'This is not authentic history though,' warned the officer-in-charge, an old man, surrounded by a group of younger officials, none of whom had any work. 'All the information we have about this saint is through folk stories.'

In our modern understanding of history, we give little importance to oral versions of history, which are not authenticated by the written word. We have inherited this academic attitude from the British, who are a product of the written word. Historically, in South Asia, oral transmission of history has been much more important than the written version. We have been recording versions of history in our folk tales, legends, myths, songs, names and other such sources, which an academic historian who tends to favour the written word might reject as apocryphal. Records of ancient mounds can be found in folk tales long before they are discovered by professional archaeologists. For example, at the shrine of Shahjamal in Lahore it is said that the saint buried an entire city under his foot in wrath long before it was discovered that the location of his shrine could be the site of a mound with archaeological importance. Similarly, in

Taxila much before the British discovered the ancient Gandhara cities: there were local myths and stories about a mound of dead kings.

The folk story of Baba Naulakha might not give us an accurate account of the events in this case, but that is not what I am searching for in this tale. It is enough for me to know that there is a reference to Guru Nanak in the life of this saint. The fact that a Sikh author, Harish Dhillon, claims that Mata Triptaji used to visit a Hindu temple on the mound outside of Talwindi also reinforces my perception that Mata probably visited this mound where there must have been a temple and where now lie the sacred rocks of the saint.

On our way back from Shahkot, Iqbal Qaiser and I discussed if this could have been a Hindu temple prior to becoming a Muslim shrine. We concluded that this must have been a shrine dedicated to the Hindu goddess, Durga. This is because in the folk story of Baba Naulakha Hazari it was stated that he used to ride a lion, like Durga does in Hindu iconography. We assumed the footprint we saw on top of the mound must have been shown to Hindu devotees as the footprint of the goddess herself or that of her lion.

Given that the shrine was located on top of an archaeological mound it was perhaps then an ancient temple. It must have been a sacred space not only for Hindus but also for Muslims of the neighbouring regions. Most of these Muslims were Hindu converts anyway, and for a lot of them this temple must have remained important even after their conversion. In my travels around Pakistan I have seen this phenomenon more than once. A Hindu shrine at Ram Thamman at Kasur remained sacred for Muslims even after Partition. The shrine of Hardo Sahari in Kasur district also has a similar story. In Bhera, I visited a Hindu temple where Muslims still lit lamps believing that now a Muslim saint occupied that temple. In Lahore, I found that Muslims and Christians, whose ancestors were once Hindus, continue to visit a Hindu temple their ancestors visited. Perhaps the most popular example is that of the shrine of Sehwan Sharif, one of the most important Muslim shrines in Sindh, which was once a Hindu temple dedicated to Lord Shiva.

Similarly, it is likely that the shrine of Naulakha Hazari could have been a Hindu temple once, which must have been sacred to Muslims as well. After Partition as the religious divide between these two groups became sharper, the temple was converted into a Muslim shrine to adjust to the changing religious landscape of the country.

In this context, it is safe to assume that Baba Naulakha Hazari must have been one of the many Muslim ascetics who regularly visited this temple. He must have been a Malamati Sufi, who refuse to follow any religious order and do not distinguish between different religious traditions. After his death he must have been buried at a little distance from the temple and over the years a shrine must have come up around it. After Partition, the Hindu temple vanished and this shrine became the sole source of the religious identity of the mound.

ੴ

The white dome of the gurdwara was visible from afar. A potholed road led to the village. Around us were newly built houses of former agriculturists, who had sold their lands to developers and earned millions. Their wealth was displayed ostentatiously in their gaudily done-up houses.

'There was a lot of pressure on the Government of Pakistan from Sikhs living in Canada, England and America to renovate this gurdwara after my book came out,' said Iqbal Qaiser. We were driving on the edge of the village on a road that led straight to Gurdwara Janamasthan Bebe Nanaki at the village of Dera Chahal. 'It was in a horrible state when Meraj Khalid ordered its renovation. Even then, only its external structure was spruced up. The gurdwara remained shut to the Sikh community. Only recently has the government allowed pilgrims to visit this gurdwara when they come to Pakistan for festivals. Now on those occasions, prayers are offered here. This has become a gurdwara once again.'

Malik Meraj Khalid was born in 1916 to a poor agricultural family of this village. He worked hard to continue his education. He later joined the Pakistan People's Party and continued to serve it till his death. He served twice as the National Speaker, once as the Chief Minister of Punjab and once between November 1996 and February 1997 as the interim Prime Minister of Pakistan. One of his first orders as the Prime Minister was the approval of funds to renovate this historical gurdwara at his village. Being a son of the soil, he understood the importance of this shrine, which is so embedded in the history of his village, even though he was not Sikh.

I parked the car under the shade of a *peepal* tree and climbed the stairs to the gate. A saffron flag rose from behind the wall testifying that there were members of the Sikh community living here. Behind the tree was a pool of water where buffaloes wallowed. It was once the sacred pool of this shrine. Next to it was a mosque which was being expanded.

Gurdwara Bebe Nanaki is named after Guru Nanak's elder sister. According to tradition, she was born in a house that was situated where the gurdwara now stands. Guru Nanak's mother Mata Tripta belonged to this historical village of Dera Chahal, located on the Bedian road; now flanked between DHA Phase Five, Six and Seven. Mata Tripta came here from Talwindi before the birth of her first child as was the tradition at the time. According to tradition, Nanak was named after his sister Nanaki.

Since this was Nanak's maternal home he often came here. Later, his followers built a gurdwara here to mark the spot. When Maharaja Ranjit Singh became the sovereign of Punjab at the end of the eighteenth century he spent large amounts of money on the renovation and expansion of many gurdwaras, including this one. In addition, he attached vast tracts of land to these gurdwaras, so that the revenues from the lands could facilitate their functioning. This was also believed to be a kind of religious service, made mandatory by Guru Nanak himself. As long as the Sikh community was present here, the affairs of the gurdwaras and the property associated with them were managed by their administrative bodies. After 1947, these buildings were abandoned and like orphans, their properties were snatched away from them. Many gurdwaras were taken over by refugees from the other side of the border and slowly, their historicity eroded.

When the Evacuee Trust Property Board (ETPB) was created along with the Auqaf Department in the 1960s, it brought under its control various neglected gurdwaras. However, in most cases official apathy and a religious bias against these buildings resulted in further deterioration. Newly appointed officials looked the other way as the land mafia took over their properties, amounting to thousands of acres all across the country.

Something similar happened in the case of this historical gurdwara. About a year prior to our visit to this shrine I read in the newspaper that Ghulab Singh, a Pakistani Sikh who happens to be the first Sikh police officer in the revamped traffic police of Lahore, filed a case against ETPB in the Lahore High Court for the alleged sale of agricultural land associated with Gurdwara Janamasthan Bebe Nanaki. Ghulab Singh claimed that the ETPB was illegally selling land connected to this historical gurdwara. Just a few days before my visit, the Supreme Court of Pakistan took cognisance of the case and after going through the evidence asked the construction companies to pay Rupees 986 million as surety while the hearings proceeded.

I wanted to talk to Ghulab Singh about the case. However, there seemed to be no way of getting in touch with him. I got his mobile number from mutual friends at Nankana Sahib, but that number remained switched off for days. In desperation I decided to visit the gurdwara where Ghulab Singh stays when he is in Lahore. We were now standing at the threshold of the gurdwara hoping that he was inside.

We were led inside by a young priest named Daleep Singh. I could see Ghulab's official bike parked in the courtyard accompanying the gurdwara. 'That used to be the *langar* hall (where free food is prepared and served to those in need),' said Iqbal Qaiser. Now it is a lawn with a few rooms around it.

'I am not sure if Ghulab will agree to an interview,' Daleep warned me, as we sat down in his room. 'It is not because of the case per se. It's something personal. I'll try talking to him and might be able to convince him to do the interview. If he agrees, he can show you documents that prove the corruption of the ETPB. Asif Hashmi (former head of the ETPB) has earned billions in his tenure of five years,' he added. In April 2016 Asif Hashmi was arrested in Dubai for his alleged corruption as the chairman of the board.

'What about the Pakistan Sikh Gurdwara Prabandhak Committee (PSGPC)?' I asked him.

The PSGPC is another government institution, which was formed in 1999 to look after the Sikh gurdwaras of Pakistan. Prior to its creation the Shiromani Gurdwara Parbandakh Committee (SGPC) based in Amritsar used to collect offerings from these gurdwaras in Pakistan and take them back to India. The PSGPC was created with the intention of keeping within the country the revenue created from the gurdwaras in Pakistan. Several people whom I interviewed at Nankana Sahib felt that PSGPC was not representative of the Sikh community in Pakistan. They felt that they were cronies of the government, who are also involved in corruption themselves. 'All of them are in on the deal,' said Daleep. 'They required signatures of the members. For that they were provided kickbacks. But you know now the case has gotten really interesting. Ghulab Singh has presented the Gurdwara Act of 1925 along with his papers. According to this act only those Sikhs who have been Sikhs for three generations can take part in the organization of the gurdwaras. This means that all the members of the committee would be removed,' he said with a wink. The Gurdwara Act of 1925 was a British legislation that firstly legally defined the Sikh identity, identifying it with the Khalsa of Guru Gobind Singh, and also brought the control of the gurdwaras under a Sikh body, which was before that controlled by members of the Udasi. The Udasi sect is believed to have been founded by the eldest son of Guru Nanak, Sri Chand. Ignored by his father when it was time to appoint the next Guru, Sri Chand founded his own religious sect. Throughout his lifetime he had an uneasy relationship with the rest of the Sikh Gurus. It is alleged that some members of the PSGPC are not Sikhs but Muslims pretending to be Sikhs at the behest of the government so that they can be manipulated easily.

The windows of his room were open and a soft breeze blew in keeping the temperature low. From the mosque the *moulvi* started a sermon, which blared out of the loudspeakers. Behind the once-sacred pool now occupied by buffaloes is the agricultural land in dispute in the courts. From the window I could see a new block of apartments built recently to cater to the growing demands of urban Lahore.

The intensity of the sermon increased with time and soon it was impossible to conduct a conversation. 'Let's go into the gurdwara,' suggested Daleep.

Walking into the shrine, Daleep bows in front of the Guru Granth Sahib placed in a wooden Thara Sahib, while I stand next to him, unsure of myself. Iqbal Qaiser also doesn't bow given his Muslim background. We sit next to the Thara Sahib and the discussion resumes.

Daleep is a well-read young man in his early thirties and is particularly interested in the history of religion. Inside the shrine, we do not talk about the controversy of the alleged property sold but about the origin and development of Sikhism.

'I believe that Nanak was influenced immensely by Islam,' I said. 'You should keep in mind that his time was the later fifteenth century and the Islamic culture of the time was not that of today. It was at its zenith. Just as an intellectual of today cannot ignore Western humanism and liberalism, a scholar from that era could not keep his eyes closed to the Islamic intellectual environment.'

'I agree,' said Daleep. 'I would say that seventy-five per cent of Nanak's teachings are similar to Islam. But I would not use the word influence. This is the eternal truth that is acquired intuitively through the guidance of the Divine. Let me tell you something interesting. I don't leave the gurdwara much but people come and visit me here. There is a Muslim shrine not far from here called Peepali Pir. The guardians of that shrine came to meet me and told me that their shrine was also as old as this gurdwara. According to their elders, Guru Nanak used to come to this village often and would also visit their shrine while he was here. I am not denying their claim but we have no evidence to verify their statement. I asked them if they have any relic or object that was given to them by Nanak but they said no. Had there been any such object I could have confirmed whether it belonged to Guru Nanak by looking at it. As it stands, their claim cannot be justified.'

'It does sound likely though,' I added. 'That was how Nanak operated. Whenever he would visit an area he would visit its religious shrines, Muslim, Hindu and of any other denomination and would engage in religious discussions there. You are a religious historian and I understand your need to verify claims. However, I am more interested in folklore. For me it is important that a Muslim shrine here in Pakistan claims that Nanak used to visit their shrine and as I see it, this is a matter of pride for them. This has its own significance, irrespective of historical veracity, given that Partition occurred on the basis of religion and Pakistan was created.'

Iqbal Qaiser was conspicuously quiet. Turning towards him I asked, 'So is this gurdwara built on the exact spot where Nanak's maternal family home used to be?'

'Yes,' he said.

I looked around the place trying to imagine what the house would have looked like. The gurdwara was one big hall with a small balcony opening towards the centre of the hall from the first floor.

'I am also interested in the history of parallel Guru movements along with the conventional ones. I am interested in understanding the dialectic between religion and politics,' I said to Daleep.

'There is no politics. There was only religion. I wouldn't call them parallel Guru movements,' he said.

'Sects?'

'No. They were not sects either. I would call them anti-Guru movements. There were several of them. Maybe Iqbal Qaiser would be able to tell you more about them.'

'The first one was started by Sri Chand with his Udasi sect. He was the son of Guru Nanak,' said Iqbal Qaiser.

'So he never accepted the Gurudom of Guru Angad Dev?' I asked.

'No,' said Daleep.

'Then there was one that was started by Prithi Chand, the brother of Guru Arjan,' continued Iqbal Qaiser.

'I remember that one,' I said. 'We visited his *samadhi* (tomb) a few years ago. The shrine he built was also next to it. It's not far from here, next to the village Heir.'

'Really?' asked Daleep. 'It cannot be here. Since he wanted to rival the authority of the Golden Temple, he would have constructed his shrine on the route from Lahore to Amritsar.'

'Exactly,' said Iqbal Qaiser. 'The Bedian road is the old route to Amritsar. There is also a *baradari* (building or pavilion of twelve doors) constructed by Shahjahan in that village. This was constructed to commemorate the time when the Emperor was passing through and stopped at the village for a little while. It has been converted into a *madrassa* (a Muslim educational institution). Prithi Chand's in-laws were from Heir which is why he came and started living here after he rebelled against his father and brother for the Gurudom.'

'Did the building have a pool?' asked Daleep.

'Yes,' I said. 'But now it has been filled.'

He asked me a few more questions about the architecture of the structure but I could not answer the technical questions. 'I'll email you some of the pictures of the samadhi,' I promised him.

'Do you know that one of the movements also started from this particular gurdwara?' said Iqbal Qaiser.

'Really?' asked Daleep.

'Yes. It so happened that Guru Arjan asked one of his followers to go to Lahore to bind the Adi Granth. The Kashmiri binders who used to reside in Lahore were known for their meticulous binding. Bhai Bannu was the name of the devotee who was assigned this job. We even visited his gurdwara at Mandi Mangat.'

A few months previously, while driving from Bhera towards Gujrat, we had stopped at Mandi Mangat to explore the abandoned gurdwara built by Bhai Bannu. It was a beautiful structure with elaborate frescoes on its walls. It was taken over by an influential landlord from the city and he was using it as his *dera* (a place where men meet and socialise).

'Bhai Bannu came and stayed at this gurdwara during his trip to Lahore. While he was here he prepared another copy of the Adi Granth without the Guru's permission. The Granth which was not sanctioned by the Guru had some additional verses which the Guru rejected eventually. That Granth was kept at the Gurdwara of Mandi Mangat till Partition, after which it was taken to India.'

'Is there still a group of followers who continue to recite that Granth instead?' I asked.

'Yes,' said Daleep. 'But it's such a small number that it is negligible. This is true for all the other anti-Guru movements. They remained confined to a small group of followers.'

The conversation had prolonged our stay at the gurdwara much longer than we had anticipated. My primary purpose was to talk to Ghulab

Singh and get details about the case, but my conversation with Daleep had also provided me with a lot of information. Daleep assured us that he would try to get Ghulab to agree to the interview but remained sceptical.

We had to head down the Bedian road to visit two other shrines associated with Guru Nanak. This was the month of June and as the heat during the day was unbearable, we had left at six in the morning. Our target was to finish the tour before midday and head back home for lunch. We had spent about two hours here and were now behind schedule. Abruptly ending our conversation, I reminded Iqbal Qaiser about our itinerary and off we went to our next destination.

2
Walking with the Guru

I first met Iqbal Qaiser six years ago. He had come to my university in Lahore to give a lecture on Sikh architecture. A few days before his lecture, posters were put up around the university that the author of *Historical Shrines of Pakistan* would be speaking. I read his book later and was immensely impressed by his work. Iqbal Qaiser was doing what I wanted to do, travelling to historical places and witnessing the unfolding of history with his imagination.

The book itself is divided according to the gurdwaras of the ten Sikh Gurus, beginning with Guru Nanak and ending with Guru Gobind Singh. All of these gurdwaras were constructed to commemorate the visit or some other important event from the life of one of the ten Gurus. There are 174 gurdwaras recorded in the book out of which the majority are associated with Guru Nanak. In the book, each gurdwara and its history has been sketched, along with a photograph that Iqbal Qaiser himself took. To research the book he laboured for five years, travelling the length and breadth of Pakistan, from Gilgit to Karachi, from Lahore to Peshawar, on public transport. While travelling, he often did not even know if the gurdwara he was going to would still be extant or not. At the time, Iqbal Qaiser was a schoolteacher and so most of his travels took place during the three-month summer vacations, under the scorching sun.

Now when I look back, it seems like a rather odd coincidence that

I was reading a book on Guru Nanak when I met Iqbal Qaiser. After my graduation, I started to meet Iqbal Qaiser regularly, insisting that he show me places of historical importance around the country. Most of the places we visited were either Hindu or Sikh shrines because these were the places that were in the most vulnerable states. Iqbal Qaiser insisted that I write about these places and thus began my career as a writer. It has turned out that our short meeting at university has changed the course of my life.

Over the years I have become increasingly fond of my mentor. While his formal education was only till High School, he has read extensively and now guides doctorate students. It would not be an exaggeration to say that I have learned more from Iqbal Qaiser in the past few years, travelling across the country, than I did as a formal student. Our journeys are marked by intense conversations about the history of Punjab and particularly the Sikh religion for which I have developed a special fascination. During our journeys we discussed Nanak and his poetry, the subsequent Gurus, Mughal and Sikh conflicts and Maharaja Ranjit Singh.

It was through Iqbal Qaiser that I was able to understand the Sufi concept of *murshad* and *mureed*, teacher and student. It is believed in the Sufi tradition that one needs to have a teacher to get education. This concept of teacher cannot be understood through our contemporary education system, which is about one teacher and many students. In the Sufi scheme of things, it is a one-to-one relationship like the relationship between Rumi and Shams Tabriz or Bulleh Shah and Shah Inayat. Even in Nanak's poetry there is frequent reference to the need to have a teacher. Iqbal Qaiser has more than once said to both my family and his that I am his spiritual son and hence more real to him than his own son. For me, Iqbal Qaiser personified more than one relationship. He was a father-figure whom I would call up whenever life threw something unexpected at me. He was my best friend with whom I could share anything under the sun. He was my travel companion, my teacher, my muse and my mentor. Bulleh Shah used the word 'love' to describe his emotion towards his teacher. Rumi does the same. I believe that in those societies where the categorisations of the industrial world had still not

taken root, only that one word could encapsulate all these relationships
with Iqbal Qaiser that I have described above.

Having made the effort to drive to the edge of Lahore to visit the
Gurdwara Dera Chahal on the Bedian road, Iqbal Qaiser insisted that
we visit two more gurdwaras associated with Guru Nanak. On one of
his visits to his maternal home Nanak had visited the two places where
we were headed.

'Do you know that the name Bedian road comes from the village of
Bedian, which is not far from here?' asked Iqbal Qaiser, as we headed
further down the road. To our left was a hollow structure built of thin
bricks, standing on a vacant lot behind which was a government school.
On the right was an open sewer dissecting the village of Heir.

This abandoned structure was once meant to rival the religious and
political significance of the Golden Temple in Amritsar. It was built by
the elder brother of the fifth Sikh Guru, Guru Arjan, after his father,
Guru Ram Das, appointed his younger son as the next Guru as opposed
to him. He formed his own sect, referred to as an 'anti-Guru movement'
by Daleep. He was succeeded by his son Meherban, who built a huge
shrine on the outskirts of Chunian. Meherban also wrote a version of
the Janamsakhi of Guru Nanak that describes events from his life and
is one of the primary sources for Guru Nanak's life story.

It is interesting to note that this particular sect also drew its legitimacy
from the first Sikh Guru, Guru Nanak, claiming to be his true followers.
Sikh scholars point out various discrepancies in the Janamsakhis
attributed to Meherban. For example Meherban claims that Guru Nanak
was born in Dera Chahal and not Rai Bhoi di Talwindi which later
became Nankana Sahib. It further states that the young Guru spent his
early childhood there. Other writers of Janamsakhis and Sikh scholars
though are unanimous that Nanak was born in Rai Bhoi di Talwindi
where there are several gurdwaras marking events from his childhood.

'Bedian village was occupied by the descendants of Guru Nanak
before Partition. They were called Bedi, hence Bedian. They were referred

to as Bedi because in ancient times they used to recite the Vedas, from which they earned the title of Vedis or Bedis,' continued Iqbal Qaiser. 'Baba Nanak had two sons, Sri Chand and Sri Lachman. Sri Chand became an ascetic and never married but Sri Lachman did and had children. Baba Nanak's lineage is therefore preserved through his younger son. During the tenure of Maharaja Ranjit Singh, there was a man called Baba Sahib Singh Bedi who was respected widely because of his piety and religious lifestyle. Ranjit Singh allotted him vast tracts of land around the cities of Gujranwala and Lahore. It was on this land that Sahib Singh Bedi founded the village of Bedian near the city of Lahore. Here he also founded a religious centre that would preach the teachings of Guru Nanak. He chose this spot because he wanted to counter the propaganda being spread by the sect founded by Prithi Chand at Heir, which as you can see is not far from Bedian. When the British took over Punjab they allowed the Bedi community settled here to retain their land. At the time of Partition all of them migrated to India to be replaced by Mewatis and Arains from Amritsar. There is also a large Christian settlement next to this village. Before Partition, these Christians were *Mazhabi* Sikhs. Do you know who Mazhabi Sikhs are? When untouchable Hindus converted to Sikhism they were referred to as Mazhabi Sikhs just like you have *Musali* and *Deendar* in the Muslim community.'

'But I thought there is no concept of caste in Sikhism?'

'Caste system also doesn't appear in Islam but you know it exists. The Syeds because of their direct lineage from the Prophet of Islam hold a special place in the caste hierarchy and the Musalis and Deendars continue to be treated as untouchable Hindus despite their conversion. This is a cultural thing and not religious. Something similar happened in Sikhism, where the Bedis because of their lineage from Guru Nanak came to be considered as special people while untouchables retained their social stigma in the form of Mazhabi Sikhs.'

'Guru Nanak would have objected to this classification of castes,' I said.

'Yes. But whenever a religion travels further away from its source in terms of time, it also travels away from the essence of the teachings of the source. This phenomenon can be observed in all religious traditions.

Buddha was an iconoclast, while today you have giant golden statues of Buddha in Buddhist temples. Anyway, let me complete the story of this village. So at the time of Partition when the Bedi Sikhs were migrating to India they asked their servants who were Mazhabi Sikhs to stay back and look after their property since they believed that these riots and the division was a temporary phenomenon and sooner or later they would return to their ancestral villages. When the riots spread to this region and these Mazhabi Sikhs felt that their life was threatened because of their religious identification through a beard, *kirpan* and turban, they removed their turbans and cut their hair. They then converted to Christianity which was a neutral religion at the time of Partition. The Christians living at Bedian now are the descendants of those Mazhabi Sikhs who served the Bedis.'

'There must have been important Sikh shrines at the Bedian village?' I asked Iqbal Qaiser.

'Yes there were. I have seen the land revenue reports of that region and learned that there were two gurdwaras inside the village while there were a few samadhis of prominent Bedis outside the village.'

We had now reached the canal that sprouted from Bambawali-Ravi-Bedian (BRB) and fed the area around the village of Bedian and other regions in Kasur. The road took a T-shape here. To our right was the historical village of Bedian and the road to the left would have taken us to Jhaman, a border village where there is a gurdwara built in memory of Guru Nanak's visit to the village. On a field next to the turn, a few women were sowing rice seeds in the marshy fields. Bending as they moved around slowly, they were making sure that the seeds spread over a wide area. They would remain in that position the entire day.

'Should I take a right then? I would like to visit Bedian,' I suggested.

The summer sun which had been tamed by the early arrival of the monsoons was once again emancipating itself from its fetters. It was about nine in the morning. It was still pleasant because of a gentle breeze, but the temperature had risen considerably since morning and we could anticipate that in a few hours it would get much worse.

'There is nothing to see at Bedian. The gurdwaras were allotted to the refugees who have destroyed the original structures and made new homes for themselves, while the samadhis have also been razed. Let's go to Jhaman instead.'

The single lane overshadowed by eucalyptus trees was beautiful. Occasionally motorcyclists and rickshaws passed us. There were agricultural fields flanking the road, which had been watered and left alone for the time being. White cranes hopped in them, searching for insects. The musical call of the cuckoo bird wafted through the air. Shrubs and oddly shaped trees stood comfortably around the fields. These are a few examples of the indigenous trees of this area which are now being replaced by imported ones in the developed areas of Lahore. Indigenous birds which only rest on particular trees have also had to migrate outside the city after their natural habitats were replaced. Here, civilization in the form of 'development' has not arrived and therefore one finds trees that would have inhabited this region for centuries and still hear the sounds that must have greeted pilgrims travelling through these regions.

Small potholes marked the road. Soon they became larger, forcing the car to slow down considerably. The signals on our phones also started to fluctuate before completely disappearing. Small mounds that run all along the border appeared in front of us. Within them were plastered bunkers with numbers painted at the entrance. These were signs of the approaching border.

'Why aren't these border roads ever renovated?' I asked Iqbal Qaiser.

'The army doesn't let the government do it,' he replied. 'This entire region is under their control. Till sometime ago they would not even allow farmers to till the lands which were too close to the border. That has changed now and agricultural activities can now be found all the way up to the zero line. However, they still don't allow much development to take place here, especially the construction of roads, because they feel that paved roads will facilitate the movement of enemy vehicles. What they don't understand is that better roads would also mean that they can move quickly as well.'

We took a right turn on this road and started driving on a road running parallel to the embankment with bunkers. These embankments were constructed during the 1965 war between India and Pakistan to ward off a tank attack from the Indian side. A small canal was also dug under them which once contained water with an electric current running through it. There are three such embankments at the border.

'The art of warfare has progressed much,' I said to Iqbal Qaiser. 'I don't believe you need embankments or water with electricity to protect your borders anymore.'

'Wars are now fought from rooms by pressing buttons,' added Iqbal Qaiser.

Driving into the village of Jhaman which is situated on a small mound, I asked one of the locals about the way to the gurdwara. 'You mean Gurdwara Sahib,' he asked me. 'Keep on following this road until it leads you out of the village. You will see the Gurdwara Sahib in front of you.'

I was pleasantly surprised by his reference to the gurdwara as the Gurdwara Sahib. 'Sahib' in the South Asian tradition is a suffix that is used after a name to suggest respect. A majority of the historical gurdwaras have been bestowed names which end in 'Sahib'. For a Muslim from Pakistan to use this word of honour for an abandoned gurdwara was new to me.

Jhaman, located about twenty kilometres from the DHA Phase V, dates back to ancient times. According to the Archaeological Survey of Pakistan, there are three ruins here which date back to the sixth and seventh century CE. The village that stands today was first established in the thirteenth century by a man who had arrived here from the region of Malwa, located in Madhya Pradesh, according to the land revenue records collected by the British in the middle of the nineteenth century. The records further state that for some inexplicable reason, this village was abandoned and then repopulated around the middle of the seventeenth century. During the raids of the Afghan marauder Ahmad Shah Abdali in the eighteenth century, this village was subject to his wrath.

According to Sikh tradition, Guru Nanak visited this place thrice in his lifetime. Instead of staying in the village Nanak, along with his companion, Mardana, chose to stay outside the village on an abandoned mound.

Since there were shards of pottery and other archaeological artefacts found in large numbers here, the name of the gurdwara that was built here later, to commemorate the visit of the Guru, became Gurdwara Rori Sahib. 'Rori' in Punjabi is used to refer to pieces of a broken utensil or small rocks. Later, when these pieces of pottery were inspected by the British it was learned that this mound was actually an ancient archaeological mound. It was never excavated, as a splendid gurdwara had been built on the spot. It is believed that Nanak, along with his companion Mardana, rested here under a tree. Nanak made a *rubab* for his friend out of the branches of this tree. (The rubab is a traditional stringed instrument which was fairly popular around the time of Nanak. This instrument has acquired a particular significance in the Sikh tradition because of its association with Mardana, Nanak's companion.)

As we drove into the village, I saw several remnants of historical *havelis* (palatial houses). The structures had been wiped out but their walls were still intact. 'You should also write about this village in connection with Bhagat Singh,' said Iqbal Qaiser. In 1931, when the young revolutionary Bhagat Singh, along with his comrades, Rajguru and Sukhdev, were hung at Lahore jail, there was widespread unrest. In order to avoid protests, the British Government banned demonstrations in large cities, as a result of which villages became the focus of attention. The Naujawan Bharat Sabha, the political organization of Bhagat Singh, had an office in this village. It held a meeting here after the assassination and a demonstration was organised, which at that time was reported to be the largest protest rally held in India against the assassination.

The gurdwara presented itself to us as soon as we left the village. It was a sad sight. A square structure built with small bricks, on top of which was a white dome; it was a picture of neglect. Parts of the protective wall had crumbled, while several bricks from the structure had been robbed. Next to it was a bunker. Behind the gurdwara was the last embankment on the Pakistan side, beyond which lay India.

'Have I told you the story about what happened to me the last time I came here?' asked Iqbal Qaiser. Without waiting for me to reply, he continued, 'This was in 1993. The Pakistan Rangers (who are responsible for monitoring the India-Pakistan border) had set up a base inside this building. To cover this place they had surrounded the place with trees. I wanted to photograph the gurdwara for my book so I went up to them and asked for permission. The officer on duty told me that he could not allow that and that he would have to ask his superior. The superior was not at the post so I was asked to wait for him. He returned after a couple of hours, while I waited here. He did allow me to take one photo eventually but only if I promised to follow his guidelines. He told me that I could only shoot from one particular angle which didn't show much of the building. He also told me that the flag of Pakistan which was hoisted on top of the gurdwara could not be shown.'

The photograph for which Iqbal Qaiser had to wait for several hours has been immortalised in his book. One can only partially see the gurdwara behind the trees.

This was not my first visit to this particular gurdwara either. I had come here earlier, in November 2008, a few days after the Mumbai attacks by Pakistani terrorists, as a result of which both countries were on the brink of war. While I was exploring this area, Indian jets were flying overhead, clearly violating Pakistani airspace. This issue was taken up by Pakistani media and there were discussions about shooting down the Indian planes. Before that could happen, the Indian Air Force put an end to their foray into Pakistani territory and a war was avoided.

During the wars of '65 and '71, this village was attacked by Indian forces. It was worse in '71 as at that time the Indians had managed to even occupy it. Before they took over, the locals fled and the Indians were left with an abandoned village. Several houses were destroyed but as was expected, no damage was wrought to this gurdwara.

I parked the car at a little distance from the building and we climbed the small mound on top of which the shrine was located. A few buffaloes were grazing in the land around the gurdwara. The property of the gurdwara is now under possession of ETPB (Evacuee Trust Property Board) and controlled by no one. The herdsmen, young boys from the villages, were exploring the dome of the gurdwara. There were a few buffaloes wallowing in the cool water of a large pond behind the gurdwara. This was once the sacred pool attached to the shrine. Stairs descended into it from behind the building; it was now a pool of stagnant water, suitable only for animals.

There were huge holes in the ground inside the gurdwara at the place where the Thara Sahib was kept and also around it. In the craziness that followed Partition, several Hindu temples and Sikh gurdwaras were desecrated in this manner in the search for buried treasure. At the entrance, graffiti in black read, *Subhan Allah, Ibadat sirf Allah ki karein* and *Allahu Akbar*. Its neat calligraphic style proved that this could not have been done by villagers but by professionals. Perhaps when the gurdwara served as the office of the Pakistan Rangers, some passionate young personnel had this done. This doesn't come as a surprise as since the Islamisation of Pakistan under General Zia-ul-Haq in the eighties, training and courses in the Army have increasingly started using religious symbols and discourses. This has created a breed of officers who are much more ardent Muslims than their predecessors.

We took the stairs to the top floor. Here, the herdsmen had grouped around trying to decipher the Gurmukhi writing on the dome. The writing was accompanied by pictures. The faces on these frescoes had been wiped out while the bodies of the figures had been left unharmed. This too was perhaps done during the time when the shrine served as a base for the Rangers. I asked Iqbal Qaiser to translate the text for me while the group of young boys gathered around us, eager to learn more about the writing on the wall.

The writing made it clear that these were pictures of the Sikh Gurus. Beginning from Guru Nanak it went all the way to the sons of the tenth Sikh Guru, Guru Gobind Singh. Nanak's message of *Tauhid* or monotheism was noted next to his picture, though the face had been wiped out. The figure was of a Nanak sitting on the ground in a blue cloak, accompanied by the Muslim rubab player Bhai Mardana and Bhai Bala. I wondered if the culprits who had defaced this structure knew about Nanak's insistence on monotheism.

Similar to teachings in Islam, Nanak felt a kind of disgust towards polytheism and insisted that there was only One God, who is the Ultimate Truth. However, this message of Nanak was lost on the Muslims who had wiped out his face. For them this gurdwara was not a symbol of Nanak or his teachings but of Sikhism, of the same Sikhs who had killed thousands of innocent Muslims at the time of Partition.

Following Nanak's picture, there were names of Guru Harkrishan, Guru Ram Das, Guru Arjan Dev, Guru Gobind Singh in battle and then Guru Gobind Singh along with his sons, Jujhar Singh and Fateh Singh. 'Where exactly is the border?' I asked one of the young herdsman. 'Do you see that pole?' he said. 'That is in Pakistani territory. And that pole behind it, the longer one, is in Indian territory.'

It wasn't even a kilometre from where we were. Had Nanak rested a few kilometres further ahead, today his shrine would have been a thriving place. Devotees in colourful turbans and women with their hair covered in dupattas would have been sitting here right now, reciting the Granth. In the langar hall several more would have been eating. There would have been an entire market town around this shrine, selling religious paraphernalia. Various guesthouses and hotels would have been offering cheap accommodation to pilgrims coming from regions far away. This world existed only in my imagination. The truth was that Nanak, unaware of the historical consequences of his action, rested on what eventually became the wrong side of the border, and today this shrine is in shambles.

As we descended the stairs and headed towards our car, I saw three young men wearing pyjamas and T-shirts walking towards us. AK-47s were slung across their shoulders. 'These are personnel of the Pakistan Rangers. Their duty is to walk all across the border region throughout the day,' whispered Iqbal Qaiser.

I expected them to come to us and ask us for the reasons for venturing this close to the border but they didn't. They turned towards the gurdwara instead and entered it. Did the Rangers still have some control over the gurdwara?

ੴ

From Jhaman, we set off towards another small border village called Ghavindi, about ten kilometres from Jhaman. Near a small enclosure on the embankment that would have allowed us to get closer to the most dangerous border in the world, I stopped next to a herdsman, as Iqbal Qaiser peeped out of the window. 'Son, outside the village of Ghavindi there is a small lone structure from the Hindu era. Do you know where it is?'

'I wouldn't,' he spoke in stilted Urdu, with a Pashtu accent not common in areas around Lahore. I then noticed his eyes, which were hazel in colour, another feature associated with the inhabitants of Khyber Pakhtunkhwa. His brown kameez and a white *dhoti* with polka dots on it were neatly ironed. He had tied a cloth around his forehead. There was a small herd of buffaloes next to him which he was supposed to be looking out for.

'We are from the army,' he added. I further noticed a group of tall and broad-shouldered Rangers lazing around on a single *charpoy* behind him. What was he doing dressed as a herdsman?

'Members of the intelligence agencies usually live undercover in these border villages to monitor the activities of the locals and others visiting,' said Iqbal Qaiser.

Even though they attempt to camouflage themselves, pretending to be a shop vendor or a buffalo herder, they are usually easily identifiable. The locals always know who they are and keep their distance from them.

Was he noting down the number of my car? Would he later inform his superiors about two strange men, one young and one old, roving around this area, searching for an abandoned Hindu building at the border? I tried deciphering his activities from the rear-view mirror but there was too much dust behind us to make sense of the scene.

Up ahead, we stopped an old man riding a bike to ask for directions. He guided us well and then asked us about our whereabouts. His friendly demeanour and local Punjabi accent reassured us and we shared our information candidly with him. 'Why don't you come and have food with me?' he asked. 'At least come for tea,' he persisted, but we turned down the offer.

This is traditional rural hospitality, a phenomenon that has disappeared from the cities. I tried imagining what the situation would have been like five hundred years ago, when Nanak stayed on the outskirts of this village. Nanak, unlike other ascetics, was strongly against the idea of begging for food, and instead preached that if someone chose to extend their hospitality out of their own free will, only then was it permissible to take food from them. Otherwise, it was preferable to remain hungry. Nanak too was a product of this Punjabi rural environment in which the concept of hospitality is deeply ingrained. Such a philosophy and an assurance that one would not go without food for long must have developed out of this environment, which was displayed by the old man offering us food.

Similar to what he had done at Jhaman, Nanak preferred to stay on the outskirts of the village of Ghavindi. This is a recurrent theme in Nanak's travels. Wherever he went, he chose to stay aloof from civilization, yet he was always close enough, that he did not completely abandon it. This is also in tune with his philosophy that preached moderation in religious endeavours and worldly affairs. He believed that a human being should follow a middle course. This philosophy, like Nanak's monotheism, is similar to Islamic beliefs. Muhammad (PBUH) taught that one should not spend one's life in the wilderness as the Eastern Christians of that time did, but to live a truly religious life, one should engage with the world, yet take care not to get too drawn into materialism. Such similarities between Nanak's ideas and the teachings of Islam led me to believe that he was aware of this concept in Islamic thought and must have given it enough consideration to incorporate it into his religious philosophy.

While we were passing through the village of Ghavindi, little naked children started running in our path. Vendors attending to customers stopped as they stared at us. For the short time that we were there it was as if the entire life of the village had come to a halt and all attention was fixed on us. 'If our brief passage through this village in such a day and age has the potential to attract so much attention, what do you think the situation would have been at the time of Nanak?' I asked Iqbal Qaiser, and then without waiting for him to reply, said, 'Nanak and Mardana must have attracted a lot of attention. Word would have spread like fire that two fakirs have settled outside the village.'

The carpeted road soon turned to one made of bricks. We were heading towards a grove of *lahura* (desert teak) trees, hidden in the middle of which, away from our gaze, facing India, perhaps in longing, was the building commemorating the spot Nanak and Mardana had sat in.

On the same trip that he visited Dera Chahal and Jhaman, he came here and then left for Sultanpur, which is now on the Indian side of the border. It is widely believed that it was in Sultanpur that the religious life of Nanak began, which inspired him to travel in all four directions, along with his Muslim companion, Mardana, from Rai Bhoi di Talwindi. Nanak first travelled east, going all the way to Bengal. He then travelled south, going to the island of Sri Lanka. Back in Talwindi, he then headed north, which included the regions of Kashmir, Nepal and Tibet. Upon his return he decided to go west to Mecca and returned to settle at Kartarpur. Nanak covered most of this distance on foot and this took him about twenty-four years.

It was after the return from his trips to the East and South that Nanak decided to visit his sister, Nanaki, at Sultanpur, for which he travelled from Nankana, stopping at Dera Chahal, Jaman and Ghavindi.

The brick road was replaced by a road filled with sharp stones that threatened my car tyres. This was a clear indication that we were close to the border. I parked the car and Iqbal Qaiser and I completed the rest of the journey on foot.

The gurdwara was a lone white structure with a dome on top. Inside were two plinths meant to represent the seats of Guru Nanak and Bhai Mardana. Nanak's was higher than Mardana's. Placed on top of them were packets of salt and on the floor there were straws of sweep.

'Do you know what this means?' Iqbal Qaiser asked me. 'It means that the locals still come here. They bring salt for a special prayer whereas straw from a sweep is used to get rid of black magic.' The neighbouring village of Ghavindi was once dominated by Hindus and Sikhs. The demographics have changed after Partition. Who then was still praying at this shrine?

When we visited this shrine in 2008 after our visit to Jhaman, Iqbal Qaiser and I spotted a well next to this building. This time, we searched for the well but it was nowhere to be found. 'In just five years it has disappeared,' said Iqbal Qaiser.

'How long do you think this building will last?' I asked.

'By the looks of it, not very long.'

Facing the building was a bunker for the Rangers, while next to it was a small mound that had within it the remains of the other buildings constructed around this shrine.

We drove back to the village of Ghavindi from where we were to head to Lahore. Iqbal Qaiser made me stop in front of a wall made of thin bricks while the rest of the structure was made with thicker ones. A green board next to it pointed out that this building belonged to the government's Department of Union Council.

'This was the gurdwara built in memory of Nanak,' said Iqbal Qaiser, pointing towards the building. 'Nanak and Mardana stayed at the spot we just visited but a gurdwara was also built within the village. Nothing but this wall remains of it now,' he said. I drove past the blue metal gate of the building and sneaked a look inside. The structure had been divided into several houses. There were newly plastered walls and recently renovated rooms. All traces of the gurdwara had been erased.

As we moved away from the border region, our mobile phone signals reappeared and Iqbal Qaiser's phone started to ring incessantly. Later, I asked him about the story of Nanak's visit to Ghavindi. Putting his phone down, he began narrating the story.

ੴ

Walking from Jhaman, Nanak decided to rest for a little while, next to a small settlement of gypsies. He was on his way to Sultanpur where he wanted to visit his sister, brother-in-law and his friend Nawab Daulat Khan Lodhi. He came and sat under the shade of a grove of lahura trees. Nanak was a naturalist. He regarded the beauty of the world to be a manifestation of the Divine. For example, he says:

> *The sky the salver, the sun and moon the lamps,*
> *The stars studding the heavens are the pearls*
> *The fragrance of sandal is the incense*
> *Fanned by the winds all for Thee*
> *The great forests are the flowers.*
> *What a beautiful aarti is being performed*
> *For you, O Destroyer of fear.*[2]

---

[2]Taken from: Harish Dhillon, *The First Sikh Spiritual Master: Timeless Wisdom from the Life and Teachings of Guru Nanak* (Woodstock, VT: SkyLight Paths Pub., 2006), page 89

Do you understand what Nanak is trying to say here? Nanak is criticising the act of performing of aartis within Hindu temples. He is trying to say that God doesn't reside just in temples, mosques or shrines, but in nature. Nanak is saying that when God resides everywhere why should we, as devotees, limit our aarti to temples? The entire world is our temple and everything in nature is performing the act of aarti. But all this talk is a distraction from our story. I was telling you about Nanak's visit to this forest on the outskirts of the village of Ghavindi.

Nanak and Mardana stopped here for a little while. While Nanak meditated, Mardana said that he was hungry. Nanak told him there was a small village nearby, where a child has been born to a particular family and the family was celebrating its birth.

'Go there and get some food for yourself,' he instructed Mardana. One thing that I find fascinating in the Janamsakhis is that Nanak is stripped of all his human characteristics. He is depicted as a saint who never gets hungry, feels tired, cold, hot, etc. Bhai Mardana on the other hand is prey to these human weaknesses and throughout their journeys he is the one who feels homesick, tired, hungry, etc. I also feel that in the Janamsakhis Nanak and Mardana are probably used as symbols for religious and worldly life, where Nanak depicts the former and Mardana the latter. Nanak is above all worldly needs, whereas Mardana is engaged with the world and that often gets him into trouble. Anyway, where was I? Yes. So Mardana went to the village to get some food for himself. More importantly, Nanak instructed Mardana not to beg for food and that he should partake of it only if offered by the family without having asked.

So Mardana reached the village where the festivities for the first born son were in full flow. He stood next to the mendicants and beggars who were also waiting for the celebrating family to offer them some food. But so lost was the family in its jubilation that it forgot to give them food. Mardana was under orders not to ask so he returned empty-handed and complained about the situation to Nanak. In the meantime, the child whose birth they were celebrating died by an act of God. Soon the celebration turned into mourning. It was then that the family realised why the curse of God had fallen upon them. To make up for their mistake they approached Guru Nanak and asked for his forgiveness. There is a poem in the Guru Granth Sahib that records what Nanak said to the villagers on that occasion.

ੴ

In the first watch of the night, O my merchant friend,
You were cast into the womb, by the Lord's Command.
Upside-down, within the womb, you performed penance, O my merchant
friend,
And you prayed to your Lord and Master.
You uttered prayers to your Lord and Master,
While upside-down, and you meditated on Him with deep love and
affection.
You came into this Dark Age of Kali Yuga naked,
And you shall depart again naked. As God's Pen has written on your
forehead,
So it shall be with your soul.
Says Nanak, in the first watch of the night, by the Hukam of the Lord's
Command,
You enter into the womb.

In the second watch of the night, O my merchant friend,
You have forgotten to meditate.
From hand to hand, you are passed around, O my merchant friend,
Like Krishna in the house of Yashoda.
From hand to hand, you are passed around, and your mother says,
This is my son.
O my thoughtless and foolish mind, think:
In the end, nothing shall be yours.
You do not know the One who created the creation.
Gather spiritual wisdom within your mind.
Says Nanak, in the second watch of the night, you have forgotten to
meditate.

In the third watch of the night, O my merchant friend,
Your consciousness is focused on wealth and youth.
You have not remembered the Name of the Lord, O my merchant friend,
Although it would release you from bondage.
You do not remember the Name of the Lord, and you become confused by
Maya.

*Revelling in your riches and intoxicated with youth, you waste your life
uselessly.*
You have not traded in righteousness and Dharma;
You have not made good deeds your friends.
*Says Nanak, in the third watch of the night, your mind is attached to
wealth and youth.*

In the fourth watch of the night, O my merchant friend,
The Grim Reaper comes to the field.
*When the Messenger of Death seizes and dispatches you, O my merchant
friend,*
No one knows the mystery of where you have gone.
So think of the Lord!
No one knows this secret,
Of when the Messenger of Death will seize you and take you away.
All your weeping and wailing then is false. In an instant,
You become a stranger.
You obtain exactly what you have longed for.
Says Nanak, in the fourth watch of the night, O mortal,
The Grim Reaper has harvested your field.[3]

ੴ

Leaving the forlorn parents and other family members of the deceased
child, Nanak and Mardana moved towards their next destination,
Sultanpur Lodhi, where both of them had spent several years. The city
is a hundred-odd kilometres from this gurdwara, a journey of a couple
of hours by car. Today, heavily weaponized armies guard the border on
both sides, making sure that a journey that Nanak and Mardana took at
that time is no longer possible. Sultanpur Lodhi is now in India.

---

[3]Guru Nanak, English translation by Dr Sant Singh Khalsa MD, Guru Granth
Sahib, www.srigranth.org, pages 74–78, http://www.srigranth.org/servlet/gurbani.
gurbani?Action=Page&Param=74&g=&h=0&r=1&t=1&p=0&k=0&fb=0

3
An Encounter with Divinity

The call of the *muezzin* pierced the sky. Almost on cue, the colour of the sky changed from a harmless blue into a burning pink. The last streaks of the sun petered out and the sky turned a barren black. Emerging from his thoughts, Nanak observed the birds coming back to their nests ready to feed the young ones who had been waiting the entire day. Sitting under this *waan* tree, whose canopy-like protection covered him from the cruel sky, he too longed for his family. A labyrinth of branches surrounded him. On some of them he noticed pieces of cloths tied as supplication. His home was about two furlongs from here (about half a kilometre), yet he sat in the company of these holy branches, as an unwelcome guest, wondering how to return home to the embrace of his mother and sister.

From another section of the town the sound of a bell tolling could be heard distinctly. Nanak picked up the beat of a bass drum accompanying it. In a Hindu temple it was time for the evening prayers which would include the singing of *bhajan*s.

How come mosques and temples, Hindus and Muslims, have such differences when they both engage in worship in a similar manner, at the same time, whose testimony is also furnished by nature, Nanak wondered to himself. Why do Muslims complain about Hindus singing bhajans at the time of their *azaan* when they too insist upon making their call for prayers when nature is in the act of worship? Is it not all the same? The entire world, all its experiences, converging towards a focal point. Divinity.

Is the chirping of the birds also not a call of prayer? Is the humming of a song not an act of worship? Is working in the burning hot fields in summer to supply children with food not a supreme act of devotion? Why then does divinity need to be divided and distributed as *tabarak* (blessings) and prasad only from temples and mosques? Why can't divinity be found in the smile of an infant or the fear of a calf separated from its mother? Is divinity not present in the multifarious colours of the world—the starving sadhu, the overfed Brahmin, the lecherous *mulla*, the innocent giggle? Is this also not an act of divinity, the way two different sounds of different origins merge to become one with the Supreme One?

Years later, Nanak composed a poem which gave words to the emotions he had experienced sitting under this tree:

> *All the sounds we hear are but a part of the mighty roar of Thy torrent,*
> *All the sights we see are but a part of Thy vast creation,*
> *Thou art the taste*
> *Thou art the fragrance*
> *O mother of mine! no other hath these qualities.*
> *My Master is One*
> *He is One, brother, the only One.*[4]

Tears streamed down his cheek. This was followed by a feeling of happiness rising from within Nanak's soul. He too was part of divinity. His body, the soul, the tired legs and the weary eyes, all connected to the cosmos; every movement of his, part of a divine plan, in which every element of nature was incorporated. He noticed how the crying of the birds became his voice in the form of a single tear shed. He knew that far away his mother felt his pain. He had not shed tears in vain. He rose to go home, to face the consequences of his actions.

'If this is what is ordained for me then I should not try to avoid it,' he thought to himself. He rose to his feet and felt an unusual weakness in his knees. His head touched the canopy of the overarching tree. As soon as he got up, he sat down again, feeling the weakness in his feet. He almost fell to the ground as he lost control over his legs.

---

[4]Khushwant Singh, trans. *Hymns of the Gurus* (New Delhi: Viking, 2003), page 99

His mind wandered off to the encounter earlier in the day with the naked ascetics in the jungle of Chuhrkhana. The lessons imparted by their old teacher resonated in his mind. He thought about the concept of purity of the body.

'The human body is a piece of art, whose creator is the Sole Creator. Look at your fingers and the protruding veins at the back of your hand. Have you noticed how your stomach churns when someone tickles your feet or how there is a strange sensation in your chest when you dip a finger in your navel? The human body is the ultimate machine and is in a state of perfection. You compose verses, don't you, young boy? How would you feel if I were to alter your words? How would a painter feel if someone smears more colours on a completed picture? The human body also works in the same manner. God doesn't want us to make changes in His art. Our bodies are beautiful as they are. We don't need to wear fancy clothes or jewellery, or cut our hair, or remove our lice to become beautiful. Our purity lies in our "imperfection". We were born naked and naked we will be when we are cremated. Why then do we in our journey through life corrupt our bodies with needless ornamentation?'

The concept of the purity of the human body had touched a chord within Nanak. He could not summon any arguments to counter the leader of the ascetics. He had decided a few years earlier that he would incorporate any point of view into his philosophy if he could not counter it with an argument. On the other hand he was willing to shed any established tradition or belief system if he could not find within himself a rational reason for it. This is why, when his father and the local priest of Rai Bhoi di Talwindi suggested that he take up the sacred thread (*janeu*) to purify his body and differentiate his caste from lower ones, he refused to do so. Later, he would compose a poem which explained his reasons for defying this ancient holy tradition.

From the cotton of compassion,
Spin the thread of contentment,
Give knots of continence and twists of Truth;
This is the sacred thread of the soul—
If thou hast one such, O Brahma, then put it on me.

It will not snap, nor soil; nor will it be burnt or lost
Blessed is the man, O Nanak,
Who wears such a thread around his neck.[5]

His defiance of this sacred ritual which had been upheld by Brahmins and Kshatriyas for centuries caused a furore in the traditional society of this small town. Respectable Hindus started to avoid the Bedi family, causing much grief to Nanak's father. Nanak held himself responsible and slipped further into melancholy.

How easy it would be to abandon everything; his family, social status, social obligations, and become an ascetic, Nanak wondered. It was an appealing idea given his state of mind. But then the face of his mother and sister formed in his head and he began challenging the idea. Wouldn't it be much more spiritually difficult and hence rewarding if one strove to tread the path of piety while engaging with the world?

This was not the first time that these thoughts had come to his mind. He had been grappling with the idea since his childhood. Often when he would visit the mound outside of Talwindi he would ask Hindu yogis and Sufi dervishes this question but he had yet to receive a satisfactory answer. He was pulled towards the reasoning of his mentor Sayyed Hassan, a Muslim Sufi, who lived near his house. He was told that it was unacceptable to repudiate social life in search of religiosity. Sayyed Hassan would often condemn the Sufi mendicants who would roam around wearing tattered clothes, living on the generosity of people.

'Islam teaches one to adopt the middle path,' he would argue. 'The Quran says that one should not seek Allah in abandoned caves and jungles but one should instead live as a member of society so that a believer is able to inspire others around him.' At a young age, Nanak was exposed to the philosophy of his Muslim mentor and hence the idea of naked ascetics abandoning the world for a life in the jungle disgusted him. Repulsed as he was, he was nonetheless impressed by some of their ideas. Besides the concept of the purity of the body he also appreciated that unlike other ascetics these naked yogis did not beg for food.

---

[5]Dhillon, *The First Sikh Spiritual Master*, page 32

The chirping of the birds died down and night subdued the activities in the town. Across the city lay Nanak's home where his mother, Mata Tripta, sat in front of her pantheon of Hindu deities, praying for her son's safe return. Her husband, Mehta Kalu, was pacing up and down the courtyard with his hands held behind his back. Nanak had left home in the morning after his father had given him the hefty amount of twenty rupees to visit the market town of Chuharkhana about twelve kos (forty-five kilometres) from here and purchase something worthwhile to trade. The eighteen-year-old Nanak should have returned by now. Nanak's sister, Bebe Nanaki, brought her anxious father a glass of hot milk mixed with almonds. She knew better than her mother that underneath the anger her father was actually worried about the safety of his son.

'This boy cannot do anything right,' grumbled Mehta Kalu as he took the bronze tumbler from his daughter and sipped the milk.

'He will be alright, *Bapuji*. He is a very sensible person,' Bebe Nanaki defended her brother.

'What sensible? Is it sensible to not return home after the sun has gone down? You know well enough how dangerous these jungles are. I am sure that he is once again in the company of those no good ascetics discussing useless things. What does he find in them? Look at all the other boys of his age. Nawarang was born around the same time as Nanak. He has now completely taken over his father's cloth business. Rajat on the other hand, has started maintaining the accounts for his family's vast agricultural lands. Bebe Nanaki, you know we don't have vast agricultural lands or a thriving business. I am an accountant. It's not a hereditary occupation. What will happen after I die?'

'Don't say such things, Bapuji. Please!'

'Nanak needs to take up a trade, a profession. I know you and your mother think that I am unduly harsh upon him but one day you will realise how important this training is for him. He cannot be a buffalo herder for the rest of his life. It is below his status. We are Bedis. We are the ancient orators of the Vedas. Is this how we want to pay tribute to the memory of our forefathers?'

Mehta Kalu handed back the empty tumbler to his daughter and laughed sarcastically. 'How can Nanak bring shame to our family by becoming a buffalo herder? To be honest he cannot even do that. Remember when I once asked him to look after our buffaloes? He fell asleep and the animals entered the fields of Raj Kumar. Had Rai Bularji not intervened in time and agreed to pay the amount lost, we would have suffered a major loss.'

'But father, you have to understand. Our Nanak is not like ordinary people. He is sensitive and observant. He thinks and talks about topics that ordinary people cannot even fathom,' said Bebe Nanaki.

'All sisters think their brother is special and all mothers think their child is special,' he replied mockingly. 'Nanak has extraordinary intellect but he needs to use his intellect in practical matters. How will he survive in a world like this if he continues to talk about spirituality and metaphysical matters all the time? He needs to learn accounts and other things which would be useful for him to make a living. How will he make a living from religion?'

Finishing her prayer Mata Tripta emerged from the room. 'Nanaki, go get an earthen-pot from the kitchen and fetch water from the well. There is no water in the house for the night.' As Bebe Nanaki left, Mata Tripta asked her husband, 'Any news of Nanak?'

'No, nothing yet.'

There was a knock on the door. Mehta Kalu rushed to it and opened it to find a young boy, slightly older than Nanak, standing outside the door. 'We've found Nanak,' he said. 'He is hidden in the grove of waan trees outside town.'

'But why is he hiding?' Mehta Kalu asked and without waiting for an answer headed out of the house. He called his employer and friend, Rai Bular, and together they left to get Nanak.

They found Nanak sitting under the trees sobbing softly. His white clothes were covered in mud. Mehta's initial thought was that Nanak had been robbed on the way. Rai Bular, who had been fond of pious Nanak for a long time gently placed his hand on top of the boy's head and asked, 'What happened, son? Why didn't you return home?'

'Because I am afraid of Bapuji.'

'Why are you afraid of me?' asked Mehta, his voice rising in anger.

'Please, Mehta. Let me talk to him,' intervened Rai Bular, aware of the complicated relationship between father and son.

'Why are you afraid of your father? Have you done anything wrong?'

'I have done nothing wrong,' replied Nanak. 'In fact, I have done a good deed. But I know that what I have done will not please my father. I have disappointed him, which is not a good deed. I am confused about this relationship between good and bad.'

'What good have you done?'

'As you know, Bapuji gave me twenty rupees to do an honest trade this morning and I headed towards the market of Chuharkhana. There is a jungle on the way which I am sure you have seen many times. In the jungle I came across a strange sight. There were a group of ascetics lost in mediation. They were naked, all of them. They had matted hair falling on *both sides of their shoulders.* Their leader was a wise man called Santrain. I knew that I should not stop and that I should continue my journey and complete the responsibility that my father had given me. I knew that if I stopped I would engage in a philosophical discussion with them and then I would lose track of time. Yet, I still couldn't help myself. It was a strange sight indeed. Some of them were standing on their heads, while there was one resting in a meditative pose inside the recesses of a banyan tree. So lost were they in their thoughts that they did not even realise I was passing by. I walked up to their leader and asked them about their beliefs. They belonged to a group which refers to itself as Nirbani. The leader of the group told me that they had not had food for several days. 'Why haven't you?' I asked them. 'Because our beliefs forbid us to engage in the material world hence we have no money to buy food, neither do we have any land on which we can grow our own.' 'Why don't you go to the town and beg for food like all the other ascetics?' I asked him. 'Begging is forbidden as per our beliefs,' he told me.'

'Why were they naked?' Rai Bular felt himself being drawn towards the story, while Mehta listened indifferently.

'They say that their bodies are pure, a boon to them from the Divine. By putting on clothes they would disrespect that boon. Unlike jogis they don't even pierce their ear because they believe that they have to return their body to the Divine in the same state as it was given to them. That is their idea of purity.'

'If I wanted to listen to the nonsense of ascetics, I wouldn't travel to

Chuharkhana for that. There are plenty who pass through Talwindi. I would ask them. Where did the money go?'

'I tried giving the money to Santrain but he refused. He said that it was against his religion to take money. He told me that if I wanted to feed them I should buy them food instead. So when I reached Chuharkhana, instead of buying profitable goods I bought food for the ascetics and fed them. That was my honest trade.'[6] Mehta Kalu could not control his temper and despite the presence of Rai Bular, whom he respected immensely, slapped Nanak. An already shaken Nanak started to cry.

'Mehta!' shouted Rai Bular. 'Control yourself! This is no way to treat a grown-up man.'

'A grown-up man doesn't go around wasting his father's money. He earns his own. Since this was the hard-earned income of his father, he found it easy to give it away to the ascetics. I would love to see him do that with his own money, given that he chooses to earn someday. I cannot believe my misfortune. I waited so long for a son, a successor. Had I known that this was how he was going to turn out, I would never have spent those nights in prayer and given all those gifts to the temple in hope of a son. I would have lived my life without any male progeny and instead allowed my lineage to fade away. With the direction that this young man has taken, our lineage is already threatened.'

'If Nanak pains you so much then why don't you allow me to adopt him as my son? From today, you are relieved of all of your responsibilities as his father. He is my son now,' said Rai Bular.

The relationship between father and son deteriorated further after this incident. Even though they lived in the same house, they never spoke. Nanak became increasingly aloof from his family and started to spend more time at the abandoned mound on the outskirts of Talwindi. Soon after, Nanak's only supportive family member, his sister, also got married and moved to Sultanpur. This further alienated father and son.

Seeing the condition of her brother, who was lost within himself, and would not take any interest in the house or in any profession, Nanak's

---

[6]This incident is known as *Sacha Sauda* (honest trade) and is one of the most important events from Nanak's early life.

sister, on a visit to Talwindi, suggested that he get married. At this point, Nanak was spending all his time in the jungles around the city and Bebe Nanaki felt that with the responsibility of a wife, he would spend time at home. When she broached the topic with her mother she too felt that this was a good idea. Bebe Nanaki had already identified a girl. Her name was Sulakhni and she was the daughter of Moolchand Khatri from the village of Pakhoke near Gurdaspur.

Bebe Nanaki had interacted with the young girl and had found her to be well-suited to take up the role of daughter-in-law at the Bedi household. She was respectful towards the elderly and knew about her responsibilities as a woman.

Mehta Kalu too was thrilled by the proposal. When Nanaki talked to Nanak about the marriage proposal, he accepted it quietly. It was not as if Nanak was eager to marry. He simply couldn't think of any other option. He was inclined towards spirituality and was attracted towards asceticism but he did not want to live the life of a celibate, like them. He knew that he wanted to continue to engage with society and so thought that a marriage would be a step in the right direction.

The proposal was then extended to Sulakhni's family by Bebe Nanaki and they accepted it immediately. They knew that the Bedi family was a respected family and that their daughter would be protected in their house. Marriage dates were decided by the priests and a modest ceremony was organised.

Marriage had the desired effect on Nanak and he started to spend much more time at home than he did earlier. He would continue to meet the ascetics and Sufis on the outskirts of Talwindi, but there was moderation in his behaviour now. The relationship between father and son also improved slowly as Sulakhni acted as a bridge between the two. Soon after their marriage the young couple was blessed with a son who was named Sri Chand. Nanak had never been happier in his life. Mehta Kalu started believing that Nanak was now completely cut off from the spiritual matters.

One day when Bebe Nanaki and her husband, Jai Ram, were visiting Talwindi from Sultanpur, Mehta Kalu broached the topic of Nanak's profession with his son-in-law, who was well established in his job in the court of Nawab Daulat Khan, the Governor of Sultanpur. Jai Ram suggested that Nanak be allowed to come with them to Sultanpur where he would find him a reasonable job. Tripta and Mehta Kalu were shocked by the suggestion. Never before in the history of the Bedi family had a son lived with his sister after marriage, but they eventually agreed because never before had a son like Nanak taken birth in the Bedi family. Nanak, after the birth of his first child was also much more aware of his responsibilities, which is why he readily agreed to accompany his sister and brother-in-law to Sultanpur. Here, his brother-in-law got him a job with the Governor of Sultanpur as a manager of the Nawab's provision store. Nanak enjoyed his new responsibilities.

Soon he was joined there by his wife and first son. A year after Sulakhni moved in with Nanak at Sultanpur, they were blessed with another son, whom they named Lachman Das.

ੴ

'Iqbal Sahib, I feel that after the incident of Sacha Sauda, young Nanak must have been in a lot of anxiety,' I said, glancing at my older companion as I navigated the car through the rush of this market town called Farooqabad.

'I remember reading in Nanak's biography, written by Trilochan Singh, the one that you recommended, that from this point on, till the time he left for Sultanpur where he stayed with his sister, Nanak was very distressed. This must have been a formative period in his career as a spiritual reformer. Imagine an eighteen-year-old boy who doesn't know where his life is heading, while those around him neatly fit into their roles as landlords and government officials. His father is a regular reminder to him that he is not doing anything constructive. It is but natural for anyone in this state to feel vulnerable. Perhaps Nanak felt that he was worthless at that point.'

'Of course, it must have been tough,' said Iqbal Qaiser. 'Things got so bad for him that he had to go and stay with his sister. In our culture that is the lowest act a person can engage in. There is a proverb in Punjabi about brothers who live with their sisters after marriage. "A brother living in a sister's house and a husband living in the house of his wife is the same as a dog".'

'But then Nanak was someone who challenged religious and social boundaries. Do you think living with his sister was another way in which he mocked social convention?'

'Even if that was the case one can imagine that the people of those times must have said terrible things and that must have bothered Nanak. He was after all a part of society.'

Iqbal Qaiser is someone who is all too familiar with being mocked as useless. His father was a businessman and a disciplinarian. When during the Zia era his business started to suffer due to the economic sanctions placed on the military regime, he forced his eldest son, Iqbal Qaiser, to quit his studies and join the business.

'I was put in charge of accounts,' Iqbal told me once while laughing at the memory. 'Something happens to me when I see numbers. They start jumping around the page. I would always make mistakes. Eventually, my father kicked me out of the business. For years I felt worthless. Even today, none of my family members take me seriously. My opinions are conveniently ignored. I am too much of an idealist, I am told.'

Till the time of her death, Iqbal Qaiser also had a bitter relationship with his wife, who was constantly troubled by his interests. She was bothered by his unorthodox religious views. To her, Iqbal Qaiser was a Sikh. Once when he put up a poster of Nanak in his room, his wife immediately took it down thinking that it would be a sin to have a picture of a Sikh saint in a Muslim household.

I too have gone through similar incidents of being labelled a Sikh or biased against Muslims, because of my fascination with Guru Nanak. Often, my family members, my students and my friends say in a derogatory manner that I am a Hindu or a Sikh, implying that I was somehow inferior to them. My mother and sisters have told me several times to write about Muslim saints and buildings instead of our Sikh or Hindu heritage. In a country where everyone is researching Islam, it seems there is no space to do any research outside the fold of Islam.

Following his failure in business, Iqbal Qaiser dabbled in literature and history. Today, he is the author of fifteen books, a majority of which are of Punjabi poetry. His most celebrated work is *Historical Sikh Shrines in Pakistan*. This book brought him international acclaim as it was popular with expatriate Sikhs living in America and Canada.

'Imagine, had you never written, you would have spent your entire life thinking that you were not capable of doing anything,' I said.

'Yes,' he concurred. Sighing deeply, he raised his head only slightly, throwing his shoulders back. He was a proud man and wished that his father could see this aspect of his son's achievements. And then suddenly his shoulders dropped again and he stared at the ground, not willing to be disturbed at this moment. His father still doesn't hold his 'kind' of work in much regard. For him the world of business and money is the only correct use of one's time.

We drove over a small bridge. A canal teeming with water trying to escape its banks flowed under us. It was the monsoon season and the rains had arrived early this year. There were potholes on the road, full of water. I drove carefully around them, trying to avoid splashing water on the people walking and riding on cycles or motorbikes on the side of the road. This also being Ramzan, there were several fruit vendors on both sides of the road, selling overpriced fruit to reap the full benefits of this holy month under their makeshift tents. The market was busy.

'Do you know the name of this market?' asked Iqbal Qaiser.

'Farooqabad.'

'Yes. That is the new name. Do you know its historical name?'

'No.'

'Chuhrkhana.'

'Really?' I looked around once again as if trying to spot its historicity amidst its busyness. It couldn't have been very different when Nanak visited this place. There must have been similar makeshift tents selling lentils, sugar, vegetables and other goods on this road.

'This is still a *mandi*,' said Iqbal Qaiser.

'How far is it from Nankana Sahib?'

'Well, if you go in a straight line it's not that far. About forty-five kilometres, I think. Do you know how it came to be called Farooqabad?'

'No.'

'During the Zia era, there was a man called Farooq Dogar who happened to be a resident of this town. He was elected Member of Parliament when we had non-party based elections in the eighties. In the assembly, he supported the military dictator. While in office, he was killed over a personal feud and the name of this town was changed from Chuhrkhana to Farooqabad in his honour.'

'What does Chuhrkhana mean?' I asked him.

'Traditionally there were two bangles that were worn with regular bangles. One of them was worn at the start while the other at the end. Those two bangles were known as *Chuhr*. This is a Sanskrit word which means to lead. Take a left from here,' he said pointing towards a horrible road that was covered with slushy mud. Muttering a silent prayer, I turned left.

At a little distance from the main road, was the Gurdwara Sacha Sauda. It was a splendid structure, recently renovated. All around it there was a protective wall covered with barbed wire on top. I was about to turn in the direction of the gurdwara when Iqbal Qaiser asked me to keep driving straight. We drove next to the wall of the structure. I thought Iqbal Qaiser was taking me to the rear gate of the gurdwara but when the boundary wall ended, I turned towards him with a puzzled expression.

'We will come here on the way back. Let us go see Gurdwara Sachkand first.'

ੴ

It is believed that Nanak was sitting in the forest when a trader passed him. His mules were laden with goods. 'What is it that you carry?' asked Nanak. The trader, anticipating evil intentions behind the question replied, 'You mean this? Oh this is nothing. Just some mud.'

'Mud, is it? Must be mud if you say so,' said Nanak.

The truth was he was carrying sugar and other sweets. It so happened that when he reached his destination he found out that his sugar and gur (jaggery) had turned into mud. He understood what had transpired, so he returned to the Guru who was still sitting there and repented. In this way his mud became sugar and gur once again.

ੴ

The story of Sachkand and Sacha Sauda seem to merge with each other. The former, it seems, is an extension of the latter. Even though the Janamsakhis relate them as two different incidents, I have no doubt that his devotees saw the story of Sachkand as an extension of Sacha Sauda. Needless to say, it is impossible to determine the historicity of either event.

ੴ

Iqbal Qaiser and I stopped in our tracks when we saw a dog resting in front of us. It was a white dog while another brown one slept next to it. Behind it was the Gurdwara Sachkand, a white structure. 'Allah' was clumsily inscribed on it with charcoal. The white dog stared at us for a little while and went back to sleep. They looked harmless enough but we were still scared to go through.

'Oh, this is a new development,' said Iqbal Qaiser. 'The gurdwara has become a shrine.'

'It wasn't the case, the last time you came?' I asked.

'No.'

'Let's go inside. The dogs won't do anything,' I suggested.

'No. Let's wait here for someone else to come.'

I stood there wondering how long it would take for another soul to emerge to release us from this dilemma but it wasn't long. Within the next few minutes a motorcycle stopped next to our car. One of the occupants walked towards us while the other disappeared into the fields around the shrine, perhaps to relieve himself.

'*Assalamualikum*,' he said. He was an old man who must have been in his late sixties or early seventies. He was wearing golden spectacles while his moustache and hair were jet black, recently dyed. 'I have come here to see Sheikh Saad. I am the brother of his father-in-law. I have been told that he is often found at this shrine. He smokes up here.'

'Let's go in together and find out where he is,' suggested Iqbal Qaiser.

We walked carefully around the dogs, who were unperturbed by our presence. Next to them, facing the white gurdwara was the grave of the Muslim saint whose shrine this abandoned gurdwara was now on the way to becoming. The grave, situated under the shade of a tree, was made of mud and covered with glittery shawls. There was a boundary around it made out of bricks to maintain the sanctity of the place. Next to the grave were a few rooms which looked recently constructed. There was no sign of activity within those rooms.

'Come in straight,' instructed a voice from behind the gurdwara.

There were a group of people sitting on a mat. There were several trees around us. This was a shady spot. We took off our shoes and joined these men who were serving the shrine of the Muslim saint.

Before Iqbal Qaiser and I could introduce ourselves, the man accompanying us who was in search of Sheikh Saad told them about the purpose of his visit. He was from a neighbouring village and his name was Mohsin. There was immediate recognition and the next thirty minutes were spent talking about people who were mutual relatives of the different parties in conversation here. It turned out that the person who had welcomed us in, an old man in his seventies, wearing a white *kurta* and *dhoti*, was also the father-in-law of Sheikh Saad's brother. His name was Furqan.

'I have come with my murshad (teacher). He is a *Syed Badshah*,' said Mohsin. (The Syed caste in South Asia derives their ancestry from Prophet Muhammad {PBUH} and thus enjoy a unique privilege in Islamic spirituality.)

'*Jazakallah* (May Allah reward you with goodness). Where is he?' asked Furqan.

'He is just coming.'

This group of people, which besides Mohsin and Furqan, included four more, showed no interest in us. In a pause in their conversation about relatives and extended family I asked someone to tell me about the saint who was buried in front of the gurdwara. It was Furqan who decided to share the story of the saint.

Listening to his interpretation of the Muslim saint, I could not help but draw comparisons between the ascetics that Nanak met and Pir Munawar, which was the name of the saint buried here.

'He would never ask for food and would only eat what was offered to him.'

'He stood in the canal for twelve years and used to eat rocks.'

Despite the centuries separating the two, one could still trace a continuity of religious tradition. It can be argued that Pir Munawar's asceticism was a continuation of a tradition whose roots were buried in antiquity and whose practitioners were also yogis and *tantrics* (followers of Tantrism) from the Hindu tradition.

'Do you know whose gurdwara this is?' I asked.

'Yes,' answered a man who was sitting in front of Furqan. He was younger than the rest of them. He was squatting on the floor. He also held a sickle in his hand which meant he had returned recently from working in the fields nearby. By now Mohsin had forgotten about Sheikh Saad and was listening to our story.

'This gurdwara is called Sachkand. It belongs to Guru Nanak.'

'Do you know why it is called Sachkand?' I asked.

'When Guru Nanak came of age his father gave him a few rupees and asked him to buy something useful from the market and then trade the goods. He travelled to this mandi. When he reached here he found a group of yogis lost in mediation on top of a mound. The mound is where the big gurdwara stands. Guru Nanak saw that they were in a horrible condition. They were all skin and bones. They hadn't eaten for days. Guru Nanak asked them why they hadn't eaten. They told him that they were yogis and they didn't beg for food. Guru Nanak asked them if he could buy them anything to eat. They said yes. So when Guru Nanak went to the market, instead of buying goods for trading he purchased food and gave it to the yogis. However, after he had spent all his money on buying the yogis food, he became distressed because he didn't know what to say to his father anymore. Guru Nanak came and sat at this spot, which is the Gurdwara Sachkand,' he said, pointing with a sickle towards the gurdwara.

He was a good storyteller, pausing in the middle to add emphasis and locking eyes with different people at different times during the narration.

'In the meantime, his father in Nankana Sahib became worried as it was night. He sent his men to find Guru Nanak. Guru Nanak was found sitting in the jungle at this spot. When they were about to leave for Nankana Sahib, Guru Nanak piled his mules with mud from the ground. At Nankana when his father asked him what trade he had done, he replied that he had bought sugar and gur. Nanak was scared that when his father would open the bags he would learn the truth and would be angry with him; however, when his sister opened the bags on the mules she found that the mud had actually been changed into sugar and gur.

'*Subhanallah!*'

'*Mashallah!*'

'Guru Nanak was a true devotee of God. He was a rightly guided soul,' added the story teller.

This version of the story was different from the one that is recorded in the Janamsakhis. But to determine historical accuracy was not a concern. I was intrigued that a man who looked 'uneducated' and who was a Muslim knew about the story of Guru Nanak and regarded him as a true devotee of God.

'How did you learn of the story?' I asked him.

'Our elders told us. They used to live with the Sikhs before Pakistan was made. The Sikhs used to tell them stories of Guru Nanak.'

Finally, the Syed murshad of Mohsin arrived. Furqan stood up to greet him while the rest remained seated. He took out his cigarette pack and offered cigarettes to everyone present. Everyone took one. It was the month of Ramzan and eating in public was forbidden according to the laws of the country during the time of fasting. Yet here, those social conventions didn't apply. This was the shrine of a dervish, and dervishes are generally considered to be outside the orthodoxy of religiosity. The same rules apply to his followers.

We took our leave to head to Gurdwara Sacha Sauda. Before leaving, we entered Gurdwara Sachkand. In front of us was a picture of the Muslim fakir wearing a green shawl and sporting a beard, sitting inside this gurdwara. There were posters of Kaaba and Masjid Nabwi on the walls, while there were other inscriptions on the walls professing the Muslim identity of this building.

'Something needs to be done about this,' said Iqbal Qaiser as we walked towards the car.

'Why?' I asked. 'I think it's really interesting that Muslims of this area have still preserved the legend of Guru Nanak. You can tell that they still respect him by the way they narrate the story. You don't find that in the Muslims of Nankana Sahib.'

'That's true,' he said. 'That's because the Muslims of this area are those who were the inhabitants of this place before Partition. Therefore they had a relationship with the Sikhs and also associated with the legend of Guru Nanak. The majority of the Muslims in Nankana Sahib are those who migrated from the other side of the border following Partition. They lost their homes and family members at the hands of Hindus and Sikhs. Their attitudes are therefore shaped by those experiences. The Muslims in this village were responsible for all those atrocities on Hindus and Sikhs.'

'That makes sense but why are you worried about Muslims taking over the gurdwara and converting it into a Muslim shrine? In this manner, at least the sanctity of the place would be preserved, if not as a Sikh shrine then at least as a Muslim shrine. Besides, we saw how these people regard this place to be a gurdwara first and a Muslim shrine later,' I argued.

'All of that is true, but that is the case right now. Ten years down the road the followers of the Muslim *pir* (a Muslim saint) would claim that there was no gurdwara here and that this was their shrine. Then there will be a conflict.'

'So what you are saying is that we could have a situation similar to Gurdwara Shaheed Ganj here?'

'Precisely.'

Some time ago, Iqbal Qaiser had narrated the story of Gurdwara Shaheed Ganj to me.

ੴ

I wasn't directly involved in the issue of Gurdwara Shaheed Ganj. This was an old issue that started about two centuries ago. The area the gurdwara stands in was a vacant plot of land. No, this is not the walled city of Lahore. This is outside Delhi gate. This area is known as Naulakha Bazaar.

Do you remember why it is called the Naulakha Bazaar? I told you the story when we drove around the railway station the other day. Prince Dara

Shikoh had his Naulakha palace here. How different the history of this region would have been had Dara Shikoh become the Emperor instead of Aurangzeb. Maybe there would have been no Partition. Who knows?

What was I saying? Yes. Naulakha Bazaar. So this was a vacant piece of land where there was a small mosque. Sitting in that mosque, the Qazi would announce punishment to criminals. Yes, you have guessed it right. This is also where innocent Sikhs were punished. Thousands of them, men, women and children alike were slaughtered and thrown into a well here on the orders of the Governor of Lahore, Moin-ul-Mulk also known as Meer Manu. A room was constructed here where the prisoners were kept before they were executed.

The mosque was small and was never used as a place of worship. During the tenure of Maharaja Ranjit Singh, the Sikhs took over the mosque, placed the Guru Granth Sahib inside it, converting it into a gurdwara. The Muslims could not do anything then.

It was during the British era that this issue first came to light. The Muslims filed an application in court that this was a mosque and that it should be returned to them. The Muslims argued that the Court should look at the architecture of the building to judge that this was indeed a mosque. The Sikhs on the other hand argued that this had been a mosque once and that now it had become a gurdwara.

The Lahore High Court, where the case was presented, asked if there was anyone alive who could testify that he had seen that building used as a mosque. Naturally, there was no one. So the court decided in favour of the Sikhs. After the judgment the Sikhs who had control over the gurdwara decided to raze the building because they thought that it was because of the architecture of the building that this issue had come to the forefront.

The building was demolished. This led to rioting between Muslims and Sikhs. It was actually the British who were responsible for these riots. It goes back to their policy of divide and rule. Even Muhammad Ali Jinnah and Allama Iqbal got involved as they tried pacifying the Muslims. I have seen one photograph of Jinnah standing on a chair, speaking to a crowd of people at the Badshahi Mosque at the time of this riot. Nothing emerged out of the protest and the gurdwara remained a gurdwara.

After Partition, when the Auqaf Department was created, this issue of the gurdwara was raised yet again. This time, people believed that since the

Sikhs had migrated and the gurdwara had been abandoned, the court would allot it to the Muslims but that did not happen. The Lahore High Court decided once again that this would remain a gurdwara. When was this you ask? Around 1957-58.

The issue about the property of this gurdwara or mosque was raised once again in the late 1980s. Some petitioners appeared in the court and asked for the judgment to be reviewed. This time the judge ordered that he would convert this gurdwara into a mosque if the petitioners brought forth even one person who had prayed at the mosque. That did not happen and the status of the gurdwara remained as is.

In about 1994-95, the Kar Sewa Committee of England asked the Pakistan Government for permission to renovate this gurdwara. The government was reluctant initially but eventually gave permission. There is a man named Avtar Singh Panghedha in the Kar Sewa Committee. I stayed with him when I went to England and when he came to Pakistan, he stayed with me. He asked me to supervise the construction of the gurdwara for them. So all the money, the contracts, each and everything concerning the gurdwara went through me. I opened up all the accounts, paid everyone, etc.

I can't even describe the things we saw when we were constructing this building. We would dig into the ground and skeletons of children and adults would emerge. These were the remains of the Sikhs who were killed here on the orders of Meer Manu.

When it was mentioned in the newspapers that the Gurdwara Shaheed Ganj was being reconstructed, the Muslims tried once again to create an issue. This time they wanted the local people living around the gurdwara to get involved and halt the construction of this shrine. There was a man named Rana who was an ironsmith outside the gurdwara. You must have seen the various ironsmiths next to the gurdwara. He was one of them. He was a wise man. He told his fellow businessmen that the construction of the gurdwara would help them. He told the traders that the gurdwara would attract foreign pilgrims and it would be beneficial for everyone. He argued that if the gurdwara was not constructed, this place would remain vacant and that would serve no one. With his efforts the local businessmen and traders of Naulakha Bazaar became stakeholders in the construction of the shrine and in this way this gurdwara was eventually constructed in 2004.

When this gurdwara became functional and pilgrims started visiting, the Government of Pakistan woke up to the potential of Sikh pilgrimage tourism. It has now invited the Sikh community living abroad to invest in the renovation of any Sikh gurdwara in the country.

'I saw this gurdwara for the first time in 1993 when I was researching my book,' said Iqbal Qaiser. The Gurdwara Sacha Sauda was in front of us once again.

'I was accompanied by Ilyas Ghuman. The condition of the shrine was miserable at that time. Buffaloes were tied in the courtyard while drug addicts and gamblers had occupied the rest of the space. At that time there was a man from this area who was referred to as Shah. I don't remember his real name. He had taken it upon himself to preserve the sanctity of the gurdwara. He pleaded with the drug addicts and gamblers to abandon this space. Instead, they beat him up and broke his head. The fight was taking place when we arrived here. We took Shah to the nearest hospital and got his head bandaged. Then we went to the police station and filed a report against the culprits. After that the issue appeared in a few national newspapers. It was then that the Department of Auqaf woke up from its slumber and came to find out about this gurdwara. They asked for Shah and appointed him the official guard of this place. In subsequent years, the gurdwara was renovated and now it is one of the major shrines that is visited by pilgrim tourists who come to Nankana Sahib and Hassan Abdal.'

'This means that you played a major part in the renovation of this gurdwara, like in Shaheed Ganj?' I asked him.

'Yes.'

We parked our car in front of the iron gates of the shrine. There were two security men sitting inside the gate while a policeman sat next to them with his gun resting on his shoulder.

'These are new boys,' said Iqbal Qaiser. 'They don't recognise me. Otherwise they would have allowed us to take the car inside.'

'My name is Iqbal Qaiser. I was responsible for getting this gurdwara renovated,' said Iqbal Qaiser to a young boy who had left his seat and walked across the gate to enquire about us. He gave us a puzzled look. 'Is Boota Singh inside?' asked Iqbal Qaiser.

Before coming here he had found out through his contacts in the Sikh community that Boota Singh was the name of the *sewadar* (one who serves in a gurdwara) appointed here by the Auqaf Department.

'He is. But who are you?' asked the boy, who showed no intentions of allowing us inside. 'Do you have his number? Why don't you call him and ask him to come to the gate?'

'I don't have his number. It was in my old phone but I lost that one and this is a new one. Do you have his number? Give it to me, I'll call him,' said Iqbal Qaiser.

Dialling his number, Iqbal Qaiser walked away from both of us. He returned shortly and gave the phone to the guard, who after talking to Boota Singh, allowed us to enter.

Boota Singh was waiting for us at the entrance to the gurdwara. He was about forty years old and was wearing a green shalwar kameez with a green turban. His youngest son, about ten years old, who wore a shirt and jeans stood next to him. Boota Singh was an extremely shy person who avoided any eye contact while speaking. While conversing, when Iqbal Qaiser got a bit close to him, he moved back, trying to reclaim his personal space. In this manner he almost went a full circle around Iqbal Qaiser during the course of the conversation, with one trying to get closer while the other moved away. I wasn't sure if Iqbal Qaiser observed his peculiar behaviour.

His son, though, looked us straight in the eye. '*Pranam*,' he said, with his hands joined together.

As Boota Singh led us in, Iqbal Qaiser whispered into my ear, 'I have met this man many times but we have never really talked. I have always come here with a *jatha* (a group of Sikhs) and he shows us around.'

We walked through the portal and entered a courtyard, at the centre of which stood a white gurdwara. Next to it were a few waan trees enclosed by a small boundary. The gurdwara, the courtyard and the trees were situated on an ancient mound, which was the highest point in and around the city. 'It was under these trees that Nanak discoursed with the leader of the yogis,' Iqbal Qaiser told me.

A few trees in the middle of a marbled courtyard were the last remnants of the jungle that used to exist here. According to legend, a few yogis were hanging from the trees while there were others who were sitting within an empty trunk when Nanak passed through. I stared hard at the trees, picturing Nanak observing their practices. I was drawn towards it. I touched one of the trees in the hope that through physical contact I would be able to transcend the boundaries of time and space and enter the world of Nanak and those naked ascetics.

I was there.

Nanak sat here, his legs folded under his knees, while in front of him Santrain sat in a yoga position. Nanak was young but looked much wiser than his age. There was curiosity in his eyes as he listened with rapt attention.

'This gurdwara was constructed to commemorate the event.' Iqbal Qaiser's words disrupted my thoughts.

We entered the shrine, which was like any other Sikh shrine. At the centre was a wooden palanquin in which the Guru Granth Sahib was placed. In front of the palanquin there was a space where a couple of swords were placed. Iqbal Qaiser took out a ten rupee note and placed it there. He then walked around the palanquin. Picking up a flying-whisk he fanned the Guru Granth Sahib. I mimicked him.

'We have constructed a new *sukhasan*. Let me show it to you,' said Boota Singh, with excitement in his voice. He took us behind the gurdwara where a room had been reserved for the Guru Granth Sahib. It was neatly carpeted while the walls had been done up in wood. There was a split air-conditioner on the wall which was turned off at the moment as there was no electricity. Under the air-conditioner there was a wooden bed with intricate patterns on it. There was a blanket towards the rear of the bed. 'It is beautiful,' said Iqbal Qaiser, more out of courtesy than genuine appreciation. 'Did you have this bed made in Amritsar?'

'No,' replied Boota Singh. 'It was made in Nankana Sahib.'

I wondered what Nanak would have felt at this ritualistic veneration of the Guru Granth Sahib. According to tradition, the tenth Sikh Guru, Guru Gobind Singh, concluded the institution of Gurudom by declaring that the Guru Granth Sahib was the eternal Guru. The book

contains the spiritual poetry of the various Sikh Gurus, including Guru
Nanak and other spiritual teachers like Bhagat Kabir, Baba Farid and
Bhai Mardana. The Sikhs now treat the Guru Granth Sahib as a living
Guru. A room like this one is constructed for the Guru Granth Sahib
at every gurdwara, where it is laid on a bed at the end of the day and the
air-conditioner is turned on if it is summer and the heater if it is winter.
In a ritualistic procedure at the conclusion of the evening prayer each
day, the *Granthi* carries the Guru Granth Sahib on his head and brings
it to this room while others follow.

Guru Nanak spoke vehemently against religious institutions and
rituals. At Hindu temples, he challenged the concept of aarti. Nanak's
philosophy is centred on the concept of redefining the sacred and the
profane. Through his actions he recasts the sacred as profane and vice
versa. For example, he chooses to associate himself with people of
lowercastes, terming them people of God, while he criticises high-caste
landlords and government officials as exploiters. According to legend,
Nanak once travelled to Mecca where he performed *Hajj*. While on Hajj,
once at night he slept with his feet pointing towards the *Kaaba*. A Muslim
preacher woke him up and rebuked him for showing disrespect to the
holy shrine. It is said that Nanak turned his feet in the other direction
and as he did so, the Kaaba miraculously turned towards his feet. 'Put
my feet in the direction where God does not reside,' Nanak said to the
Muslim preacher. Instead of believing the miracle that is narrated to
us, I often wonder what really happened in Mecca. Of course, any such
thought is premised upon conjecture. What is important in this story is
Nanak's criticism of the concept of a 'sacred space'. Every place is sacred
as far as Nanak is concerned.

With his head bowed and hands clasped in front of him, Boota
Singh walked out of the sacred room backwards, making sure that at no
point did his back face the Guru Granth Sahib. Iqbal Qaiser exited in
a similar manner. I followed.

We sat in the porch, within sight of the gurdwara and the trees in
front of us. Boota Singh's son served us tea. 'Iqbal Qaiser, can you help
me renovate a particular gurdwara?' asked Boota Singh.

'Which one?'

'There is a gurdwara at the village of Nena Kot in Faisalabad district.'

'The Gurdwara of Baba Budha?'

'Is that the Gurdwara of Baba Budha?' asked Boota Singh.

Baba Budha is an iconic Sikh saint who became a disciple of Guru Nanak and continued serving five Gurus after him. He had the unique role of applying the tilak on the forehead of five Gurus after Guru Nanak, therefore appointing them as the next Guru.

'Yes. He was from a village which lies on the other side of the river. That side is now in India. But his gurdwara happened to remain in Pakistan.'

'Iqbal Sahib, you know more about our history than us,' said Boota Singh. He then looked at me and said, 'Do you know he has done a great service to the Sikh community? His research and work are phenomenal.'

I nodded in agreement and said, 'Why don't you first work on the renovation of the Gurdwara Sachkand? It is close to you and Sacha Sauda is already prominent. It will be easier to get attention for that gurdwara than any other right now.'

'Yes,' jumped in Iqbal Qaiser. 'You should focus on this gurdwara first. The problem is that a few dervishes have taken over and built a shrine. In the next few years they will erase any signs of the gurdwara and claim that there was no gurdwara there.'

Boota Singh showed no interest in our suggestion. His eyes remained glued to Iqbal Qaiser's feet as he spoke to him.

'Iqbal Qaiser, you've done so much research on Sikh buildings and gurdwaras, you should also do some research on the sewadars. I have been working here for the past twelve years. There are so many other such stories,' he said.

'When did your family move to Nankana Sahib from the Tribal Areas?' Iqbal Qaiser asked him.

'We are not from the Tribal Areas. We are Punjabis,' replied Boota Singh with a shy smile on his face. He was the first Pakistani Punjabi Sikh I had interacted with. Earlier, I had only encountered Pathan Sikhs who had moved to Punjab in the past few years. 'I am from the village of Nena Kot,' he continued. 'The gurdwara that I was telling you about is in my village.'

'Oh, you are from that village?' said Iqbal Qaiser with surprise. 'That gurdwara is being used as a school, if I am not mistaken.'

'Yes it is. I studied in that school.' Memories of his childhood lit up his face. 'I have so many memories associated with that gurdwara. It is still being used as a school. I want the sanctity of that gurdwara restored. I want it to be used as a gurdwara once again.'

'Were you the only Sikh family left in your village after Partition?' Iqbal Qaiser asked.

'Yes.'

'Did you ever face any difficulties living as a Sikh minority in a Muslim majority area?' I jumped into the conversation.

'Not really. My grandfather had good ties with everyone living around us. That is why he stayed. His Muslim friends didn't allow him to leave. They told him that they would protect him, which they did. It was only during the 1965 war that things got a bit difficult for us. A Gujjar family from the neighbouring village took over our lands. However, my grandfather managed to get through to the Martial Law Administrator in Faisalabad, who sent an army official with us and got us our land back. The army official also announced in the village that our family has to be protected and looked after at all costs. People then realised that we were not helpless and had the backing of the army. No one dared trouble us after that.'

'Did you ever feel treated unjustly as a child?' I asked him.

'What he is trying to ask is whether your class fellows or your teachers ever treated you as someone who was not one of them,' elaborated Iqbal Qaiser.

'Never. I was friends with everyone. In fact, I was the most hardworking student in my school. That is because unlike other children I knew that if I was to achieve anything in life I would have to work hard. All the teachers liked me. It used to upset me though that the gurdwara was being used as a school. I would wonder why all the Muslim students walked inside with their shoes on. Why couldn't they take off their shoes here as they did at a mosque? But these were childish thoughts and I never spoke to anyone about them. Now, however, I am determined to restore the sacredness of that gurdwara.'

It was then that I realized that the seeds of being an introvert were laid in Boota Singh's personality in childhood. The way he avoided eye contact and moved away if someone got a little close was perhaps a side-effect of repressing his emotions in childhood. I wondered how being a religious minority in a Muslim majority area shaped his psychological foundations? How different would his personality have been if he were a Muslim?

ੴ

'This is a newly constructed road that connects Chuhrkhana with Nankana Sahib,' Iqbal Qaiser told me. We were driving on a well-laid road at the speed of a hundred kilometres an hour. 'This has been constructed to facilitate Sikh pilgrims.' Earlier, pilgrims had to travel to Sheikupura and then head towards Chuhrkhana, a route which added several kilometres to the journey. Now it takes only about twenty minutes. 'Look at what all a primary school teacher has done,' Iqbal Qaiser commented with pride. He was talking about himself.

After his book was released, a debate raged about the renovation of a number of gurdwaras, one of which was the Gurdwara Sacha Sauda. Once the gurdwara was constructed, this new road also had to be made to connect it to Nankana Sahib. It was truly amazing what Iqbal Qaiser has managed to achieve through the power of his words. Nanak too became immortal because of the power of his poetry. All his ideas, philosophies and experiences would have died with him if he had not recorded them in his words.

Nanak acknowledges the power of words when he says:

By hearing the word
  One sounds the depth of virtue's sea.
By hearing the word
  One acquires learning, holiness, and royalty.
By hearing the word
  The blind see and their paths are visible.
By hearing the word
  The fathomless becomes fordable.

And,

O Nanak, the word hath such magic for the worshippers,
Those that hear, death do not fear,
Their sorrows end and sins disappear.[7]

On another occasion he says:

Though there is no count of Thy names and habitations,
Nor of Thy regions uncomprehended,
Yet many there have been with reason perverted
Who to Thy knowledge have pretended.
Though by words alone we give Thee name and praise,
And by words, reason, worship, and Thy virtue compute;
Though by words alone we write and speak
And by words our ties with Thee constitute;
The word does not its Creator bind,
What Thou ordainest we receive,
Thy creations magnify Thee,
Thy name in all places find.
What might have I to praise Thy might?
I have not power to give it praise.
Whatever be Thy wish, I say Amen.
Mayst Thou endure, O Formless One.[8]

Nanak must have followed a similar route on his way back from
Chuhrkhana to Nankana Sahib, which at that point in time was still
known as Rai Bhoi di Talwindi. What took us only a few minutes would
have been a journey of hours for him, walking in the company of mules.
Instead of the agricultural fields, he would have encountered a vast jungle
that existed then between Nankana and Chuhrkhana.

Not knowing what to do after he had spent all his father's money

[7]Singh, trans. *Hymns of the Gurus*, pages 10–11
[8]Ibid., pages 15–16

on a good deed, Nanak looked for sanctuary in a group of waan trees that existed outside the town. Those trees still exist and are held sacred by Sikh devotees. Next to the trees is a small gurdwara, a yellow single storied structure. Behind it are two large hostels used by Sikh pilgrims at the time of the largest Sikh festival in Pakistan—the birthday of Guru Nanak, celebrated in November every year. Pilgrims tie pieces of cloth onto the branches of these stooping trees as a supplication. This entire complex is known as Gurdwara Tambu Sahib, the name derived from the *tambu* (tent) like trees under which Nanak hid. Like Nanak, we were heading in the direction of those trees where Iqbal Qaiser's Sikh friend, Jatha Singh, the self-appointed caretaker of the gurdwara, had invited us for lunch.

We sat in his room, which was located in one of the rooms of a hostel, while he was busy arbitrating between two feuding families of the city. To my surprise, both families were Muslim. As in-charge of the vast property associated with the gurdwara, which was allotted to it by the Sikh ruler of Punjab, Maharaja Ranjit Singh in the nineteenth century, Jatha Singh enjoys considerable economic influence, which often translates to political influence. He also receives millions of rupees in donations from Sikh expatriates residing in first world countries, which he is responsible for spending on the upliftment of the gurdwara and the Sikh community in Nankana Sahib. He is a well-known name in the regional police stations, which he calls up regularly to facilitate the affairs of friends amidst the red-tape and corruption of police proceedings. For the Sikh community in Nankana Sahib, which amounts to about two hundred-odd households, he has for several years played the role of a leader. But the fact that today he was acting as an arbitrator between two Muslim families came as a surprise.

While we sat in his room waiting for him to emerge from his meeting we were served langar, vegetables along with lentils and hot *rotis*. This was our first meal since the morning. A young Sikh boy, wearing a pyjama and a T-shirt with a black *dastaar* (Sikh headgear) on his head served us. 'May I offer you some yoghurt?' he asked, as soon as we were finished with lunch. '*Lassi?* Water?'

'Have you seen the movie on Milkha Singh?' asked Jasdeep, a young

Pathan Sikh boy, a resident of Nankana Sahib. Jatha Singh had asked him to keep us company while he was engaged in political matters. Jasdeep is enrolled in the M. Phil. programme in Punjab University, Lahore. He also teaches at the Government College at Chunian. He is one of several recipients of Jatha Singh's generosity. Only recently have the Sikh communities in the various cities of Pakistan, including Eminabad, Nankana, Gujranawala and Lahore been able to exert themselves in a way that was unthinkable earlier. An increasing number of people are now enrolled in universities and many have their own cars. This was not how things were even a few years ago.

'No. Have you?' replied Kulan, the young man who had been serving us.

'It is nice. If you want to see it I can give it to you. It's on my laptop. Do you have a USB?'

Handing his friend his red USB, Kulan commented, 'I am looking forward to watching this movie. Bollywood is dominated by the Hindu lobby. They always show the Khalsa in a bad light.'

On a normal day I would never have interrupted this conversation, but that day I did so as I felt that his analysis of the Indian film industry was a little harsh. 'How so?' I asked.

'They are always shown as drinking beer and cutting their *kesh* (hair).'

'Isn't that how it is?' I wanted to ask him. Alcohol sales in the Indian state of Punjab is one of the highest compared to all the other states. Also, a large number of young Sikh boys are increasingly abandoning the symbols of the Sikh religion. Before I could reply, Jatha Singh entered and the atmosphere in the room became sombre. I also knew that for Jatha Singh and many others who grew up in the days of the Sikh insurgency of the eighties, the Indian government was a Hindu lobby.

'Have they made a movie on Milkha Singh?' asked Jatha with astonishment. 'Do you know what they called him?'

'The Flying Sikh,' answered Jasdeep with excitement. 'Ayub Khan gave him that title,' he added, his knowledge freshly learnt from the movie.

'He once came to race in Pakistan and after the race was over, Ayub Khan said to him, "I have never seen anything faster than you. You are a Flying Sikh''' Jatha said, ignoring the fact that Jasdeep had already answered for him.

'Did you ever meet him?' I asked Jatha.

'No. But we used to follow his races. He was popular in those times. I once read an interview in which he said that there were only two times in his life that he cried. One, when his parents died at the time of Partition and second, when he lost in the Olympics in Rome. You know he would have won that race had he not looked back and seen where the rest were. He was leading when he looked back and all the others were able to cross him right at the finish line.'

'I wanted to see the movie but it has been banned in Pakistan,' I complained.

'You know it is an Indian movie. The directors, the producers, the actors, all are Hindus. They have to add *masala* (spice) in a movie.'

'Akram is calling you again, sir,' said a dark-skinned turbanned Sikh peeping through the bedroom door as if scared of Jatha's reaction.

'What does he want now? Tell him I am coming. Iqbal Sahib, I recommended a driver to this Muslim house. After a little while that Muslim driver eloped with the daughter of the cook of that house. Now the father of that girl has come to me. I have told him that I will go to the police station with him and file an FIR against Akram. What else can I do? But he doesn't want that. I have told him that in that case he should forgive his daughter and let the couple settle. Let's see what he wants to say now. I'll return in a short while.'

Jatha followed the servant out of the room. Eager to take his place with the elders, Kulan too followed him.

'Iqbal Sahib, in my free time I write poems. Can I recite them to you so that you could give me feedback?' asked Jasdeep.

'Sure.'

Jasdeep recited a spiritual poem that criticised the dogma of religion. It also challenged the institutionalisation of religion. Later, during a conversation, Jasdeep told me that he lived at the Gurdwara Patti Sahib. This small gurdwara is only a few metres away from Gurdwara Janamasthan. It was here that Guru Nanak got his early education. Here, he wrote his first poem which is recorded in the Guru Granth Sahib.

... O foolish heart, why do you forget Him?
When you render your account, O brother,
Then alone will you be among the educated.[9]

During the early days of Sikh migration to Nankana Sahib after the wars of 1965 and 1971, a lot of Sikh families from Khyber Pakhtunkhwa and the Tribal Areas found refuge in Gurdwara Patti Sahib. Here, a teacher by the name of Giani Pratap started teaching young Sikh children the Gurmukhi alphabet and the Guru Granth Sahib. He was an Indian citizen who visited Pakistan sometime during the sixties for a pilgrimage to Nankana Sahib. After looking at the dilapidated condition of the shrines here he decided to stay and look after these holy buildings. That was the first time someone had taken the initiative to take care of the gurdwaras in Nankana Sahib after Partition. Jasdeep was also educated in Sikh precepts at this gurdwara. Listening to Jasdeep's poem, I wondered if Guru Nanak had inspired the poet within him. As a child, he must have heard countless tales about the Guru, one of which was that Nanak composed the above-mentioned poem in the same building where he lived, as a young child, and impressed his teacher, Pandit Gopal.

ੴ

There are a total of six gurdwaras associated with Guru Nanak at Nankana Sahib. The grandest of them is the Gurdwara Janamasthan, a splendid structure spread over a vast area constructed over the place that was once the house of Mehta Kalu. The actual shrine is a small room in the middle of a spacious marble-floored courtyard. At the centre of this room is Thara Sahib, where the Guru Granth Sahib is recited. According to tradition, Guru Nanak was born here. Next to this shrine is a well, a board next to which says that it belonged to the household of Guru Nanak.

Gurdwara Patti Sahib is near Gurdwara Janamsthan. A few feet away from Gurdwara Patti Sahib is Gurdwara Bal Lila. According to Sikh tradition, this was once an open field where Guru Nanak used to

---

[9]Dhillon, *The First Sikh Spiritual Master*, page 25

play as a child. Every year on the occasion of Lohri, sports competitions are arranged for children within the premises of this gurdwara, to mark the event.

The gurdwaras known as Kiari Sahib and Malji Sahib are the furthest from Gurdwara Janamsthan, while Gurdwara Tambu Sahib lies in between Janamsthan and Kiari Sahib and Malji Sahib. Gurdwara Kiari Sahib is said to mark the spot where Guru Nanak's buffaloes spoilt the fields of a local farmer who is reported to have complained to Nanak's father. It is believed that Guru Nanak once fell asleep while his buffaloes were grazing nearby at the spot that Gurdwara Malji Sahib was constructed. While he was sleeping, the sun changed direction so that Nanak's face was directly under the sun. Miraculously, a cobra emerged at that time and extended its hood, protecting the Guru from the sun while he slept.

ੴ

'Let me show you the ancient mound of Nankana Sahib before we go,' said Iqbal Qaiser as we drove out of the blue gate of Gurdwara Tambu Sahib. 'It is an archaeological mound. The settlement there was destroyed after which Rai Bhoi di Talwindi was constructed within a boundary wall.'

'So Nanak was born in the new Nankana?' I asked.

'Yes.'

We passed through the small market of Nankana, heading towards the Gurdwara Janamasthan. Most of the shops were run by Muslims but there were a few Sikh-owned shops as well. We drove around Gurdwara Janamsthan and went around the back where the ancient mound now rests, away from the hub of the new settlement.

'Was this also the mound that Nanak used to come to as a young man?' I asked.

'Yes.'

Still not sure about his religious conviction and purpose in life, a young Nanak used to spend a lot of time in conversation with yogis, sadhus and dervish who would pass through Talwindi. Since this was an abandoned area next to the town, high enough to provide a panoramic view of the surrounding area, secluded enough not to be disturbed by civilization and close enough to the town if need be, most of them gathered here. Here, Nanak would sit next to them, often posing questions to them. He spent his formative years here, engaging with representatives of different schools of spiritual thought. What he learnt here must have played an important role in the career of the reformer Nanak.

We parked the car at a little distance from the mound and decided to climb it. It was a steep climb with no proper path to the top. It was at least twenty metres from the ground. Once on top, the slight pain caused by the effort to get here quickly vanished as one was absorbed into the serenity of the surroundings. The mound was covered with small shrubs of *karir* (*capparis deciduas*), another ancient Punjabi species of plant that is no longer found anywhere except in abandoned places.

As we walked around the mound, I noticed a colourful bird flying around us, jumping from one shrub to the other. It was a magnificent red, blended with yellow, with a long tail that was longer than its body.

Iqbal Qaiser and I sat on a rock. The fertile fields of Punjab were stretched out in front of us. Fresh from a monsoon shower, it glimmered in the rays of the sun. There was no sadhu or dervish around us as there must have been at the time of Nanak. We sat silently, lost in our own thoughts. We meditated with our eyes open, observing everything that this scene had to offer. At our feet were shards of broken pottery and other mud utensils. The earth here had absorbed an ancient city in its bosom just like it was embracing us at that moment.

The exercise was cathartic and strangely uplifting. One can understand why a young Nanak would come here often. It is believed that in the years between the incident of Sacha Sauda and his migration to Sultanpur, Nanak started to frequent this place. The serenity of this place must have provided him solace from the turmoil in his mind. That period of six to seven years was a rough ride for him and this ancient mound sheltered him from the storm that was brewing within and without.

'Iqbal Sahib, while we were at Chuhrkhana I was thinking about something and wanted to share that with you,' I said. Iqbal Qaiser listened patiently. 'I find it contradictory that Sikhism today has become an institutionalised religion. I feel that Nanak's entire struggle was against the rituals revolving around organised religion. Today, however, if you walk into a gurdwara, there is a strict code of conduct. There are proper rituals that are followed. I remember, once I was sitting at Gurdwara Janamasthan with my back towards the main shrine when a Sikh man came up to me and told me to not sit with my back towards the main shrine. I wanted to narrate the incident of Nanak at the Kaaba to him at that time but refrained from doing so. I feel this incident is symbolic of what became of Sikhism eventually. I think the subsequent Gurus missed the essence of Nanak's movement when they institutionalised the religion. My question to you is—do you think Guru Gobind's teaching was different from Nanak's?'

4

Guru Gobind Singh

My first impression of Guru Gobind Singh came from Gurdwara Janamasthan when I was there for the annual celebration of Guru Nanak's birthday. In front of the building was a huge banner with pictures of all ten Sikh Gurus. There was Guru Nanak on one side, wearing his saffron chola and raising his right hand in blessing. There was serenity in his eyes. At the other end of the spectrum was Guru Gobind Singh, a young, good-looking man, wearing a silk gown and several pearl necklaces. Whereas Nanak's head was covered with a simple cloth, Gobind was wearing a tiara adorned with beautiful jewels. An eagle (*baaz*) rested on his right hand and the quiver on his shoulder was full of arrows. The images of the other Gurus were placed in smaller sizes in-between these two.

In Sikh iconography, Guru Nanak and Guru Gobind Singh are arguably the two most prominent personalities. Traditionalists would argue that every Sikh Guru is equally significant and that would be true as far as theology and legend is concerned. But as far as the development of the Sikh religion is concerned, it is Guru Nanak and Guru Gobind Singh who have played the most important roles.

Whereas Nanak is considered to be the founder of the Sikh religion, Guru Gobind is seen as someone who completed Nanak's mission. Nanak discovered the path, which was then traversed by the other Sikh Gurus. It was Guru Gobind who led the Sikh community to its destination and gave it its current character. He codified the teachings of Nanak and founded the Khalsa. Sikhism at the time of Guru Gobind Singh emerged as an independent religion, separate from Islam and Hinduism. In the modern religious battles of the Indian subcontinent, it became the third force.

At the time of Nanak's death, his followers came from all kinds of religious traditions. Nothing illustrates the religious beliefs of Guru Nanak better than when Bhai Bala and Bhai Mardana, a Hindu and a Muslim respectively and both companions of Nanak, asked him what religion they should adopt to follow the religion of Guru Nanak. Nanak himself had been born into a Hindu household and was then educated in a Muslim milieu; however, he was neither a practising Muslim nor a Hindu. His entire life was a struggle to dilute the differences between these two religious communities. Everywhere he travelled, he offended both Hindus and Muslims by stating that there was no Hindu or Muslim. This statement did not mean that he believed in a third religious force. It was a rejection of any sort of identity that different groups used against each other to ferment hostility.

Answering his companions, Nanak replied that if one is a Muslim then one should be a good Muslim and if one is a Hindu then one should be a good Hindu.[10] This statement shows that Nanak believed in the universality of all religious traditions. He believed that any religion followed in its essence will lead one towards the Truth, a journey that Nanak himself traversed throughout his life.

Centuries later, Gandhi and Abdul Ghaffar Khan personified what had been stated by Nanak, when the former used Hinduism to lead his non-violent political movement, while the latter used Islam. These two proponents of religion were able to do this at a time when the political and cultural differences between Muslims and Hindus had been much accentuated, especially around the time of Partition. Using Hinduism, an iconographic religion, and Islam, an iconoclastic religion, both Gandhi and Ghaffar Khan were able to reach the same conclusion. Such results can only be achieved if one is able to appreciate religions beyond their

---

[10]Haribala Rani Kaur Vaid, *The Sikh Religion: An Introduction* (New Delhi: Star Publications, 2007), page 77

rituals and be able to feel the message of a religion in one's soul. Nanak was able to achieve that and hence that became his message.

Building upon Nanak's message that there is no Hinduism and Islam, Guru Gobind came to the conclusion that both Hinduism and Islam were flawed religious traditions as the true message of God had been tainted by the promoters of these religions. He believed that in both these religions the messengers had become more important than God, which is why a true devotee could never traverse the path of truth using either Islam or Hinduism.[11] This path, he said, could only be achieved by following the message of Guru Nanak and the subsequent Sikh Gurus, for they understood in its essence the message of Guru Nanak and hence, like Nanak, could pave the way towards Absolute Truth. He categorically stated that any follower of Nanak who refused to obey the commandments of the subsequent Gurus was not a Sikh.[12] This exclusivist approach followed by Guru Gobind Singh can be understood in the political context of the era he was living in.

Appointed as the leader of the Sikh community at a young age, Guru Gobind Singh's stint as Guru was beset by several problems after the assassination of his father Guru Tegh Bahadur, the previous Guru. The gravest threat came from his uncle Ram Rai, who was the disgruntled son of Guru Har Rai. When Ram Rai's younger brother Harkrishan was appointed the Guru instead of him, he revolted against his father and approached Emperor Aurangzeb, who was positively inclined towards him, for help. According to J. D. Cunningham's *A History of the Sikhs*, the machinations of Ram Rai played an important role in the execution of Guru Tegh Bahadur.[13] Ram Rai also had cordial relations with the various chiefs of Punjab, who surrounded Guru Gobind's abode in Anandpur. Thus, the hostility of the local Punjabi chiefs also threatened the young Guru.

---

[11]Surjit Singh Gandhi, *History of the Sikh Gurus Retold* (New Delhi: Atlantic Publishers & Dist, 2007), page 768

[12]Ibid., pages 774–775,

[13]Joseph Davey Cunningham and H. O. Garrett, *A History of the Sikhs, from the Origin of the Nation to the Battles of the Sutlej* (New Delhi: S. Chand, 1966), page 109

Guru Gobind Singh rose to power after the execution of his father by the Mughal Emperor Aurangzeb. This was perceived to be a religious martyrdom. The symbolism of martyrdom played a critical role in the development of Guru Gobind as a Sikh Guru and also that of the Sikh religion. Like Shiaism within the tradition of Islam, Sikhism too induced passion in its followers through the iconography of the sacrifice of the Gurus. Guru Tegh Bahadur was not the first Guru to be persecuted at the hands of the Mughals. Before him, Guru Hargobind had been incarcerated by Emperor Jahangir. Jahangir was also responsible for the execution of Guru Arjan. As the character of Nanak is now used in Sikhism as the founder of this religion, his encounter with the first Mughal Emperor Babur was also interpreted to mark the beginning of this antagonism between the Mughals and the Sikhs.

All incidents were stripped of their political contexts and presented as a fight between religions. As the successor of such a violent legacy, Guru Gobind was a passionate leader who successfully tapped the emotions of his followers and prepped them to become a political group ready to sacrifice themselves. For a community mired in violence it was no longer possible to remain as a diffuse group situated between the identities of Hinduism and Islam.

On the first of *Vaisakh*, 1699 (14 April 1699), while addressing his followers at Anandpur, a city that had been founded by his father, Guru Gobind Singh asked if there was anyone in the gathering who was willing to give his head for the Guru. One by one, five volunteers offered themselves. They were then taken behind a tent by the Guru and a few minutes later, the Guru emerged alone, with his sword smeared in blood. The impression that the Guru gave was that he had killed his followers, but in reality, it was a goat's blood. The five devotees who later became famous as the *Panj Pyare* or the five beloved, were safe behind the tents. The Guru had simply wanted to test the spirit of sacrifice in his community and he was happy. The Sikh community was now ready to become the Khalsa or the pure ones. Receiving instructions to observe the five Ks (*kangi, kesh, kirpan, kachcha* and *kada*) of Sikhism, the Sikh community became the Khalsa. The Sikh attire which now included a turban to hold the uncut hair (kesh), a sword (kirpan), a steel bangle (kada), short drawers (kachcha) and a comb (kangi) was to become the source of their separate identity.

This transition to Khalsa was not easy. There were several communities who believed in the teachings of Nanak and that of the other Gurus including Gobind Singh, but refused to abandon their former religious beliefs and take up the five Ks of the Khalsa. In Sikh records it is recorded that those communities that were further away from the centrality of the Guru at Anandpur were the most reluctant to take up the Khalsa. Tales of discrimination at the hands of the Khalsa against those who refused to follow this latest order of the Guru are also recorded. The Guru himself was not very tolerant of those who refused to take up the Khalsa. In this righteous battle between 'right' and 'wrong', between the Sikhs and the Mughals, the Guru had no space for dissenters.[14]

Guru Gobind Singh had become Guru at the age of nine in the year 1675. He was assassinated at the hands of Pathan horse traders in the year 1708. Sikh theology regards Gobind as the ninth incarnation of Guru Nanak himself. It is believed that the flame of the lamp of Nanak was passed from one Guru to the next and in this way the spirit of Nanak remained alive in all the subsequent Gurus. According to this logic, all followers of Nanak were also urged to become followers of the rest of the Gurus. In the Guru Granth Sahib, the poems of the rest of the Gurus are recorded, not in their own names but in that of Guru Nanak, in such a way that Arjan becomes the fifth Nanak while Gobind becomes the tenth Nanak. Despite such a clear link depicted between the Gurus, there are several devotees of Nanak who refused to join the Khalsa of Guru Gobind Singh. They continued calling themselves 'Sikh', a term that was derived by Nanak, but refused to be called Singhs, those who are baptised into the Khalsa of Guru Gobind Singh. There are thousands of such Sikhs living in Khyber Pakhtunkhwa, Punjab and Sindh in Pakistan, and they are referred to as Nanak Panthi Hindus. In their temples, along with pictures of Hindu deities, one also finds a picture of Guru Nanak.

For devoted Sikhs (those of the Khalsa), there is no contradiction

---

between the teachings of Guru Nanak and that of Guru Gobind. It is believed that Guru Gobind only took forward that which was initiated by Guru Nanak. However, even the most ardent of followers cannot deny the differences in the lifestyles of the two Gurus. Guru Nanak was a fakir or a jogi who spent his entire lifetime in a few clothes and travelled between different villages and cities singing his songs of peace. Guru Gobind Singh, on the other hand, lived like a sovereign. He lived in a regal tent which was adorned with beautiful carpets and furniture.[15] He dressed like a prince. He was in command of a standing army, whose weapons were procured through the offerings of devotees or through raids upon neighbouring villages. He also had a war drum, which at the time was the sole prerogative of a sovereign. He was referred to as Sacha Padshah, the True King, and his court was referred to as *Sacha Darbar*, the True Court. The chiefs of the neighbouring states viewed him more as a political contestant than as a religious personality. Guru Gobind regularly dabbled in the local politics of his region by throwing his weight behind particular chiefs in times of interstate rivalries.[16]

Guru Gobind Singh was particularly fond of warlike exercises. He wanted to instil discipline in his followers and therefore made war exercises an essential part of their routine. He urged his followers to offer weapons at the court of the Guru so they could be used in the army of the Khalsa.[17] The chiefs of the states surrounding Guru Gobind Singh followed these developments with some trepidation. He was also fond of hunting and spent a lot of his time hunting dangerous game. At heart Guru Gobind Singh was a warrior and it is for this reason that on the occasion of his birthday his devotees pay tribute to him by enacting scenes of war exercises.

To imagine Guru Gobind Singh purely as a warrior would be to undermine his personality. He was fond of literature and was adept in Persian, Arabic and Sanskrit. In his court, he is said to have invited poets,

---

[15]Gandhi, *History of the Sikh Gurus Retold*, page 698

[16]Cunningham's account of Guru Gobind Singh in *A History of the Sikhs*

[17]This was a practice that was started by Guru Hargobind but then reinforced by Guru Gobind Singh

writers and artists from all over.[18] He was well-versed in ancient Hindu texts and rewrote some of these tales with a focus on stories that told legends of deities defeating demons and restoring the moral balance of the world. Perhaps Guru Gobind saw his own destiny in these legends. In his writings, Guru Gobind also justified the rise of the Sodhi caste to become the Gurus of the Sikh community, replacing the Bedis.[19] Guru Nanak belonged to the Bedi caste. At his deathbed, he did not appoint his son as the next Guru but one of his favourite disciples, who became famous as Guru Angad. Guru Angad also followed the tradition of Nanak by bypassing his progeny and appointing a disciple. However, soon after, the appointment to the seat of Guru became a family affair, in which the Sodhi caste dominated. Using ancient history, Guru Gobind Singh explained how the Sodhis replaced the Bedis.

The Guru does so in his work called *Vichitr Natak* which forms a portion of the *Daswan Padshah ka Granth*.[20] In this, Guru Gobind Singh talks about how there was a descendant of the earlier rulers of India, called Sodhi Rai, whose descendants came to be known as Sodhis. Some of their descendants, who engaged in conflict but survived, went to Kashi to master the four Vedas and came to be known as Bedis.[21] Once, the Bedis were invited by the king of Madar Des which was ruled by the descendants of the Sodhis. Here, the Bedis recited the four Vedas. The King was so impressed by their recitation that he renounced the throne in their favour. The Bedis, in response, vowed they 'would return the compliment in Kaliyuga when their descendant Nanak would raise the Sodhis to a prime position in the world'.[22]

Along with the formation of the Khalsa, Guru Gobind Singh is also credited with completing the compilation of the living Guru, the Guru Granth Sahib. It is said that after the completion of the compilation the Guru himself bowed in front of the book and instructed his followers

[18]Cunningham, *A History of the Sikhs*, page 121–131

[19]Grewal, *Four Centuries of Sikh Tradition*, page 163

[20]Cunningham, *A History of the Sikhs*, page 114

[21]Ibid., page 163

[22]Ibid.

that after his death the living word of the Gurus compiled in the Granth would be the eternal Guru of the Khalsa. Through this, Guru Gobind ended the long line of Gurus.

Every time I come across a poster that contains the pictures of all the Sikh Gurus I cannot help but notice the evolution of the seat of Guru through generations. In all the pictures I have come across, Nanak and Gobind are always the most prominent ones with the size of their images bigger than that of the other Gurus. Going one by one through the pictures of each individual Guru, one cannot help but notice how the garb of subsequent Gurus changed. The simple clothes of Nanak and Angad slowly make way for the elaborate silks of Hargobind and Har Rai. The prince of princes is Guru Gobind Singh, at the end of the line, the ninth incarnation of Guru Nanak.

5
The Journey Begins

Nanak's eyes fell on the worn-out clothes of the carpenter. His shirt was tattered and patched with mismatched pieces of cloth. The turban on his head was soiled. He wore no shoes. Sweat glistened on his forehead. Nanak looked past him, into his house and saw that there was no window. The emptiness of his house stood out in the darkness that surrounded it. The carpenter was holding a hammer in his hand and was older than Nanak. His moustache was untrimmed, while stubble from the past several days sat like an unwelcome guest on his face. Nanak was delighted to find his man.

'We are travellers,' interjected Bhai Mardana, trying to break the awkward silence. 'Would it be possible for you to provide us with food and a place to stay for the night?'

The curiosity in the carpenter's eyes intensified. Without saying anything, he moved away from the door, allowing his guests to enter. He knew that he had neither food nor enough bedding for the three of them but he still couldn't help but let these holy men in.

Nanak and Mardana stepped into the darkness of the room. It took them a few minutes to be able to see clearly and when they saw that there was no furniture but a charpoy resting on one of the walls, a rolled up mattress next to it and a few clay utensils in a niche in the wall, there was no doubt in their minds that they had arrived at the poorest house at Saidpur.

While walking into this ancient city, both Nanak and Mardana were surprised to see the magnificent houses and havelis all around. These were unlike any they had ever seen. There were huge temples, their tall structures decorated with gold tridents rising from the middle of these structures. This was a busy city, with buyers and sellers haggling over prices. It was from here that trading goods spread into the other regions of the Punjab and went further east. In every shop, Nanak noticed the idols of Hindu gods. Laxmi, the goddess of fortune was the most popular, followed by Ganesh, the son of Lord Shiva. Throughout the negotiations, the traders kept referring to the gods and goddesses to make false promises about their profit margins and the quality of their material. In the evening, after closing their shops, most traders would visit their favourite temples to thank the gods for their blessings. In return for their favour the traders would donate exorbitant amounts of money to these temple complexes.

Saidpur was an ancient city. No one could date with any authority the origin of this city, but there were legends that the temples here had been built thousands of years ago, long before the birth of Islam. Over the years, these temples had been renovated and expanded. By the time Nanak and Mardana arrived, they had become huge complexes that included not only the shrine but also rooms for pilgrims and shops that had been leased out to traders. Cows and other animals were tied up in the stables of these temples and there was an army of servants employed to make sure that these Houses of God were well looked after.

There was always a long line of devotees waiting to be ushered into the temples. These comprised the gentry of Saidpur, the aristocrats and traders. Despite their remarkable material success, here at the temple, they were treated as ordinary citizens. If anyone broke the line, they were strongly rebuked by the assistants of the Brahmin pandits. Here, the Brahmin pandits were the bosses. Vast quantities of clothes, food and jewellery was offered at the temples, the majority of which was kept by the temple and distributed to its workers; the remaining was sold to make sure that the running cost of the temples was covered.

Outside each of these temples, Nanak and Mardana noticed an even larger line of naked and starving beggars. Devotees returning from the temples offered them some charity. There were a few guards outside each temple who made sure the naked and starving beggars did not enter the premises of the temple and tarnish its sanctity.

This was a Hindu-majority city with a few Muslim households. Most of the Hindu occupants here were traders, while the Muslims were aristocrats. It is for this reason that over the years Saidpur had emerged as one of the most important trading centres between the Chenab and the Ravi. After Delhi and Lahore, this was the most important stop for traders. Traders and travellers arriving from the West also made sure that they stopped at Saidpur, which had some of the tallest temples in the Punjab and also the most beautiful courtesans.

Walking through the streets of Saidpur and observing the religious practices of its people, Nanak realised that religion here was another commodity that was sold. The businessmen and traders who had amassed extraordinary profits after exploiting the farmers and labourers bought their piety from the threshold of these temples, while the Brahmins sold it. There were many mendicants, ascetics, fakirs and Sufis roaming around the streets, singing their religious songs. They too flocked around rich merchants every time they left their shops or exited the temples. In this city of business, Nanak knew that it would be almost impossible to find honesty. He knew that he, like these fake fakirs could flatter one of the rich merchants and get food and a place to sleep for the night, but that's not what they had left their home for. Nanak wanted to search for honesty in this dishonest world and it was for this reason that he decided to knock on the poorest house in Saidpur, where he knew that even if they didn't find lavish meals or comfortable bedding, they would at least find sincerity, humility, hospitality and honesty.

Nanak and Mardana seated themselves on a floor mat that the carpenter had spread on the floor for them. Nanak told him they were travellers in search of honesty, which had brought them to this city and his house.

'I used to be in charge of the food store at the court of the Diwan of Sultanpur before I realised that life in this world was a temporary state and therefore should not be wasted in amassing wealth, which is eventually of no use to the person. After having realised this, I decided to quit my job, take up this garb and travel the world in search of Truth,' said Nanak.

During the conversation, Nanak learnt that the name of the carpenter was Lalo. Lalo could not read or write but was eager for education. Often, as a child, he had wished that he had been born into the household of a rich man in one of the many havelis that stood tall in Saidpur, to be taught Persian and Arabic like the children of the aristocrats. He would stare at their carriages as they left their shiny houses and entered the houses of their rich teachers, in longing. Often as a child, he would make an excuse to his father who had started training him to be a carpenter and loiter outside the havelis of the rich teachers, hoping to catch the sound of a lesson that he could memorise. His father, either aware of his son's curiosity or out of sheer indifference, allowed Lalo to shirk work.

With age, Lalo's dreams of getting an education receded to the background. As he learned to make beautiful furniture out of plain wood, he also learned to shape the audacity of his dreams to settle in line with the realities of his life. He submitted to karma, so to say. Passing each day against the odds of poverty and all its proxies became his sole ambition.

In his lifetime Lalo had come across several dervish and jogis but never anyone like Nanak. Firstly, he had never had such a comprehensive encounter with any. They ignored him every time he walked around the streets of Saidpur. Songs and lectures would usually stop when Lalo was around, not because they didn't want him to hear it, but because he was invisible to them, cloaked as he was in poverty. They would respond with a smile when once or twice Lalo put in a coin or two into their begging bowls. That's all the interaction he ever got.

While Lalo sat there listening to Nanak's discourse about caste and the 'business' of religion, he tried figuring out Nanak's religious denomination. Usually by looking at the clothes of a dervish, one could identify his religious identity. Red was preferred by Hindu ascetics; while Muslims wore green. Muslims wore a skull cap while Hindu ascetics left their hair open. Nanak on the other hand, wore a long *choga* (cloak) just like the Muslim dervish but it wasn't green. Instead, it was red. There was a white belt around his waist similar to the dress of the fakirs, while there was a cap on his head, partially covered by a turban. He wore wooden sandals, something that was favoured by religious men of all denominations. Looking at his garb, Lalo could not figure out if the person standing in front of him was a Hindu or a Muslim.

It was actually a conscious effort by Nanak to dilute his religious identity, which is why he had adopted a garb that incorporated symbols from the clothes of all religious traditions. During his time at Sultanpur, Nanak had realised that it was these distinctions between different religious traditions, particularly Hinduism and Islam that produced such tension in society. At Sultanpur, his philosophy had caused much controversy.

He had been sent to Sultanpur by his father on the request of Bebe Nanaki and her husband; there he was able to secure the job of the storekeeper at the court of the Governor of Sultanpur, Daulat Lodhi Khan. Nanak's hard work and honesty had earned him respect in the eyes of the governor but there were other powerful nobles in the court who wanted to get rid of him. So when they found out about Nanak's unorthodox statement, 'There is no Hindu, no Muslim', they were quick to pounce on it and create all sorts of controversies. Initially, Nanak was able to ward off the blows but eventually these attacks became much more personal. A couple of times it was alleged that Nanak was stealing from the treasury of the governor, but when an audit was conducted, the accounts were shown to be in perfect order.

In the meantime, Nanak, having experienced travel and a professional life, also came of age, and his philosophy attained a greater stability and coherence. Soon after his arrival at Sultanpur he was joined by his best friend from Talwindi, Mardana, a Muslim *Mirasi* (a community of genealogists and bards) who had ignited within Nanak a passion for music. Initially, Nanak's and Mardana's friendship had caused a lot of anxiety to Nanak's family, who regarded Mardana as an untouchable Mirasi but given that the list of 'disappointments' from Nanak was long, this was a minor issue.

At Sultanpur, both Nanak and Mardana started a ritual together which was to become a daily feature for them for the rest of their lives and also for the Sikh community. Every night after work, Mardana would pick up his rubab, while Nanak would sing his poetry to the classical tunes that the Muslim bard played.

It was also in Sultanpur that Nanak became much more confident as a poet and started composing and reciting regularly. Initially, he wouldn't share his poems with anyone, but gradually on Mardana's insistence, who detected poetic genius in the young poet, Nanak began singing in public.

Nanak's popularity as a poet and spiritual guide spread through the streets of Sultanpur and to smaller villages and cities on the outskirts. Every night, the audience around Nanak and Mardana grew. His audience included both Hindus and Muslims. Nanak was becoming increasingly aware of his purpose in life.

On the one hand, his popularity was spreading, on the other hand, the Muslim nobles at the court of the Governor, who were already upset about Nanak's high status in court and his unorthodox religious views, started to plot against him. They thought of several schemes to get rid of Nanak but all of them failed because Daulat Lodhi Khan had immense respect for him.

However, as his audience grew, Nanak realised that nothing brought him more joy in life than this spiritual quest that Nanak and Mardana had begun through their spiritual songs. His interest in his work decreased and he soon came to the conclusion that it would be unfair to the governor to keep on continuing in this half-hearted manner. He decided to head back to Talwindi with his best friend, Mardana.

At Talwindi, Mehta Kalu was disappointed that his son had abandoned such a lucrative job. He could not understand his son's new-found passion for singing his religious songs in every corner of the world. Mehta Kalu wanted to scold him and forbid him from doing so but he was also aware of the fact that Nanak was no longer a boy but a fully grown man and such harsh methods would achieve nothing but alienation. So, a few days after his arrival at Talwindi, when Nanak expressed the desire to leave for his religious journey, Mehta Kalu said nothing.

Nanak would have liked his father to bless him on his new-found mission in life but he was also willing to accept his silence as long as he did not show vehement opposition. In this way, soon after their return from Sultanpur, both Nanak and Mardana left on another journey. They had no idea where they were going, when they were going to return or

what they would eat or drink. They were leaving from Talwindi with
nothing but a small bundle thrown over their shoulders.

In this situation, all Sulakhni and her two children could do was
stand at the threshold of their home watching Nanak and Mardana
walk away. Sulakhni wanted to run to her husband and beg him not to
abandon them, but she couldn't do that. Mehta Kalu and Mata Tripta
were standing next to her, crying quietly. Both Sri Chand and Lakshman
Das were unaware of the gravity of the situation. They were eager to go
back into the household and play with their toys but their mother had
forced them to say goodbye to their father. Reluctantly, they stood there
at the threshold of the door, watching their father leave while the rest of
the household cried quietly.

It was as if Sulakhni, Mata Tripta and Mehta Kalu wanted to keep
their tears hidden from each other. Even though none of them fully
supported what Nanak was doing, they all understood his passion and
free-spirited soul. They knew that this was a big step for Nanak and felt
that they should not make this auspicious day an inauspicious one by
their tears.

Both Nanak and Mardana did not know that they would not return
to a sedentary life for twenty-four years and that they would travel
thousands of kilometres, that too on foot. They had no idea that they
would become two of the most widely travelled people not only of their
era but even the modern era. They especially did not know that through
the course of their journey they would change the history of the world,
giving birth to a new religious movement that would eventually have
millions of followers. Had they known the gravity of their undertaking,
perhaps, they would never have set foot outside Talwindi. They were able
to achieve greatness only by remaining in the dark about their destiny.
Even at the time of their deaths, Nanak and Mardana did not know
what they had achieved.

As younger men, both Nanak and Mardana had wanted to visit
Saidpur, a city they had heard so much about. This was the city with
the grandest Hindu temples. The priests here were said to be the wisest.
The idols here were the most expensive. The prasad at these temples was
rumoured to be the sweetest. It is for this reason that Nanak first decided
to head towards Saidpur after leaving Talwindi.

'Is there anything to eat, Bhai Lalo?' Mardana asked, interrupting Nanak's speech. Nanak did not seem to mind the interruption and looked towards Lalo as if he too was asking for food. Lalo went to one corner of the house where he busied himself searching for something. After a little while Nanak realised that there wasn't really anything to eat in the house and Lalo was using the time to come up with a reasonable excuse.

'Why don't you serve us that dry roti on top of that cloth?' said Nanak, pointing to something near where Bhai Lalo was sitting.

'Please, Guruji. Don't embarrass me. I'll make you fresh roti with some *daal* if you could only allow me some time to look for the flour.'

'No, Bhai Lalo. I insist that you give us that dried-up roti. That is all we need.'

Without further arguments, Lalo served his guests two dried up rotis and instead of daal, gave them water. Both Mardana and Nanak soaked their roti in the water and seemed to relish the meal. After they were finished Lalo dared to ask what had been on his mind since both of them had shown up at his door unannounced.

'Guruji, there are several notables living here in Saidpur. You must have seen that haveli of Malik Bhago on the way.'

Nanak nodded. The four-storey haveli known as the Shahi Qilla at Saidpur was hard to miss. Torches had been lit from the middle of the city, leading into the haveli. Bearers had been dispatched with messages from the Hindu minister that all Brahmins and members of the high castes had been invited to the haveli to celebrate the wedding of Malik Bhago's son. Curious at the proceedings, Nanak had asked someone on the street about Malik Bhago. They had told him that he was a minister of the Rai of Saidpur. From the gossip on the street he had also learned that Malik Bhago was stealing from the treasury of the King. Initially, Nanak dismissed what he heard as hearsay but when he saw the haveli he realised the reason for the gossip. It was a magnificent structure, the largest in the city. There were several frescoes on the external walls of the haveli, while guards stood at all windows and doors. Hearing about the feast, Mardana had suggested that they should also attend it, since Nanak was from a high-caste, but Nanak refused to enter Malik Bhago's haveli.

'Today is the wedding of the son of Malik Bhago and he has opened his doors to all high-caste Hindus,' continued Lalo. 'Why didn't you go there, instead of coming to my humble abode? Please don't take offence at my question. I don't suggest this because your arrival has brought me any displeasure. I am elated that I have received the opportunity to serve you. There is no one in Saidpur besides me who can boast of having hosted an honest sadhu. I only say this because I don't understand why you would want to eat dried-up roti instead of a lavish feast.'

'These people think they can buy religion by feeding a few hungry Brahmins. What should I say about the character of these Brahmins? Feeding off the money of the corrupt, they bless them, promising that all their sins will be washed away. The food being served inside is not made out of bread or other eatables. It is made out of the blood of the hard-working people who toil under the blazing sun all day to receive a paltry sum, instead of their due share. I would never be able to live with myself if I too joined these Brahmins and sold my religion at the doorstep of Malik Bhago. Maybe I'll be able to explain myself better in poetry:

There are ignoble among the noblest
And pure among the despised
The former shall though avoid
And be the dust under the foot of the other.[23]

'Guruji, please excuse me once again for I do not understand your fancy verse. I am an uneducated person. Could you please explain what you said to me in a lay person's words?'

'Bhai Lalo, you say that Malik Bhago has opened his house today for members of high castes and that I should have gone there. I have told you already that I do not believe in the institution of caste. For me all castes and religions are the same. You, Mardana and I, we are all of the same caste. How then can I pretend to be a member of a high caste just to feed my stomach? Secondly, I ask you, prior to this has Malik Bhago ever opened his doors to the starving? He has done so today because it is the wedding of his child and he needs the prayers of the Brahmins. He exhibits no compassion but rather selfish motives. Tomorrow, when

---

[23]Dhillon, *The First Sikh Spiritual Master*, page 75

his purpose is achieved, he will once again shut those doors and all those Brahmins will be thrown out. My final objection is: why doesn't he also seek the blessings of the low castes? Does God not listen to their prayers? Had he opened his doors to everyone in the city, I swear by God, I would have gone to the feast. But because this was an exclusive gathering, I did not think myself worthy of going to such a place.'

All through the evening Lalo kept asking Nanak questions and Nanak kept answering them. He asked questions about the Hindu pantheon, about Muslim Sufis, about the places that Nanak had been to, about the occult science of magic, about the jungles of Punjab and the bandits residing in them. Nanak was the perfect teacher, replying patiently, satisfied at the curiosity of his young student.

At night, before sleeping, according to the tradition that had been established at Sultanpur, Mardana took out his rubab while Nanak started to sing his poetry. Lalo felt mesmerised at the husky voice of this Bhakti saint. As the world prepared to sleep, the sound of Nanak's music travelled to every street of the city, whispering in the ears of sleeping people. 'Wake up.' 'Follow the sound,' it said, and throngs of people headed towards Lalo's house to hear the songs of Guru Nanak and Bhai Mardana.

Nanak stayed at Saidpur for a few days and every night he would sing his poems. He became the topic of conversation in the bazaar of the city. Whereas there was a group of people who could not help praise the voice and the poems of the spiritual leader, there were others who were offended by his message. 'He says that he is neither a Hindu nor a Muslim,' said one of them. 'Who is he then? He says he is a man of God but what sort of religious man is he if he does not believe in any religion? I say he is a fraud who is only here to deceive people.'

'That could be true. He chooses to live in the house of that world-rejected Lalo to attract attention. He wanted to do something odd so that he could attract the attention of people.'

The bazaar gossip also reached the ears of the tyrannical Hindu minister. As is the case with those who attempt to buy off religion, Malik Bhago too was easily offended in matters of religion. 'Bring that infidel to me,' he said to his guards.

Nanak was brought to his court and asked about his whereabouts.

'You are a Kshatriya Hindu. Why then didn't you come to my feast?' asked Malik Bhago. 'Instead, why choose to eat at the house of a carpenter?'

'That's because your food is prepared out of the blood of your subjects while Bhai Lalo's food is cooked in the milk of honesty.'

ੴ

In the Janamsakhis that record Nanak's life story, the encounter between Nanak and Bhai Lalo is one of the most important tales. The Janamsakhis were compiled at least sixty-five years after Nanak's death, and were collected by people who were devotees. It is believed that several miracles and stories were inserted into the Janamsakhis to give Nanak a larger-than-life personality. For example, the story that mentions Nanak's interaction with the Hindu minister, Malik Bhago, says that when Nanak appeared before him, he took a piece of bread from Bhago's feast and when he squashed it, blood started to ooze out of it. When he did the same with Bhai Lalo's bread, milk came out. 'That's because his food has been earned with hard work while yours has been earned by exploiting the people,' Nanak is reported to have said.

I am not even sure if Nanak ever met with Malik Bhago. For me, the personality of Malik Bhago comes across as too tyrannical to allow Nanak to leave unharmed after he had insulted him in his haveli. Perhaps this version of the story, where Nanak and Malik Bhago meet, was an insertion from one of Nanak's devotees. According to the legend, after Nanak's interaction with Malik Bhago, the minister was so humbled that he not only let Nanak leave but also realised Nanak's spiritual depth.

It is ironic to hear of stories in which miracles are associated with Nanak. Immersing myself in his philosophy, I have come to the conclusion that Nanak was repulsed by the concept of making a larger-than-life figure out of a religious leader. He spoke vehemently against miracles being associated with them. To me, he comes across as a rationalist who learnt early on in his life that most of the myths associated with saints and shrines are exactly that, myths. It is recorded that once when one of the devotees of Nanak asked him if he could perform miracles, Nanak said the following:

Dwell then in flame uninjured,
Remain unharmed amid eternal ice,
Make blocks of stone thy food,
Spurn the solid earth before thee
With thy foot,
Weigh the heavens in a balance
Then ask thou that Nanak perform wonders.[24]

The beauty of Nanak's poetry lies in his sarcasm. *Babur Bani* was the first poem of Nanak that I read. It is believed that Nanak wrote this poem when the first Mughal Emperor from Kabul crossed the Indus and attacked India. As a reflection of the devastation caused by the conquering army, Nanak writes:

As the Word of the Forgiving Lord comes to me,
so do I express it, O Lalo.
Bringing the marriage party of sin,
Babar has invaded from Kabul,
demanding our land as his wedding gift, O Lalo.
Modesty and righteousness both have vanished,
and falsehood struts around like a leader, O Lalo.
The Qazis and the Brahmins have lost their roles,
and Satan now conducts the marriage rites, O Lalo.
The Muslim women read the Koran,
and in their misery, they call upon God, O Lalo.
The Hindu women of high social status,
and others of lowly status as well,
are put into the same category, O Lalo.
The wedding songs of murder are sung, O Nanak,
and blood is sprinkled instead of saffron, O Lalo.
Nanak sings the Glorious Praises of the Lord and Master in the city of
corpses,
and voices this account.

---

[24]Dhillon, *The First Sikh Spiritual Master*, page vii (Introduction)

The One who created, and attached the mortals to pleasures,
sits alone, and watches this.
The Lord and Master is True,
and True is His justice.
He issues His Commands according to His judgment.
The body-fabric will be torn apart into shreds,
and then India will remember these words.
Coming in seventy-eight (1521 C.E), they will depart in ninety-seven
(1540 C.E.),
And then another disciple of man will rise up.
Nanak speaks the Word of Truth;
He proclaims the Truth at this, the right time.[25]

The Janamsakhis also record a meeting between Nanak and Babur and that too at Saidpur. It is recorded that Nanak was there to meet his friend Lalo when Mughal forces took over the city and Nanak, along with the other citizens of the city was incarcerated. In jail, he was given the task of working on a stone grinder. However, using his miraculous powers, Nanak caused the grinder to move by itself. When the prison guards saw what was happening, they immediately informed Babur who sent for the holy man.

'Bless me, O man of God, so that I succeed in my endeavour of conquering India,' Babur is believed to have asked Guru Nanak. 'You have come to conquer my land and you have the audacity to ask for my blessings,' Nanak is believed to have replied.

It comes across as rather odd that if this incident actually took place, Babur failed to mention it in his diary, *Baburnama*, which otherwise records meticulously every detail of his encounters. It also comes as a surprise to me that Babur allowed a man who challenged his sovereignty in court to leave without harm. That was not the way of kings then. However, in the Sikh tradition, this interaction between Nanak and

---

[25]Guru Nanak, English translation by Dr Sant Singh Khalsa MD, Guru Granth Sahib, www.srigranth.org, pages 722–723 http://www.srigranth.org/servlet/gurbani.gurbani?Action=Page&Param=722&english=t&id=31080#l31080

Babur took on a historic meaning as it was interpreted as the beginning of the long history of hostility between the Mughal Emperors and the later Sikh Gurus.

ੴ

The cone-like spires of ancient Hindu temples rose proudly amidst the houses. There were several of them, looking beautiful, in contrast to the monolithic Muslim architecture that now dominates the city of Eminabad. From afar we could tell that we were entering a city of immense historical importance. However, the dusty roads and worn down houses highlighted the fact that the city had lost its economic prowess.

Once, it was an important trading centre on the Grand Trunk Road that connected with Lahore and then Delhi, further east. Now, it was only a shadow of its former glory. The highway had shifted southwards and a new city, not far from there—Gujranwala—has replaced Eminabad as an important trading centre.

Despite being abandoned in 1947, the temple still looked sturdy. The paint had worn off and a corrosive layer had developed over the structure but other than that there was no major harm done. These temples, like so many other non-Muslim shrines, had been taken over by migrants from the other side of the border following the creation of Pakistan. As I drove past these temples, descendants of those refugees stared back at me. I wondered if in 1992, after the destruction of the Babri mosque in India, these temples had also been attacked like other temples in the country. I searched for signs of attack but found none.

We stopped at a market and asked a group of old men where Bhai Lalo di Khoi was. They guided us into an alley. Parking the car, we headed towards it. There was a lock at the entrance of the gurdwara. This was the site of the house of Bhai Lalo. Far from being a worn down place that Nanak had visited, it was now in good shape. This is one of the most popular Sikh shrines in Pakistan and is visited by hundreds of devotees of Nanak. We stood there taking photographs of the locked gurdwara as people passed us by, wondering if we too were Sikh pilgrims.

When Babur took over the city of Saidpur, he renamed it Eminabad.

It is recorded that Babur's life was saved by a woman known as Emina shortly before he reached Saidpur. He had gone hungry for several days and this woman had offered him roasted grain to eat. The city was renamed Eminabad in her honour.

'This is how the gurdwara is at all times,' said Iqbal Qaiser. 'Locked.'

The keys were probably with members of the Sikh community, residing in the nearby Gurdwara Rori Sahib.

Iqbal Qaiser writes in his book *Historical Sikh Shrines of Pakistan* that there was a Muslim migrant family living inside the Gurdwara Bhai Lalo di Khoi. In 1989, a Sikh by the name of Sardar Surjit Singh Panesar bought the property of the shrine with money collected by the expat Sikh community and renovated the shrine. It was then opened for worship and now at the time of pilgrimage several Sikhs come to this shrine to pay tribute to the memory of Guru Nanak and Bhai Lalo.

Leading the way, Iqbal Qaiser walked around the narrow alleys of the city. I marvelled at how much of the historical architecture had still been preserved. Then without warning, he stopped in front of a small house. It was an ordinary structure with a small door and a few steps leading to it. From behind its walls a pole covered with a saffron cloth rose, hoisted on top of which was a Khalsa flag. 'This is Gurdwara Chakki Sahib,' said Iqbal Qaiser. This too was locked. 'This place was used as a prison at the time of Babur. Guru Nanak was imprisoned here and was forced to work on a stone grinder.'

'Iqbal Sahib, do you think it is possible that Nanak never met Babur?'

'Yes. Very much so. I think Nanak must have been an ordinary person. I don't mean that in terms of his poetic genius. That remains, but all these stories about him meeting a Muslim saint, giving him a lecture, interacting with Malik Bhago, with Babur, etc. seem like later constructions by his devotees. For them this was a way of paying respect to their saint.'

ੴ

The gatekeeper knew Iqbal Qaiser and let us in. There were empty grounds on both sides of the path, on one side of which a few police officials lazed on a charpoy. The doorway to the shrine was a splendid construction. A verse from the Guru Granth Sahib was carved on top of it with an artistic effect of bricks. There were also several other artistic touches given to the construction by the use of bricks, giving the building a surreal effect. 'Do you know who designed the building?' asked Iqbal Qaiser, as he photographed the various intricacies of the structure.

Without waiting for me to reply, he said, 'Bhai Ram Singh. Bhai Ram Singh was also the Principal of Mayo School of Arts in Lahore. He is the one who designed the Indian gallery in Buckingham Palace. Do you know that he too is from a family of carpenters? If you observe the architecture of the shrine, you will notice that he has created the effect of woodcutting from the use of bricks. This could also be an interesting comparison for your story,' he told me.

'How so?'

'Bhai Ram Singh is of the carpenter caste and Bhai Lalo was also a carpenter. You could make a connection between the two and this region.'

'Was Bhai Ram Singh a descendant of Bhai Lalo?'

'No, that's not what I meant. They shared the same caste. That's all. But since they shared the same caste if you go high up in their family trees I am sure you will be able to make a familial connection between the two of them.'

'So if this structure was built by Bhai Ram Singh, who has also remained the Principal of Mayo School of Art, then this cannot be a very old building?' I asked.

'It was constructed around 1922–23. Before that, it was a small shrine. Only this gateway was constructed by Bhai Ram Singh.'

Next to the gateway was a small courtyard around which there were several rooms. A few Pathan Sikh children were playing in the courtyard. 'Who are they?' I asked Iqbal Qaiser.

'They are the caretakers of this Sikh gurdwara. They have moved here from Nankana Sahib.'

We took our shoes off at the portal and walked towards the main shrine. It was an ordinary room which too was locked. We didn't bother asking for keys to see the room from inside.

'So this is where Nanak was made to toil on a grindstone?' I asked.

'No, this is the place where he was picked up by the guards of Babur. This was a small mound outside Eminabad where there were several pebbles, hence the name Rori Sahib. Nanak was sitting here with Bhai Mardana at the time of his arrest.'

As we drove away from the gurdwara, I pointed towards a ruined structure standing in the middle of the ground next to the Gurdwara Rori Sahib and asked Iqbal Qaiser, 'What is that?' There were herds of buffaloes wallowing around the structure in pools created by rain water.

'That was also a part of the gurdwara. It must have been the langar hall. There was no protective wall around the gurdwara. It was only raised a few years ago.'

'What was the condition of the shrine when you first came here?'

'Oh it was horrible. The structure was standing as it is but there was no protection. A bazaar for the sale of buffaloes used to be set up inside the premises of the gurdwara. It was after my book was published that this gurdwara came into the limelight. Now it is fully restored. There are security officials here at all times and Sikh pilgrims are entertained here every year.'

6
Southwards

Nanak and Mardana walked into the caravanserai, unaware of the danger lurking behind its walls. Little did they know that buried beneath the ground they were walking on, were hundreds of bodies, of travellers like them. Wary of travelling in the night on this lonesome road, travellers thought that they would be protected in the caravanserai. However, what they did not know was that this establishment was run by two thugs named Sajjan and Gajjan, who lured travellers in by warning them about the dangers in the wilderness and then murdered them to steal their possessions.

Perhaps the best disguise these two thugs had was the vantage point of their location. Their caravanserai was located on a popular route that connected important cities, including Lahore, Satgaraha, Deepalpur, Harrapa, Multan and Uch Sharif. There were hundreds of caravanserais located here, many of which were privately owned.

While choosing to stay in one of the caravanserais, travellers were aware of the fact that there would always be the chance of being robbed of their possessions, but this was more an issue for those establishments on abandoned routes, not in the prominent ones. To add to the disguise, both Sajjan and Gajjan, who happened to be uncle and nephew, were charming hosts and generous in their dealings. They offered lower rates than the other caravanserais and also offered free food. They would spend several hours chit-chatting with the travellers, while other owners treated their guests indifferently. For several years now Sajjan and Gajjan had been running this establishment, killing and robbing their guests.

On several occasions search parties had been sent by relatives of people who had become victims at the hands of the thugs but no clues were ever found. This was a long route, surrounded by forests, infested with wild animals and thugs. There was simply no way to ascertain the truth. No one ever doubted Sajjan and Gajjan anyway. Thugs were not likely to run caravanserais. They were thought to be living as bandits in the jungle.

Usually, Nanak would never opt to stay in a caravanserai. He had not embarked on this spiritual pilgrimage to stay in the comforts of a caravanserai. This journey of his was to search for Truth. He wanted to see the world in all its splendour—all its trees, animals, insects, roads, people, rituals and religions. During his stays at Talwindi and Sultanpur, he had realised that for generations his family had been Hindus because they were born into Hindu households. Similarly, a Muslim becomes a Muslim not because of any inherent truth that he discovers but only because he is born into a Muslim household. How then can a Hindu or a Muslim say that Hinduism or Islam is the only Truth? There has to be something more out there was his feeling. He wanted to see if there was any Absolute Truth he could locate in the world.

Nanak knew that in order to discover the world one has to spend one's time in the open, which is why he preferred sleeping under the shade of huge trees as opposed to caravanserais. He knew that in such facilities he would end up encountering the problems and discussions that he had left behind in Talwindi and Sultanpur. That was also the reason he never looked for hospitality in cities or villages. He knew that just because of their garb, people would regard them as holy men and shower all sorts of gifts on them. This would weaken their resolve to find the Truth.

Mardana, on the other hand, was not as determined as Nanak. He was willing to trade life on the road for the occasional comfort of a night at a caravanserai or in the house of some villager. It was not that travel bothered him; he had spent his entire childhood in transit. Belonging to a Mirasi background, who were the keepers of tradition, Mardana, along with his clan, often travelled from one city to another, singing songs of the bravery of the local chieftains to their descendants. The current landlords would shower companies of Mirasis with gifts for memorising and spreading the stories of the deeds of their forefathers. Mardana also knew by heart several folk stories of Hindu deities and Muslim saints that he would sing during different festivals of Punjab.

Unlike Nanak, Mardana was not on a quest for the Truth. He was content with his life. However, when he first met Nanak at Talwindi, when both of them were young boys, he was moved by Nanak's simplicity. Nanak was inquisitive, as well as a good listener. He would ask questions about the various local chieftains, about whom Mardana used to sing and also about Hindu deities and Muslim saints. He would then ask questions about Mardana's travels, about the different villages and cities, the different tribes and castes, the various temples and shrines and diverse religious practices.

While interacting with Nanak, Mardana realised that Nanak was completely unaware of his caste and prestige in society. He spoke with Mardana as if he were an equal and not a lowly Mirasi. He would express his fascination for the knowledge that Mardana had, a knowledge that Mardana did not think was very valuable. Mardana, like others of the society of his time, had grown up believing that knowledge was what Hindu Brahmins possessed in Sanskrit or Muslim Maulvis in Arabic. Nanak made him realise that the knowledge that Mardana had was as valuable as any other and that it didn't matter if this knowledge was available in Punjabi.

Through his innocent questions and simple observations that captured the hypocrisy of society, Nanak had lit a lamp within Mardana's soul and without even being aware of it, Mardana had become Nanak's devotee. Mardana was a proud Mirasi but whenever he was in the company of high-caste people he would adopt a subservient manner. That was the way of life he had been taught. He had also welcomed Nanak into his house with that assumption, but Nanak challenged the concept and taught him to value himself no matter what.

'You are a proud race,' Nanak would say to him. 'All these landlords who regard you as a lowly Mirasi would be nothing if you refused to record their deeds.'

Nanak was highly impressed by the musical skills of his friend. He would sit for hours with him at Talwindi learning the basics of music. For Mardana, music was a way of worship. However, lurking at the back of his mind was the idea that music was un-Islamic, a criticism that came from the more puritanical sects of Islam. These were a minority but they had a powerful voice. For this reason, Mardana, while taking pride in his skill, was also apologetic about his talent. Nanak assured him that his talent was worth more than the skill of a Mullah in leading prayers.

Once Nanak went to Sultanpur for work, Mardana followed him, abandoning his previous lifestyle. Mardana knew that he could not live without the friend who had shown him a new way of living. Hence when Nanak expressed his desire to leave on a long journey, Mardana knew that he had no other option but to follow him. He had become aware of Nanak's importance in his life.

What Mardana had not realised while preparing to leave with Nanak was that travelling with his mentor would be so tough. Many days went by without food and many nights without shelter. They had been swept away in the rain, roasted in the sun, attacked by mosquitoes and threatened by wild animals. Whereas such incidents had only strengthened Nanak's resolve, Mardana, on many occasions, regretted his decision to accompany him. And then when the untoward situation passed and they pressed forward once again, he would forget all about his lapses in commitment.

While walking on the road, the dust rising from their feet, Mardana saw a small light on top of a structure and asked Nanak if they could stay there. They had been walking continuously ever since their departure from Saidpur for an entire month, only resting at night to sleep. This was only the beginning of their journey which was why it was also the toughest part. Their bodies were still not used to the demands of the road. For years, their bodies had been spoilt by the luxuries of households, of sisters and mothers and then wives looking after all their needs; but now for the first time, they were on their own. Calluses appeared under their feet and they had suffered many scratches after rubbing against thorny bushes.

They were heading towards the historic city of Multan. Nanak wanted to visit this holy city in the southern region of Punjab before heading east towards Bengal. At that time Multan was one of the biggest cities of Punjab and was known for the religious shrines of Muslim saints, and Jain and Hindu temples. It was a sacred space for people of all religious denominations. The temple of Prahlad Bhagat was one of the most important Hindu temples there, while the shrine of Bahauddin Zakariya was one of the most popular Muslim shrines located beside the temple. Nanak was particularly fascinated by this city, because to him it signified the religious syncretism that he yearned for. Mecca was a sacred city only for Muslims, while Benaras was sacred to the Hindus; Multan was revered by all. He thought that perhaps the answers he was looking for would be found there. Later, when he visited Multan, he was disappointed to see that the religious syncretism he had imagined was non-existent. The Hindus were assured of their superiority, while the Muslims were assured of theirs.

After a month of walking, Nanak too was exhausted and would have appreciated the luxuries afforded at the caravanserai but when Mardana recommended that they go and stay there, he as expected, refused. 'Let's sleep under this tree instead,' he said, pointing towards an ancient banyan tree. They were near the village of Makhdoom Pur Pahuran and the caravanserai was in front of them. The nearest city of Tulamba, about midway between Lahore and Multan, was still a little further away.

'If you refuse to listen to me then I will refuse to accompany you any further,' said Mardana. Even though Mardana regarded Nanak as his mentor and Guru, there was a cordial relationship between them which was not constrained by formalities. Mardana could sometimes blackmail his friend into doing things he initially refused to do. Hence, due to Mardana's persistence, Nanak and Mardana entered the caravanserai of Sajjan and Gajjan.

Sajjan and Gajjan were disappointed to see their latest guests. They were used to entertaining rich merchants and royal dignitaries, who carried along with them a lot of wealth. Jogis and religious mendicants usually stayed away from such establishments and they liked it that way.

However, they did not allow their disappointment to reflect on their expressions. They welcomed Nanak and Mardana and after serving them a warm meal, showed them to their room. There were several other guests staying at the caravanserai and a lot of money was waiting to be looted. Honest hospitality in this case would do them no harm. They also thought that this act of kindness towards the holy men would purge them of some of their sins.

At night when everyone had retired to their rooms, the two thugs discussed their latest guests. 'Should we let them live or kill them?' asked Sajjan, the uncle.

'What good would come out of killing these two fakirs? I doubt they have anything we could use. Besides, I don't think they will stay here for a long time. They will leave in a day or two,' replied Gajjan.

'Gajjan, you are still a young man, which is why you are impressionable. You do not know yet the ways of these holy men. Afraid of being looted on the way, a lot of rich merchants now disguise themselves as fakirs and mendicants, so they can fool people like us. I'm sure they are rich merchants from Lahore. They are dressed up in this manner just to save the cost of hiring guards.'

'But if they are merchants, where is their baggage? They came empty-handed.'

'I am sure they have hidden it in the jungle outside, next to the graveyard.'

'I don't know, Uncle. I am sure you are judging them wrong. They look like innocent people to me. I am willing to concede to your argument and will also help you kill them, but I am afraid of the wrath of holy men. Don't you know that they know powerful spells? What if they are truly men of God? God would never forgive us for their murder.'

'Stop being stupid, Gajjan. Don't you know this is the Kaliyuga? There are no holy men left in the world. All of them are deceivers. They have made a business out of religion.'

Elated by Nanak's acceptance of his request, Mardana was once again in a jolly mood. He tried striking up a conversation with Nanak but Nanak was unresponsive. Mardana thought that it was perhaps due to his insistence on staying at this caravanserai against Nanak's will. He started to regret his decision but it was too late. He picked up his rubab from one corner of the room and asked Nanak to sing along. Nanak was always happy when he sang. This is what he sang:

Bronze is bright and shiny, but when it is rubbed, its blackness appears.
Washing it, its impurity is not removed, even if it is washed a hundred times.
They alone are my friends, who travel along with me;
And in that place, where the accounts are called for, they appear standing
with me.[26]

Nanak stopped singing after a little while but Mardana continued playing the rubab. Nanak did not look tired anymore. It was as if his words had taken away all his tiredness. Mardana had no doubt that these words were directed against him. He felt ashamed of his blackmailing. Silent tears rolled down his cheeks as he played his instrument, trying to hide his emotions in the sound of the music.

Sajjan and Gajjan had now approached Nanak and Mardana's room. It had been decided that they would torture these men, ask them where they had hidden their goods and then kill them. Outside the room they heard the sound of this song being sung.

Nanak continued after a little while:

There are houses, mansions and tall buildings, painted on all sides;
But they are empty within, and they crumble like useless ruins.
The herons in their white feathers dwell in the sacred shrines of pilgrimage.
They tear apart and eat the living beings, and so they are not called white.
My body is like the simmal tree; seeing me, other people are fooled.
Its fruits are useless—just like the qualities of my body.
The blind man is carrying such a heavy load, and his journey through the
mountains is so long.
My eyes can see, but I cannot find the way. How can I climb up and cross
over the mountain?
What good does it do to serve, and be good, and be clever?
O Nanak, contemplate the Naam, the Name of the Lord, and you shall
be released from bondage.[27]

---

[26]Guru Nanak, English translation by Dr Sant Singh Khalsa MD, Guru Granth Sahib, www.srigranth.org, page 729 http://www.srigranth.org/servlet/gurbani. gurbani?Action=Page&Param=729&english=t&id=31320#l31320

[27]Ibid.

Hearing Nanak's words, Sajjan felt a surge through his body. He felt as if Nanak was singing these words for him, as if he knew about their plan. 'The herons in their white feathers dwell in the sacred shrines of pilgrimage. They tear apart and eat the living beings, and so they are not called white.... My body is like the simmal tree; seeing me, other people are fooled.'

He realised that Gajjan was right. These men were indeed men of God and it was through divine knowledge that Nanak had come to know of their intentions. Despite possessing these insights, why did Nanak display so much humility, Sajjan wondered to himself.

Gajjan was unaware of the storm brewing in his uncle's mind. The music fell on his ears but he wasn't listening. He had forced his mind to remove any doubts about the veracity of these holy men and was now convincing himself that they were indeed deceivers and hence it was alright if they were killed.

When Sajjan opened the door of Nanak's room and stepped inside, Gajjan was preparing to attack Mardana. However, before he could do that, Sajjan bent down at Nanak's feet and started to cry. Gajjan was as shocked as Nanak and Mardana. Nanak put his hand on top of Sajjan's head and allowed him to cry his heart out. The music had stopped playing.

When Sajjan was done crying he told Nanak about their plan. He also told him about all the murders that they had committed by luring travellers with their hospitality. Nanak listened patiently, shocked at the confession of the thugs, but he did not express any displeasure with his facial expressions. When Sajjan was done confessing, Nanak told him that since he had now realised the true path he should no longer worry. He suggested that they should convert their house into a House of God where people from all creeds, religions and sects would be welcome and provided with food and shelter. The next day, Nanak and Mardana left their new followers, and headed towards Multan; while Sajjan and Gajjan converted their caravanserai into a House of God as Nanak had suggested. This was to become the first Gurdwara of the Sikh religion.

It was the second day of Eid. I woke up at five, after resting for only three hours with a terrible flu and a bad headache. I contemplated calling up Iqbal Qaiser and postponing the trip. I knew that he would be more than delighted to cancel. He had returned to Lahore a day before Eid after having completed an intensive tour of interior Sindh and Karachi. He had been gone for a month. He would have liked to spend the three days of Eid with his family while recovering from his exertions. He is almost sixty and his health is not what it used to be.

Despite his physical tiredness, Iqbal Qaiser readily agreed to accompany me to Tulamba. This would have been my first visit to the shrine of Guru Nanak there, but Iqbal Qaiser had explored the shrine and its vicinity about a decade ago while researching his book.

Often, Iqbal Qaiser's commitment towards me and my research is humbling. Not only is Iqbal Qaiser always willing to travel with me, he is also more than willing to share all his research with me, even if it is unpublished. This is very different from the erudite scholars of famous universities. I have learned through personal experience that scholars guard their unpublished research with their lives and hardly any professor makes an effort to guide a student through a difficult period.

Iqbal Qaiser is different from any such scholar. With only a matriculation degree as his formal education he is more than willing to help any student who approaches him. Most of the time, he also agrees to accompany an unknown student to a historical site if he or she expresses the desire. Many times I have called him only to find that he was on a trip with some professor or student whom he had just met and was helping with their research.

Only because he agreed to help me initially as a student and travel with me when the need emerged have I been able to complete many of my projects. I now try to adopt the same attitude that I have learned from my mentor and Guru. I try to readily help any new researcher or writer because I am well aware of the fact that I am what I am because someone agreed to help me.

During our initial travels, Iqbal Qaiser insisted that I speak to him

in Punjabi. When I explained to him that despite being born into a
Punjabi household I could not speak my mother tongue he took up the
task of teaching me Punjabi and now I have a working understanding
of the language.

In the education system that is prevalent in Pakistani Punjab, Punjabi
is looked down upon. It is considered to be a language of the boorish and
the uneducated. As a child, my elite private school had a strict policy that
any student found speaking in Punjabi, even in the playground, would be
fined. Only English was to be spoken or at worst, Urdu. Coming of age in
such an environment, the educated elite of Punjab ends up disowning, in
fact, ridiculing anything Punjabi, which includes the poetry of Baba Farid,
Guru Nanak, Shah Hussain, Waris Shah and Bulleh Shah. Whereas the
educated elite can quote verses from Shakespeare and T. S. Eliot, they
are completely unaware of their local poets.

One of the reasons I was blown away by Iqbal Qaiser and became
his student was that he introduced me to my own culture. While
travelling with him I learned to uncover the beauty of localities through
their history and heritage, localities I had otherwise dismissed as being
congested and polluted. I learnt for the first time that I could even learn
from a person who had never been to school and could only speak in
Punjabi. Once while sitting at home, my 'uneducated' guard was able to
recite to me the complete *Saif-ul-Maluk* of Mian Muhammad Baksh
whereas my 'educated' friends didn't even know who Mian Muhammad
Baksh was. The English equivalent of reciting the entire Saif-ul-Maluk
would be recalling an entire act of Shakespeare's *Hamlet*.

Ignoring the warnings of my body I lifted myself off the bed and
prepared to head south to Tulamba. It was a journey of about three hours.
Just a little ahead of the city of Tulamba we took a worn out road to head
towards the village of Makhdoom Pur Pahuran where the Gurdwara of
Nanak was situated.

The gurdwara was located in a school and there was a giant lock
on the main gate, this being a public holiday. On top of the door was a
banner describing the new policy of the Punjab government to improve
the education system in public schools. I read quickly through the rhetoric
to see if there was any contact information given for the caretaker of

the school. Next to the wall of the school was a huge playground where children from the village were playing cricket. None of them knew where we could find the guard.

There was a single lane road with several potholes running next to the school. 'This was the old Multan road,' Iqbal Qaiser told me. The new road, now a splendid highway, is about twenty kilometres from here.

'There is another serai here which is said to have been built by Sher Shah Suri. Do you know that when Humayun was chased out of India by Sher Shah, his retinue passed through this road? You can find the reference for that in *Humayunnama*.'

Having travelled more than three hundred kilometres there was no way I was going back without seeing the gurdwara from the inside. I entertained the thought of scaling the wall and jumping down, for a little while, but decided against it after looking at the height of the walls.

Iqbal Qaiser walked over to a man working in the fields next to the school. He came back with the address of the guard of the school. We drove over to his house to find that he was not home but his son was. His son walked us to the house where his father was working as a mason. Iqbal Qaiser introduced himself to the guard, whose name was Awais, and told him about his prior visit to the shrine. There was recognition and the two of them shared stories from the last visit, which had been in 1994.

Awais opened the door and led us into the school. There were models of two nuclear rockets in front of us—Ghori and Abdali, symbols of Pakistani nationalism. Behind them was the gurdwara, now converted into an office for the Principal. On the external wall of his office there were badly painted pictures of Jinnah and Allama Iqbal, while around them were Quranic verses.

It seemed as if the entire purpose of education was to instil love for one's religion and nation here. A new boundary wall had been constructed, covering the gurdwara, on which the ninety-nine names of Allah were written. On another wall, the names and deeds of 'Muslim scientists' were written as if there were no other scientists worthy of mention.

Various studies have been carried out on the biased nature of the Pakistani education system and the religious puritanism that it promotes through its curriculum. The entire school curriculum of Pakistan Studies, which is a compulsory subject till university, has been designed in such a way as to instil in the minds of young students the separateness of Hindus from Muslims and hence, justify the creation of Pakistan. There is no denying the fact that patriotism plays an important role in the education system of any country; but in Pakistan, nationalism is premised on hatred towards Hindus, which makes it dangerous. The Pakistan Project is a product of the compartmentalisation of religious identity.

Every day in this school, Muslim students are taught that their religion is the best religion in the world and that Islam brought light into this land of darkness, which was earlier dominated by Hindus. They are taught that Hindus and Muslims detested each other from the very beginning, particularly the Hindus; hence the creation of this country was essential. All traces of the Hindu past are omitted from the curriculum. Students from such government schools emerge more radicalised and susceptible to Islamic militancy than from your neighbourhood madrassas. I wondered about the contrast between Nanak's teachings and the lessons that were taught here. It is here, sitting within Nanak's memory that these students are taught to hate Nanak, a non-Muslim.

All traces of the gurdwara had been whitewashed within the principal's office. There were pictures of former principals and pictures of sacred Muslim places. There was a portrait of Jinnah behind the Principal's desk, which was placed right at the spot where once the Thara Sahib must have been kept.

'You have done a great job with the renovation of the building,' said Iqbal Qaiser to the guard. He was lying. I knew he was not pleased with the work, but he did not want to respond with derision to the hospitality shown to us.

After our short tour of the school, I went and sat with a group of men who were sitting on one side of the school, while Iqbal Qaiser took photographs. Most of them were workers at the school. 'There used to be a pool there, next to the building,' said one of them, pointing towards a vacant plot of land. It had been converted into a field. 'You can read the history of the school on that wall,' said another one, when I asked them how old this school was. I was told that hardly any Sikh ever comes here.

Before leaving, I stopped in front of the wall that recorded the history of the school. It was noted that the school began as a primary school in the latter half of the nineteenth century. There was no mention of the gurdwara. It was as if the school had been here in this building since its inception. Like the omission of Hinduism and the names of Hindu kings and queens from Pakistani history, the story of this gurdwara had also been erased.

'The school was somewhere else earlier,' Awais told me, as we headed back to his home. 'The school was shifted here during the Ayub era, after the Department of Auqaf was created.'

'What happened to all the land that was once attached to this gurdwara?' I asked.

'It was snatched by the land mafia. Now we only have a small tract in front of the building.'

'There used to be a serai here, outside of the city,' asked Iqbal Qaiser.

'Yes,' replied Awais. 'But it doesn't exist anymore. It has been converted into a primary school for girls.'

We dropped Awais and drove to the outskirts of the city, observing the buildings around us carefully to locate the lost serai. Right at the edge of the city, we came across the school. There were no signs of the older building. Next to it was an ancient graveyard.

7
Guru Tegh Bahadur

The decapitated head of the Guru hung at the Chandni Chowk of Delhi. It was the order of Emperor Aurangzeb that no one should touch the body of the Guru. It was on the Emperor's orders that the Guru had been beheaded. The Sikhs of Delhi looked in fear at the body of their temporal and spiritual leader. Then one day a dust storm gripped the city. Everything turned red and it was impossible to see anything. It was as if the curse of God had fallen upon the people of the city. When the dust storm receded, to everyone's amazement, the body and head of the Guru had disappeared.

Taking advantage of the situation, an untouchable Hindu, Jaita, had recovered the body from the chowk and presented it to Guru Gobind Singh at Anandpur, who then cremated the body as per prescribed rites. Jaita was given the title of the true son of the Guru, by the new Guru.

According to Sikh tradition, Guru Tegh Bahadur sacrificed his life for Kashmiri Pandits who had approached the Guru at Anandpur and requested him to intercede on their behalf with the Emperor. The Emperor had recently implemented the *jaziya* tax (per capita yearly tax historically levied by Islamic states on certain non-Muslim subjects residing in Muslim lands under Islamic law) on the non-Muslims of Kashmir, which had put immense stress on the Pandit community there. The Brahmins had arrived at the court of Tegh Bahadur to ask for his help. Sikh tradition points out that it was actually the young Gobind

Singh who had urged his father to come to the aid of the Pandits. 'None would be worthier than yourself, father, for such a noble act,'[28] Gobind is reported to have said.

At Delhi, when the Guru introduced himself as the Guru of the Sikh community, the Mughal officials mocked him and challenged him by saying that if he was a Guru then he should perform a miracle. Guru Tegh Bahadur wrote a magic spell on a piece of paper and attaching that to a string tied it around his neck. He then challenged the Mughal authorities saying that as long as this spell was tied around his neck, his head could not be separated from his body. Taking up the challenge, the Emperor ordered the beheading of the Guru. When the blade of the executioner cut through his neck, his head separated from his body and the Guru died. The Emperor ordered one of his officials to show him the piece of paper around his neck. It read, 'He gave his head, not his secret.'[29] The Sikhs believe that the Guru had performed a miracle while dying.

The assassination of Guru Tegh Bahadur was the second martyrdom in Sikh history. Before him his grandfather Guru Arjan had been martyred on the orders of the Mughal Emperor Jahangir. Aurangzeb was the grandson of Jahangir and Jahangir was the great grandson of Emperor Babur who had incarcerated Guru Nanak. In this long history of Mughal-Sikh conflict, Guru Tegh Bahadur was the latest victim.

The Sikhs believe that Guru Tegh Bahadur sacrificed his life for the right cause. He had decided to stand up for the protection of a persecuted community and was punished for it. Years later, when Guru Gobind Singh founded the Khalsa, he ordered his followers to keep a kirpan with them at all times for self-defence and also for the protection of the persecuted. This became a religious duty after Guru Tegh Bahadur showed the way. In Sikh history, Aurangzeb is portrayed as a bigoted Muslim who wanted to implement *Shariah* (Islamic law) all over the Indian subcontinent. This simplistic view of history assigns the role of

---

[28]Mohindar Pal Kohli, *Guru Tegh Bahadur: Testimony of Conscience* (New Delhi: Sahitya Akademi, 1992), page 1

[29]Sabyasachi Bhattacharya (ed.), *Approaches to History: Essays in Indian Historiography* (New Delhi: Primus Books, 2011), page 274

oppressor and oppressed to Aurangzeb and Tegh Bahadur respectively. The reality was a little more complicated.

Guru Tegh Bahadur was appointed as the Guru of the Sikh community in the year 1664 after the death of the child Guru Harkrishan. Tegh Bahadur was the son of the warrior Guru Hargobind and had been bypassed for the Guruship earlier. His oldest brother, Baba Gurditta, was to become Guru after Hargobind, but he passed away during the Guru's lifetime and so before his death, Hargobind appointed Har Rai, the younger son of Baba Gurditta to succeed him. Guru Tegh Bahadur accepted the ascension of Guru Har Rai to the highest seat of Sikh power and retreated to Bakala in Bari Doab, where he lived for twenty years. Here he spent his time in seclusion and meditation.

The years spent in political isolation must have played an important role in the development of Guru Tegh Bahadur's personality. It is for this reason that even after he was appointed the Guru by a strange turn of events, he remained of a deeply spiritual nature. His poetry, which is included in the Guru Granth Sahib, focuses particularly on the nature of divinity, the role of the Guru, the triviality of the world, the liberation of the human soul and detachment from the world.[30] A lot of the themes that Tegh Bahadur discusses in his poetry are those he picked up from the poetry of Nanak. Like Nanak, he too discouraged extreme ascetic practices. After a long hiatus in the poetic tradition, he was the first Guru since Guru Arjan to compose hymns.

While Guru Tegh Bahadur was reflecting on the nature of divinity and the purpose of the human soul, the politics of the Sikh community was in turmoil. Guru Har Rai's ascension was challenged by his elder brother, Dhir Mal, causing a split within the Sikh community. Another challenge came from Harji, the grandson of Prithi Chand, who was the older brother of Guru Arjan, who like Dhir Mal had refused to acknowledge the leadership of the young Guru and continued promoting his own sect. There was no doubt that the feudalization of the institution of Gurudom had been completed with various parties vying for the monetary and political rewards it brought.

---

[30]Grewal, *Four Centuries of Sikh Tradition*, pages144–146

This was the time when the Mughal princes too were fighting a battle of succession amongst each other after sidelining the ailing Shahjahan. In this civil war, Guru Har Rai decided to side with Prince Dara Shikoh,[31] who was eventually defeated and killed by his younger brother, Aurangzeb, the future Emperor. It is to be noted here that Guru Har Rai had kept the contingents that were maintained by Guru Hargobind after the assassination of his father, which he planned to use in aid of the elder prince.

After Aurangzeb established himself on the throne in Delhi, he asked Guru Har Rai to present himself and explain his political position during the civil war. Guru Har Rai sent his elder son, Ram Rai, who not only removed all doubts about the loyalty of the Guru from the mind of the Emperor but also, according to Sikh tradition, reinterpreted some of Nanak's poetry to suit the religious inclination of the Emperor.[32] Disappointed at the conduct of his son, Guru Har Rai bypassed his son when it was time to appoint the next Guru and bestowed the title of Guru upon his younger son, Harkrishan, who was six years old at the time.

Ram Rai rebelled against his father's decision and used his cordial relationship with the Emperor to get him to intercede on his behalf. In order to resolve this issue within the Sikh community, Emperor Aurangzeb summoned Guru Harkrishan to Delhi, but the child Guru died of chickenpox before he could appear at court. Before his death, he passed on the office of Guru to his great uncle, Tegh Bahadur, who was then living in Makhowal.

Guru Tegh Bahadur seized this opportunity with a vengeance. He undertook a mission of intense travel towards the east where he established connections with the Sikh *Sangat* (community). He also wrote *hukamnamas* (orders) to the sangat in Punjab and in the East. By giving powers to the local Sikh leaders there, he assured himself of their loyalty. He also established cordial relations with local leaders like Raja

---

[31]Cunningham, *A History of the Sikhs*, page 107

[32]Hardip Singh Syan, *Sikh Militancy in the Seventeenth Century: Religious Violence in Mughal and Early Modern India* (London: I.B. Tauris, 2013), page 127

Ram Singh and Nawab Saif Khan[33] to strengthen his position. It seems that the newly appointed Guru was aware of the precarious condition his office was in, due to the connivance of Harji and Dhirmal, and knew that he needed to have better relations with the Sikh sangats of different regions and also with the local chiefs.

Joseph Davey Cunningham, the author of *A History of the Sikhs, from the Origin of the Nation to the Battle of the Sutlej*, writes the following about the political manoeuvrings of Guru Tegh Bahadur:

> Tegh Bahadur followed the example of his father with unequal footsteps, and that, choosing for his haunts the wastes between Hansi and the Sutlej, he subsisted himself and his disciples by plunder, in a way, indeed, that rendered him not unpopular with the peasantry. He is further credibly represented to have leagued with a Muhammadan zealot, named Adam Hafiz, and to have levied contributions upon rich Hindus, while his confederate did the same upon wealthy Musalmans. They gave ready asylum to all fugitives, and their power interfered with the prosperity of the country; the imperial troops marched against them, and they were at last defeated and made prisoners. The Muhammadan saint was banished, but Aurangzeb determined that the Sikh should be put to death.[34]

Cunningham points out that this was not the first time that the Guru had been summoned to Delhi. Right at the beginning of his reign, Aurangzeb had asked Tegh Bahadur to present himself at court as a 'pretender to power and as a disturber of peace'.[35] He was saved by the intercession of the Chief of Jaipur who 'advocated his cause'.[36] Cunningham also cites the 'machinations of Ram Rai, and his own suspicious proceedings' as the reason for Guru Tegh Bahadur's assassination.[37]

---

[33]Gandhi, *History of the Sikh Gurus Retold*, page 634

[34]Cunningham, *A History of the Sikhs*, page 110

[35]Ibid., page 109

[36]Ibid.

[37]Ibid.

The Sikhs had found a delicate balance between a leader who was not only spiritually inclined but also someone who understood the importance of militarisation in the form of Guru Tegh Bahadur. Following the footsteps of his father, Hargobind, Tegh Bahadur continued gathering weapons and maintaining troops. He kept with himself the sword of Guru Hargobind, which he then gave to his son before he embarked on his journey to Delhi.

The steps that Guru Tegh Bahadur had taken during his tenure as the leader of the Sikh community were furthered by his son, Guru Gobind Singh, who was much more militaristically inclined than his father; however, the foundations for the formation of the Khalsa had been laid during the reign of Guru Tegh Bahadur.

8
The Inspiration

Kamal's axe fell on the bark of the *kikar* (acacia) tree with precision. He hit the same spot over and over again. The time he took between each hit was the same, creating a rhythmic sound. It was a monsoon afternoon, the weather was humid and his body was sweaty.

While his conscious mind focused on the task at hand, his sub-conscious mind wandered away into the jungle, listening to the continuous flow of the river and the sound of its journey reminding one that life never stops. The birds chirped along with the sound of the axe, as if keeping time with this eternal music of life. Sheikh Farid's most popular *qawwali* (Muslim devotional song) sprouted from the fountain of his heart spontaneously, as he started to sing loudly. This particular piece had been sung by a group of *qawwal* (those who sing qawwali) devotees who had come with the Diwan of Chawali Mashaikh the previous night.

> *I did not sleep with my love tonight*
> *And every bit of my body aches.*
> *Go ask the deserted ones,*
> *How they pass their nights.*[38]

Comforted by the solitude of the forest, Kamal sang his heart out. The birds, the wind, the trees and the river sang along with him. While

---

[38]Baba Farid, Baba Sheikh Farid, searchgurbani.com, https://searchgurbani.com/bhagats/baba_farid

singing, he happened to hear the voice of another man singing from another part of the jungle. The voice was husky but was hitting all the high notes with masterly control. Leaving behind his axe and a small pile of logs, he followed the voice to the point of its origin.

I plaited my tresses,
With vermillion daubed the parting of my hair
And went to Him
But with me He would not lie.
My heart is grief-stricken, I could die.
I wept, and the world wept with me.
Even birds of the forest cried,
Only my soul torn out of my body shed not a tear,
Nay, my soul which separated me from my Beloved
Shed not a tear.
In a dream He came to me
(I woke) and He was gone.
I wept a flood of tears.[39]

Kamal discovered the mysterious singer singing seated on a mound deep within the forest. He had heard tales about this part of the jungle. It was believed that this was the place where the spirits and djinns of the forest resided and so it was avoided by people. Sitting on top of the mound singing at the top of his lungs he saw a man who must have been in his late thirties or early forties, wearing a saffron chola. By the look of his clothes he could not tell if the singer was Hindu or Muslim. Next to him was his companion, playing the rubab. He was dressed in similar fashion. Kamal's initial reaction was that they were djinns. He wanted to run away but he could not bring himself to break off from the spell of the music. Even if they were djinns or spirits Kamal had no doubt that they were benign; in fact, they were probably holy. He sat a little distance away from the singer, far enough not to intrude into their space, but not so far as to remain invisible to them.

---

[39]Singh, trans. *Hymns of the Gurus*, pages 116–117

Beloved I cannot come to Thee,
No messenger will take my message;
Blessed sleep come thou back to me,
That in my dreams my Lover I again may see!
Nanak, what wilt thou give the messenger
Who brings thee a message from Thy Master?
I'll sever my head to make a seat for him;
Headless though I be, I'll continue to serve him.
Why then do I not die? Why not give away my life?
My Husband is estranged from me and has taken another wife![40]

As he listened to the words and allowed them to sink in, he felt as if these words had also been composed by Sheikh Farid. It felt to him as if this poem was a continuation of what he had been singing earlier. Maybe this was Sheikh Farid himself, appearing as a benign spirit and completing his poem, he thought. He had never seen a picture of Sheikh Farid and hence did not know what he looked like.

Repeating the last two lines, Nanak ended the song and opened his eyes to face Kamal. It was as if he knew that he was sitting there even though his eyes had been shut throughout the song. 'Did you like the song?' he asked him.

'I did,' said Kamal. 'But I am a little confused about its meaning.'

'You can ask me,' said Nanak, assuring Kamal.

'We are told as Muslims that our Lord loves us more than the love of seventy mothers. Why then does God sometimes become so cruel?'

'That is the duality,' said Nanak with a smile, rather impressed at the wisdom of the young man sitting in front of him. 'Everything in life works in contradiction. Evil emerges from goodness, light emerges from darkness and that is the nature of God as well. Whereas He is our beloved on the one hand, He is also our tormentor. Whereas He provides us with misery it is also Him where solace comes from. I hope that is clear?'

Kamal nodded as he continued reflecting on Nanak's interpretation.

'Tell me, young man, what are you doing in the jungle?' asked Nanak.

---

[40]Ibid.

'My name is Sheikh Kamal. I am the official scribe of Harzat Sheikh Ibrahim. He is the twelfth descendant of the great Sheikh Farid-ud-din of Pakpattan. That is what I do in my official capacity but I also have a passion for music and poetry, which is why I came towards your song like a honey bee floats towards nectar. I compose poems of my own but they are not any good as yet.'

'Sheikh Ibrahim?' Nanak pondered the name. 'I haven't heard of him but I have come across Sheikh Farid-ud-din's name while I was living in Sultanpur and also while I was in Lahore. I have been told that he was a great Sheikh and was a poet as well.'

'Yes,' Kamal smiled with pride. 'Do you want to hear his verses?'

'Yes, of course.'

On hearing this, Kamal repeated the verses he had been singing earlier. Mardana, who was listening to the conversation between these two couldn't help but notice that there was a lot of similarity between the symbolism of Nanak and Sheikh Farid. Nanak listened with his eyes closed, admiring the beauty of every single word pronounced.

'Subhan Allah! Subhan Allah! What a beautiful poem,' said Nanak, when Kamal was finished. 'There is such intense pain in Sheikh Farid's words. He must be a true Sheikh[41] indeed. Can you tell me more about him and his poetry?'

ੴ

After finishing his morning prayers, which began at sunrise and continued till noon, Sheikh Ibrahim left his meditation room and headed towards the courtyard of the shrine. From here, he could see the entire breadth of the land spread out in front of him. This was the city of Pakpattan in the middle of which the River Sutlej snaked through. This city had once been known as Ajodhan, but its name was changed to Pakpattan after the head of the Chistiyan *silsila* (religious order), Baba Farid, left Delhi and settled here. It was a small insignificant city at that time next to which on top of an abandoned mound Baba Farid used to teach his students.

---

[41]'Sheikh' is an Arabic word used for an honourable man

However after his death as his followers grew the city slowly developed into a major trading city, with the shrine at the centre of the activities. As the followers of the saint grew so did the power of his descendants who became major feudal lords and political players of the region. His shrine was in one corner of the courtyard and next to it was a beautiful tomb, which contained the graves of the descendants of the saint.

Ajodhan was a small city and this shrine was the city centre. There were several stalls around it. The city was a minor trading centre when Baba Farid moved here but over the years, as the importance of his shrine increased, so did the size of the city.

Sheikh Ibrahim was the twelfth successor of Baba Farid. Every day after his morning prayers he would spend several hours in an isolated room pondering on the poetry of his famous ancestor. He knew each verse by heart. It had been three hundred years since the death of the great Sufi but his poetry was still sung by qawwals at the shrine and by fakirs in the cities of Punjab.

There were several themes in Baba Farid's poetry that eluded Ibrahim. The tragedy was that there was no one he could approach to expound on these philosophies. Being the spiritual descendant of the great Sheikh it was believed by his devotees that he had inherited the spirituality of Farid and hence there was no one who could understand the enigmatic nature of Baba Farid's poetry better than his spiritual descendant. However, Sheikh Ibrahim was well aware of the fact that while perhaps he was the best person to expound upon Baba Farid's poetry and philosophy, there were several aspects of his teachings that even he did not understand.

As the head of this big religious institution, he could not admit to this fact. There were certain expectations from him as a descendant of the family and as much as he abhorred the institutionalisation of spirituality as was being practised in the name of his family, he could not find a way to escape it.

He was loitering around the courtyard and found himself in front of the room of the Diwan of Chawali Mashaikh. The Diwan, like Sheikh Ibrahim, was also the head of a spiritual lineage whose shrine was present at Tibba Haji Deen, the ancestral village of Baba Farid and hence Sheikh Ibrahim. This too was a Chistiyan shrine and was spiritually connected to the shrine of Sheikh Farid at Pakpattan, one of the biggest centres of the Sufi Chistiyan school of thought in all of South Asia.

The Diwan was an educated man and could talk about religious matters fluently but through conversations with him, Sheikh Ibrahim had gauged that he was not a person who could delve deep into the philosophies of Sheikh Farid. His learning was rote learning and not reflective learning. The two Sufis sat facing each other and engaged in a trivial religious discussion when Kamal came rushing in. His meeting with Nanak and Mardana had excited him and he wanted to share it with his spiritual masters.

'Are they Muslim?' Sheikh Ibrahim enquired.

'No, Master,' said Kamal. 'He says that he is neither a Muslim nor a Hindu. In fact, he says that there is no Hindu, no Muslim, but there is a Mirasi bard accompanying him. He plays the rubab while Nanak sings his poems. I heard one poem that he was singing. It was one of the most beautiful poems I have ever heard.' Kamal did not realise that while saying this he had offended Sheikh Ibrahim who took immense pride in the fact that his ancestor Baba Farid was the best Punjabi poet ever. Without waiting for Sheikh Ibrahim's request, Kamal recited the poem he had heard Nanak singing.

Mocking the enthusiasm of Kamal, the Diwan turned towards Sheikh Ibrahim and said, 'How could a person reach the pinnacle of the spiritual ladder without converting to Islam?' The words of Nanak clearly had had no impact upon him.

The Diwan continued looking at the Sheikh for confirmation but there was none. The Sheikh was still wondering about the poetry of Nanak. It sounded as enigmatic to him as that of Baba Farid. Maybe this Nanak would be able to solve the puzzle of Baba Farid's poetry for him, he thought. But he was also conscious of the status he enjoyed in society and did not want to come across as too eager to ask questions about Baba Farid to a person who was not part of the family and that too, a person who declared openly that he was neither a Hindu nor a Muslim. That would have been detrimental to his 'spiritual status'.

He also wasn't sure if Nanak actually was as profound a thinker as Baba Farid. Only one poem could not clarify that. So he sent Kamal back to him with a question. As Kamal disappeared beyond the boundaries of the city into the jungle, Sheikh Ibrahim looked down from the summit of his courtyard, wondering what Guru Nanak's reply would be.

> *There is One God,*
> *But two paths: Hinduism and Islam*
> *Which one is acceptable?*
> *Which one is to be rejected?*[42]

Kamal posed his question to Nanak. This was not the first time that Nanak was being questioned about his controversial statement that there is no Hindu or Muslim. The questioning had begun at the court of Nawab Daulat Khan Lodhi at Sultanpur. It was then asked again at the court of Malik Bhago in Eminabad. His friends and family had also asked him this question at Rai Bhoi Di Talwindi.

> *God is One,*
> *The Path is One.*
> *Accept the Path of Truth*
> *Reject all other ways.*[43]

'Subhan Allah!' exclaimed Sheikh Ibrahim when Kamal narrated Nanak's reply to him. No one had ever answered this question so succinctly. There was much simplicity in these lines, which was no longer found in religious doctrines, both Hindu and Muslim. The Path of Truth is the only truth. And what is Truth?

The Truth is what Sheikh Ibrahim had thought about several times in his meditation. It was that if he had been born in the house of a Hindu priest, he would have been one of the most ardent followers of Hinduism. Simple as the Truth may sound and easy its path, it usually falls victim to complexities of religion. Truth is an intuition that cannot die, but it can be suppressed by the burden of life and expediency. Those

---

[42]Trilochan Singh, *Guru Nanak: Founder of Sikhism; a Biography* (Delhi: Gurdwara Parbandhak Committee, 1969), page 108
[43]Ibid.

who are able to cast away the web of prudence and stare at Truth once again, as they did at the time of their birth, become Saints, Mahants, Sufis, Gurus and Bhagtis. There was no doubt in Sheikh Ibrahim's mind that Nanak too was an enlightened soul who had passed through the ordeals of spirituality to uncover the beauty of Truth in its utter simplicity.

'We shall meet this Saint who has composed such a beautiful poem,' said Sheikh Ibrahim.

'But how can you do that, Master?' objected the Diwan. 'He is a non-believer. What will your followers think if they find out that you went to meet a non-Muslim Bhagti in the jungles? They would not respect you anymore. They come to you for answers. You have all the answers. What would *you* ever ask the Bhagat?'

'The man who composed these words cannot be a non-believer. I believe you have not thought about the profound nature of this poem. The writer here is a True Believer and all Muslims should try to be like him. He believes in Tauhid, the Oneness of Allah; therefore, he is not a pagan and is to be respected according to the tenets of Islam. You perhaps may not have questions because you have shut your mind to knowledge. I, on the other hand, am a curious soul, which is a characteristic of a true believer and therefore I have more questions than answers.'

The Diwan was offended by the Sheikh's sharp reply. In the spiritual hierarchy, he was lower than the Sheikh. This status was not determined by their personal attributes but by the religious and social importance of the shrines they were the heads of. The shrine at Tiba Haji Deen was older than the shrine of Baba Farid at Pakpattan, but it was less important. The importance, in this case, was determined by the number of followers each shrine had. The Diwan respected the Sheikh and accepted him as his spiritual overlord but he was not used to being rebuked. This was the first time the Sheikh had spoken to him in such a sharp manner and the Diwan could not hide his embarrassment. He decided to stay in the shrine while Sheikh Ibrahim and Kamal left for the forest.

Sheikh Ibrahim too was surprised by his reaction. He was a true descendant of Baba Farid in his politeness. Baba Farid was known for his sweet language. Following his practice, Sheikh Ibrahim too had internalised this habit of talking sweetly to all. This was the first time

he had spoken to anyone in a sharp manner. He was well aware of the
decorum that his status demanded. Even though he disapproved of the
myths that had been created out of the life story of Baba Farid and did
not like that Sheikh Ibrahim and all Baba Farid's other descendants were
treated as divine beings, he did not object because he understood the
religious and spiritual requirements of ordinary beings. He knew that
one could uplift humanity temporarily, as the Prophet and saints did,
but after them, humanity always falls back into the same trap that these
holy men took them out of. He knew that an ordinary individual was
simply not capable of understanding the complexity of religion and the
Truth. It was for this reason that the simple nature of Nanak's message
resonated with Sheikh Ibrahim. In his philosophy, Nanak had been able
to summon all the complexities of religion that Sheikh Ibrahim wanted
to teach his followers. It was this frustration with his position in society
and the attitude of society that had resulted in an outburst.

Nanak was seated on a small mound, a few kilometres away from
the city and the shrine. From this spot, Nanak too could see the forest
around him and a few houses on the outskirts of the city. However, in
comparison, this mound was much smaller than the one on top of which
the shrine of Baba Farid was situated.

After initial greetings, Sheikh Ibrahim questioned Nanak about his
religious identity. Having grown up in an environment of institutionalised
religion, he was not accustomed to the fluidity of religious distinctions
that Nanak represented.

'If I say I am a Hindu, I would be telling a lie. I am also not a Muslim.
I don't accept the differences between Hindus and Muslims. In fact, I
do not accept any difference based on any creed, sect or religion. Isn't
the body of both Hindus and Muslims made out of the same elements?
Doesn't the spirit that pervades them belong to that One God who is
also responsible for judging everyone's deeds? He who serves One God
sincerely and truly, receives light and grace from Him. The virtues and
noble deeds of both of them are blessed by God while the wicked deeds
of both of them are condemned and punished by Him. I am a servant of
God and a brother of true devotees, no matter to which creed they belong.'

Nanak and Ibrahim continued to speak for a long time while

Mardana and Kamal listened. Sheikh Ibrahim narrated Baba Farid's poetry to Nanak, and Nanak expressed immense appreciation for the use of simple vernacular in the poetry of the Sufi. Sheikh Ibrahim had never encountered anyone who had understood Baba Farid's words with as much accuracy as Nanak. He decided to share his dilemma with Nanak. He narrated to him a poem of Baba Farid:

If someone smites your face, O Farid,
Return him not a blow for blow;
Nay, kiss his feet who smites you;
Forgive him, and go home in peace.[44]

'How, oh Nanak, can one ever be so humble?'

'What amazing words,' said Nanak. 'I have to admit that in my travels, I have never come across any Muslim alive or dead who has understood the essence of Islam as much as Baba Farid has. He is the true follower of the Prophet Muhammad (PBUH).'

'How so?' asked Sheikh Ibrahim. 'It is this humility of Baba Farid that I fail to reconcile with Islam. Islam asks us to fight oppression and always stand up for one's rights. How can one adhere to Islam's philosophy of *jihad* (struggle) and also believe what Baba Farid is saying?'

'My friend, that is because you have a cosmetic understanding of the religion. The essence of Islamic spirituality is different from what appears to the eye. Isn't it true that a pagan woman used to throw rubbish on Prophet Muhammad every day when he would pass under her house? The Prophet could have changed his route, but he did not. Why do you think he did that? Because he wanted to teach that woman through his humility the power of his faith. Had he rebuked her, the woman's hatred would have been provided with a personal reason. One day, when that woman failed to throw rubbish on him, the Prophet visited her house to find that she was sick. He took care of her, as a result of which she converted to Islam.'

For the first time, Sheikh Ibrahim was able to truly understand Baba Farid's philosophy. He was elated by the spiritual poetry but at the same

---

[44]Singh, *Guru Nanak: Founder of Sikhism*, page 109

time he realised how he had embarrassed himself by his own conduct
towards the Diwan. He decided that he would apologise to him for his
intolerance as soon as he returned.

'O Nanak, there is another poem of Baba Farid that I cannot
understand. If you may permit, allow me to recite it to you.'

> *You did not launch your boat*
> *When the weather was pleasant and calm,*
> *Impossible it is to set sail*
> *Now, when the sea waves storm and rave;*
> *Touch not the flaming flower,*
> *The flower of worldly desires.*
> *You will be burned in scorching fires.*
> *On the one hand I am weak and frail,*
> *On the other hand I am deprived of His grace;*
> *As spilt milk cannot be regained.*
> *Alas, I may not meet the Lord again.*
> *Says Farid, Listen my friends,*
> *The beloved will send a call,*
> *The soul shall have to depart,*
> *Leaving the body to mingle with dust.*[45]

Nanak contemplated the poem for a little while and then said that it was
a beautiful poem with multiple layers of meaning. It captured a message
that could only be expressed in poetry. He told him that he would not
explain to him the meaning of this poem right away, but soon he would
write a poem which would answer Sheikh Ibrahim's question.

Nanak and Sheikh Ibrahim both did not realise that the sun had
almost set as they sat there in conversation. Ibrahim invited Nanak and
Mardana to come to the shrine where they could stay for a few days.
Nanak accepted the offer and left for Baba Farid's shrine.

Here they also met the Diwan, who by the time the Sheikh returned,
had forgotten about the insult. Taking the lead from his spiritual master,
he showered respect upon Guru Nanak and even invited him to come

---

[45]Singh, *Guru Nanak: Founder of Sikhism*, page 110

and stay with him for a little while at his shrine. After a few days, when it was time for Nanak to leave, he took Sheikh Ibrahim to one side and told him that he had composed a poem that explained Baba Farid's poem. This is what Nanak recited that day before leaving:

> *Launch ye, the boat of austere contemplation,*
> *With which it is easy to cross the rough ocean;*
> *So smooth becomes life's journey,*
> *No storm, no tempest can obstruct thee.*
> *The Divine Name is the flower*
> *Of eternally fast colour;*
> *My whole being is dyed in it,*
> *O my Love, My Beloved!*
> *How can the seekers true*
> *Meet the beloved Lord?*
> *If you have some virtues,*
> *He will meet you of His own accord.*
> *He who attains this spiritual union*
> *Will never know separation.*
> *The cycle of birth and death will cease,*
> *When the true Lord is one with Thee.*[46]

Sheikh Ibrahim was delighted to hear Nanak's response to Baba Farid. He asked his scribe to compile on a parchment all the poems of Baba Farid, which he then handed to Nanak. It was through this channel that the poems of Baba Farid found their place in the Guru Granth Sahib and were preserved for posterity. Earlier, the poetry of the Muslim mystic was passed orally from one generation to another but it was through Guru Nanak that they were preserved for the first time in written form.

Maybe Nanak's fascination with Baba Farid was similar to our fascination with Nanak. Soon after his visit to Pakpattan, Nanak turned towards

---

[46]Singh, *Guru Nanak: Founder of Sikhism*, page 111

the village of Tibba Haji Deen, whose name was Kothewal when Nanak must have visited it around the end of the fifteenth century. This is where Baba Farid was born in the year 1173 CE. That house is preserved and in its courtyard are the graves of the Muslim saint's ancestors going back seven generations. Baba Farid's parents are also buried here. Here I met a man called Ghulam Shabbir, whose family has been serving this shrine for the past seven generations. Magical stories of the saint and his ancestors are passed from generation to generation in his family and narrated to the devotees. Had Nanak never recorded the poetry of the Saint in the Granth Sahib, I have no doubt that this man still would have remembered every poem by heart.

Nanak must have visited this courtyard containing the graves of the ancestors of Baba Farid and must have met an ancestor of Ghulam Shabbir as well. Perhaps they sat here discussing the poetry and philosophy of Baba Farid.

Not far from this house is another shrine dedicated to the childhood of Baba Farid. This is a well, located within a house, covered from the top with an iron cage. Devotees tie pieces of thread on this railing as supplication. A caretaker pulls up water from the well and serves it to the devotees. This is considered sacred water and is believed to cure all diseases. According to the legend, Baba Farid hung himself upside down in this well for forty days as part of his chilla, which is a Sufi rite of passage to harness spiritual prowess. Because of his presence, this well and its water became sacred.

Iqbal Qaiser and I stood there at the edge of the well, marvelling at the naiveté of the devotees and the cunning manner in which the caretakers extracted money from them after offering them sacred water. Nanak too must have witnessed a similar sight. Would Nanak have created a scene here, challenging this religious concept or quietly walked away like we did, not offending the religious sensibilities of the people here?

In a street adjacent to the shrine of the well is the Gurdwara of Guru Nanak, constructed by his devotees years after his visit to this village, to honour the memory of his arrival. At a wall next to the entrance there was a plaque which stated that the gurdwara had been renovated on the orders of the Prime Minister of Pakistan in 2008. This was another of Iqbal Qaiser's success stories that he had not known about prior to his visit. The last time he had come here, the gurdwara was in a pitiable state, divided and shared by families that had been ravaged by Partition.

I knocked on the door, not sure if I would be allowed to visit the building. An old man who must have been in his late seventies, greeted us hospitably. He told us that all the previous encroachments had now been removed and there was a single family, which was his family, living here, in a room next to the main building. They too were migrants from India and had been living here since Partition. Now they had been given the job to protect the shrine by the Auqaf Department.

'Baba takes care of his shrine himself,' he told us. He opened the door of the main shrine. Staring back at us from the darkness inside was a picture of Guru Nanak wearing a saffron chola.

'Whoever now comes and tries to sleep inside the shrine, Baba beats him up in the night. I have seen it with my own eyes,' he assured us.

Taking off our shoes, we circled the room almost religiously, as if it was an essential feature of our pilgrimage. 'I can't really imagine Baba Nanak beating up intruders with a stick,' I said to Iqbal Qaiser in a sarcastic tone. He shook his head in frustration, which he usually did when repulsed by the superstitious beliefs of people.

We climbed to the rooftop. The entire building had been covered in yellowish paint. We were standing under its canopy-like dome. There must have been frescoes here once, like at the Gurdwara of Jhaman as the architecture of this building was a replica of that one. From the roof we could see the surrounding areas of the village. In front of us was the shrine of Maha Chawar, the Hindu brother of Princess Kangna, who converted to Islam and was then persecuted by his own kinfolk.

Standing on top of the shrine, I asked Iqbal Qaiser if he too, like me, felt that people like Baba Farid, Guru Nanak, Shah Hussain, Bulleh Shah and Waris Shah have become a part of his existence, where it is difficult to differentiate between one's own personality and their influence on one's character.

'It is inevitable,' he said. 'Once you read their poetry and philosophy in such detail, they become a part of your existence. Where the self ends and they begin is hard to tell.'

Shah Hussain's verse '*I have been chanting the name of Ranjha so much that I myself have become Ranjha, call me Ranjha, there is nobody with the name of Heer here,*' had never been clearer to me. Did Farid become a part of Nanak?

Since we were here, we also decided to visit the shrine of Maha Chawar, the most important pilgrimage site of this village. We were led to one of the guestrooms behind the shrine to meet with the guardians of this shrine. The guardian, a young man in white shalwar kameez sat in one corner of the room, while his entourage sat around him. His gold watch and black shoes shone in the afternoon sun. His car was parked outside in the verandah with a customized number plate. We were told that several Sikhs had started visiting the shrine of Guru Nanak ever since its renovation. There were two festivals celebrated at the shrine, one which corresponded with the Islamic calendar and another which corresponded with the local calendar. 'I have not seen it with my own eyes but I have been told by my elders that the Sikhs also used to arrange their festival at the gurdwara at the same dates as that of the *urs* (death anniversary of a Sufi saint) of Maha Chawar. Every year there used to be a *kabaddi* (a South Asian sport) competition between the Sikhs and the Muslims.'

I wondered if the celebration of the urs according to the local calendar is a roundabout way of continuing to pay homage to the legacy of Guru Nanak, since the festival of Guru Nanak used to correspond with the festival of Maha Chawar. These were after all the indigenous people of this village and their association with the Gurdwara of Nanak went beyond the petty politics of India-Pakistan, of being Muslim and non-Muslim. After pretending for a little while that we were unaware of the history of the shrine and getting unbiased opinions from the locals, Iqbal Qaiser decided to share his knowledge about the connection between Baba Farid and Guru Nanak.

'But weren't they contemporaries? Guru Nanak and Baba Farid?' asked the government official from the Auqaf Department who too was seated there.

'Not at all. There was a difference of three hundred years between them.'

The transmission of history through the oral medium as opposed to written sources follows its own logic. Often the tales are devoid of historical authenticity but encoded within them are several themes and clues that need to be deciphered. According to this tradition, Baba Farid and Guru Nanak are presented as contemporaries, not in the dimension of their time period but because of the similarity of their philosophies. This is the traditional way of depicting their shared spiritual legacy.

In Benaras, where Guru Nanak visited, there are legends that Nanak met Kabir but that too is historically not proven. However, local legends reinforce what can also be discerned from an analysis of their poetry—a shared spiritual tradition.

There are several similarities between the poetry of Farid and Nanak. It is Farid who first uses the symbolism of a wife being abandoned by her husband to represent the relationship between devotee and deity. In Nanak's poetry, the wife as a symbol is also used several times, depicted to be dressed up for the arrival of her husband, who never comes. There is also supreme sadness in their symbolism.

Baba Farid is considered to be the first poet of the Punjabi language and at several points in his life, Guru Nanak gives the example of Baba Farid to other pretentious Sufis. He appreciates the fact that Baba Farid wrote for the people in a language that they could understand, when the language of the educated elite at the time was Persian and Arabic. Nanak, like Farid, also chose Punjabi as his medium of expression. It is for this reason that this language of peasants was given the status of a holy language after Sikhism as a religion was institutionalised.

Guru Nanak was impressed by the fact that Baba Farid lived a life of simplicity and shunned violence. Similar to Guru Nanak's poetry, one can find ideas about religious syncretism in Sheikh Farid's poetry as well. The Chistiyan school of thought in Sufism, of which Baba Farid was once the head, is one of the most syncretic sects of Islam. One of their hallmarks is the qawwali, which is the Muslim version of bhajan.

Once Baba Farid found a place in the Guru Granth Sahib, his personality and shrine became holy for the followers of Guru Nanak as well. Every year, hundreds of Sikhs and Hindus travel to Pakpattan to pay homage to the shrine of Baba Farid.

ੴ

The shrine of Baba Farid is the focal point of the city of Pakpattan. All roads lead to this spot, which also happens to be the highest point in the surrounding areas. This was an abandoned mound, probably carrying within it the secrets of an ancient city, when Farid moved here with his students. Now it is a shrine spread over a vast tract of land. One knows one is getting closer to the shrine by the names of the shops that start appearing on both sides of the road. All of them are named after Baba Farid or his title Shakarganj.

From Tibba Haji Deen we travelled to Chistiyan, a small city, which was established by Baba Farid's son and named after his school of thought, according to legend. From there, we travelled to Bahawal Nagar where we spent the night and then in the morning, headed to Pakpattan, the distance to which can be covered in an hour and a half by car. At a main roundabout which three roads dissected, we had the option of either bypassing the city of Pakpattan, travelling to the centre where lies the shrine of Baba Farid, or travel east towards the surrounding villages of Pakpattan.

'Take this route,' said Iqbal Qaiser, pointing towards the road that was in the worst shape of all of them. This was because it headed in the direction of the least important destination, at least in the eyes of the contemporary world. We were on our way to Tibba Nanaksar, a small village about five kilometres from the shrine of Baba Farid. 'This village was constructed around the Gurdwara of Guru Nanak. The gurdwara is perched on top of a small mound, which is why it is called Tibba.'

What was now thriving agricultural land was once a jungle. According to tradition, Nanak met with Sheikh Ibrahim on this mound and it was here that the latter presented Nanak with the poetry of Baba Farid.

The Gurdwara of Guru Nanak was visible from afar. It was a yellow building with a white dome. We drove all the way to the base of the mound from where the village also began. As a cloud of dust followed the tracks of my car, so did a group of children from the village, some naked, others wearing shabby clothes. They stopped next to us and started jumping in excitement at the arrival of a break from their monotonous routine.

Iqbal Qaiser was shocked to see the condition of the gurdwara. It was neatly painted, while there was a lock at the entrance barring anyone from entering. 'I believe this to be another contribution of my book,' he said in pride.

A child told us that the keys of the gurdwara were available with the family living across the shrine. We knocked for a little while but there was no answer. We walked up the street and entered a mosque which was next to the gurdwara. A few labourers were working on the renovation of the mosque while a young man was supervising the job. This mosque was built around the shrine of a descendant of Baba Farid by the name of Baba Fateh Ullah Shah Noori Chisti. We asked the young supervisor if he could help us enter the gurdwara but he was reluctant. There were clear signs of irritation on his face as soon as we mentioned that we had come to see the gurdwara.

'There was no boundary wall between the gurdwara and the mosque,' Iqbal Qaiser whispered into my ear as we left the mosque to try our luck knocking at the door of the caretakers of the gurdwara once again. 'Slowly, the guardians of the mosque were taking over the property of the gurdwara. Naturally, they are not happy that the gurdwara has been renovated and protected.'

After a few knocks on the wooden door with triangular patterns, a woman and child peeped from behind the half opened door. They agreed to open the gate of the shrine.

The gurdwara stood in the middle of the courtyard, which had also been recently renovated. It was a single storied structure with a single room. There was nothing inside it. Around it were several rooms which were once part of the gurdwara and used as a residence for pilgrims. They had not been renovated and were a reminder of how the gurdwara had once been.

'A lot of Sikhs come here,' said the woman, who had the key to the entrance. 'The gurdwara was in a bad condition but it was renovated by the Government a few years ago. Now we have been given the responsibility to look after the maintenance of the shrine.'

While walking down the mound towards the car, Iqbal Qaiser pointed to the houses that were in front of the shrine and told me that this area had once been the property of the gurdwara. The entrance to the gurdwara was right at the base of the mound. There used to be a pool within the premises and a langar hall, all of which was lost to the encroachers. What was finally salvaged and renovated by the Government of Pakistan was a fraction of the original holding.

'This was a fairly important gurdwara, which is why it has been preserved. There was a lot of pressure on the government by expat Sikhs and even by the Diwan of the shrine of Baba Farid to renovate this building, which is why the government eventually succumbed. If this has been the treatment meted out to one of the most important shrines of Guru Nanak in Pakistan, one can imagine what would happen to those which are not as important,' said Iqbal Qaiser, as we drove away on our way to Lahore, leaving behind us another cloud of dust.

9

A Cursed Lot

The dark clouds of the monsoon slowly spread over the blue sky. Then, as quickly as they had appeared, they disappeared, leaving me in uncertainty. Would it rain or wouldn't it? Would it rain in Lahore or would it rain in Kasur? Only the previous night I had arrived from Islamabad where I had recently moved after my marriage. Working while I was in Lahore was easier. I would just call up Iqbal Qaiser, tell him what I wanted to see and off we would go, the next day. Now that there was a distance of about three hundred and fifty kilometres between us, our trips had to be planned out.

It was seven in the morning and the exhaustion of my drive the previous day still lingered. However, the excitement at the prospect of travelling once again had overcome all my other emotions. I was standing on the Ferozepur road trying to gauge the intentions of the clouds, when someone knocked on my window. His unannounced entrance startled me and I have to admit that I greeted him with an unpleasant expression. He was wearing a green chola with a colourful skull cap. There was a collection of beaded necklaces around his neck and a few bangles on his arm. He had a thin white beard and in his hand he held a begging bowl.

'Go away, I don't have money for you,' I told him and pretended to observe the clouds once again.

'Give me something in the name of Allah,' he insisted.

'I don't have anything. Go away, old man,' I said politely but with a seriousness that implied that his standing next to my car was not welcome anymore.

'May God bless you,' he said, limping away. Softly singing a Punjabi song, he raised one of his hands with his finger pointing towards heaven as if to ensure that God was listening.

Only once he had left, unperturbed by my rude behaviour, did I feel guilty about what I had done. Nanak's words rang in my ears:

As a beggar goes a-begging,
Bowl in one hand, staff in the other,
Rings in his ears, in ashes smothered,
So go thou forth in life.
With ear-rings made of contentment,
With modesty thy begging bowl,
Meditation the fabric of thy garment,
Knowledge of death thy cowl,
Let thy mind be chaste, virginal clean,
Faith the staff on which to lean.
Thou shalt then thy fancy humiliate,
With mind subdued, the world subjugate.
Hail! And to Thee be salutation.
Thou art primal, Thou art pure,
Without beginning, without termination,
In single forever, forever endure.[47]

'Sorry, I am late,' said Iqbal Qaiser as he jumped into the car. He had just arrived from his farmhouse in district Kasur. He had chosen to spend the night there because our destination was closer to his farmhouse than to his Lahore house. We were on our way to Kanganpur where there is a gurdwara in honour of Guru Nanak.

'How far are these two villages from each other?' I asked him, as we drove away from the looming monsoon clouds.

'Not very far. About five to ten kilometres.'

'What I don't understand is how is it that the people of two villages

---

[47]Singh, trans. *Hymns of the Gurus*, pages 23–24

which are situated so close to each other have such different attitudes? Besides, how can everyone in a village have a similar attitude?'

'It is true that everyone in a village cannot have a similar attitude but you will have to agree that certain places have a particular attitude. It might not be the attitude of everyone there but it could be the overwhelming attitude of a village or a city.'

In my head, I was already comparing the attitudes of people in the cities of Lahore and Islamabad. It was still too soon for me to form an opinion about my new home but I could not deny the fact that there was a different feel to both the cities.

'I agree with you that different cities have different attitudes. Take Islamabad and Lahore for example. I feel that the drivers of Islamabad tend to be much more courteous than the drivers of Lahore. But then Lahore and Islamabad are about three hundred and fifty kilometres away from each other. It might as well be a different country. But in the case of Kanganpur and Manakdeke which happen to be only a few kilometres apart, how can people have such starkly different attitudes?'

'It is possible for the people of these two regions to have opposing attitudes. Kanganpur was a big village bordering a small city. That is the way it is even today. While Manakdeke was and still is a small village. People of cities and villages tend to have different attitudes.'

'That makes sense. As a city becomes part of a larger economy there is a tendency for it to become more individualistic as opposed to collectivistic. Notions of hospitality and tradition don't really matter anymore. You know what I find really interesting in this entire tale? It is that the story of Nanak at these two places is part of history now. The people of Kanganpur have forever been stigmatised because of a small incident that happened with Nanak. I feel that this was harsh on the part of Nanak.'

'Nanak could have said or done nothing. It is likely that this incident never took place,' said Iqbal Qaiser.

We skirted the old city of Kanganpur. Like the rest of the ancient cities of South Asia, its walls had been demolished. Only the arches of what once must have been entrances to the city remained. We climbed the mound on top of which the city was perched. There was a Muslim shrine in front of us. Next to it was a police station. In one corner was a dilapidated building, which was the gurdwara constructed in honour of Guru Nanak's visit to Kanganpur.

On the façade of the building, there was an inscription in Gurmukhi that recorded the name of the devotee who had paid for the construction of this structure in the nineteenth century. He too must have been from Kanganpur. Before Partition there were quite a few Sikhs and Hindus here, now it was dominated by Muslims. There are pockets of 'Untouchable' Christian quarters around the city but the low-caste Christians are politically and socially weak. On one side of the gurdwara a hole had been carved out of the wall which is now used as the entrance into the building. The name of a police inspector was written on top of the structure. 'Is this where that incident with the police inspector took place?' I asked Iqbal Qaiser.

'Which incident?'

'When the police official beat you up?' I asked.

Iqbal Qaiser often narrates to me the stories of the travels that he has undertaken. A lot of the trips were done for his book *Historical Sikh Shrines in Pakistan*. He told me that working on that book wasn't easy. 'The travel that you do is nothing compared to how I visited all these shrines. I would travel on public transport and then walk for miles to find a place. Most of the time I didn't even know if the gurdwara was still standing.'

In one of these narrations he told me that he had once visited a gurdwara. After photographing the building, which was being used as a house, from the outside, he knocked on the door to ask for permission to also photograph it from the inside. A woman emerged from the door. When she saw that Iqbal Qaiser was carrying a camera, she began shouting. Hearing her screams, a man came out of the house and without listening to a word of what Iqbal Qaiser had to say, started to beat him up. The entire village gathered around but no one dared stop the man. He even took away the camera and removed the roll of film from it. Later, another man from the village, who had witnessed the entire event, took Iqbal Qaiser to his house, where he first attended to his wounds and then offered him water and tea. He informed him that the person who beat up Iqbal Qaiser was a police inspector. He had illegally occupied the gurdwara and was running it as a brothel.

'No, that was Mandi Bahauddin,' said Iqbal Qaiser.

'That is such a disappointment,' I replied. 'Had that been this gurdwara, it would have added a really interesting twist to my story on this building.'

A few people from the neighbourhood gathered around us and started questioning us about the purpose of our visit. One of them, Aslam, who was clearly a drug addict, followed me into the building. There was hay on the ground. 'Is this for animals?' I asked him.

'No. This building is now under the control of a police inspector. Every year, he comes for the festival of the Muslim shrine next to this gurdwara. He brings other devotees along who are then accommodated in this gurdwara. The hay is used as bedding.'

'How old is the Muslim shrine?' I asked our guide.

'It's very old. It is older than the gurdwara.'

That seemed doubtful.

'Can I climb onto the roofs of one of these houses to get a better photograph of the gurdwara?' Iqbal Qaiser asked the men surrounding us. There was awkward feet shifting and reluctant replies.

'The houses are locked,' said one of them.

'The view is also not nice. It is the same as this one.'

'There are no stairs.'

'What do you expect of the people who treated Nanak the way they did?' I joked with Iqbal Qaiser as we walked away from the gurdwara, towards the alleys of this ancient city.

Chotu, as he was known to everyone, ran to his other tiny friends who were playing a game of checkers on the ground, using tiny sticks and pieces of rock. All of them were naked except for one who was wearing a lungi (a garment roughly like a sarong). All the hair on his head looked recently shaved except for a tiny lock that had been left hanging on the left side as a supplication for the well being of the child. Dust rose from the ground as Chotu's little feet stopped next to the game, carefully, so as not to mess up the arrangement of stones. 'Come quickly,' he pronounced. 'There are a couple of thugs sitting on the edge of the city. They have come to rob us.'

'Who told you that, Chotu Ram?' said Ramesh mockingly; he was the eldest of the boys in the group.

'I heard the *halwai* (sweet-maker) Krishna Maharaj saying that to the grocer Mithan who sits next to him. Both of them saw the thuggery equipment these villains are carrying with them. I also heard them saying that they know black magic and can disappear into thin air. With that magic they can enter anyone's house and take away all they want.'

'I don't believe that,' said Ramesh. 'Even if they can disappear, how can they take away all the things they steal? Those things would not disappear and how would they get out of the house?'

'If you don't believe me come see for yourself. Maharaj ji and Mithan have gone to warn the other villagers of the evil designs of these liars.'

The group of children ran towards the eastern side of the city where Nanak and Mardana were camped. They kept their distance from them as they waited for the rest of the city dwellers to gather. They observed carefully, trying to find any sign of deceit in the actions of these two men. Nanak and Mardana did not notice them. They sat under a berry tree, Nanak, with his eyes closed in mediation, while Mardana tuned his rubab. There was nothing else with them.

Only a few days prior to the visit of Nanak and Mardana, a group of jogis wearing saffron cholas had come to the village and by displaying the tricks of their religiosity had hoodwinked many innocent villagers. It was after this incident that the elders of Kanganpur decided that they would never entertain any other holy men in their village. Through the actions of the jogis they were convinced that this was Kalyug and the age of holy men was over.

'Where is their magical equipment? They look like religious mendicants to me.' said Ramesh with disappointment.

'Oh Ramesh, why do you have to act like a grown up all the time?' replied Harish, a boy who was as old as Ramesh. 'I am sure they have hidden everything behind the tree. Don't you know they are thugs?

They are pretending to be mendicants. Why would Maharaj say they are charlatans if he did not know better? I am sure he saw something.' The rest of the gang nodded and agreed with Harish.

The halwai and the grocer ran to the centre of the city where a giant banyan tree stood. Usually, a few people were always gathered there. They warned them about the thugs who had come from Kasur to rob the village. Stories were narrated about how someone had seen them flying in the air, while others had seen them disappear. Questions were raised as to whether they were holy men instead of being practitioners of evil as was being perceived but these thoughts were quickly cast away.

From the centre of the city, emissaries were sent to all corners of Kanganpur to collect more people to chase away these thugs. There was no doubt about the occult powers of these strange men, so the villagers wanted as big an assembly as possible.

Nanak and Mardana had no idea about the storm brewing against them. They had arrived earlier in the morning after visiting the city of Lahore. After completing their journey east, which went all the way to Bengal, both of them had headed south where they had crossed the sea and entered Sri Lanka. Years after they had left Talwindi, both of them decided that it was time to go back home. On their way back to Punjab they reached Lahore, from where they came to Kanganpur, which was a village near the city of Kasur, the twin city of Lahore.

Throughout their journey they had never encountered the kind of hostility that they were to face here. Nanak had ruffled a few feathers everywhere but these were usually of religious leaders who were soon won over by Nanak's mesmerising words. Never had the entire population turned against them. The opposition that he encountered throughout his journey was also different from the kind he was to receive here. During his journey, he had challenged religious dogma and ritual at Hindu temples and Muslim shrines, so the disagreement he encountered had been philosophical. Here, they were to be accused of something they had never been accused of before.

Hundreds of people headed to the eastern side of the city, picking up pebbles, rocks and anything else they could find to throw at these intruders. Children were asked to stay indoors. Some, too curious for their own good, climbed the roofs to see what was going to happen. The women of the households were instructed to shut all the windows and doors. In case these thugs performed any magic, it would not be able to enter the houses this way.

Chotu and rest of the gang hid behind a peepal tree near the spot and avoided all grown-ups. They knew that if they were caught they too would be send back.

'Go away, monsters,' came a shout from the centre of the group. 'Go away before we kick you out of this place!'

Even before Nanak and Mardana could respond to the allegations of the group, someone started to throw rocks at them. Partially bruised, Nanak and Mardana decided to leave the place where they were not welcome.

ੴ

We walked through an empty bazaar. What was once the centre of the city was now an abandoned outpost. The hub of the city had moved to the new part of the city that was constructed after the arrival of the British. The city of Kanganpur is expanding and I cannot help but wonder if Guru Nanak's prophecy is coming true.

Kanganpur is an ancient town that traces its origin back to Princess Kangna, the Hindu princess of Chunian at the time of the arrival of Muhammad Bin Qasim in the eight century CE. She is believed to have been martyred along with her brother, Maha Chawar whose shrine we visited in the last chapter, by members of her own family, after they both converted to Islam. There is a small fort on the outskirts of the city, now out of reach, because it has been taken over by the army. This fort is known as the fort of Kangana.

Iqbal Qaiser stopped in front of an old shop. There were remains of paintings on the back wall. The text underneath them confirmed that they were of Guru Nanak and Bhai Mardana. The people of Kanganpur did eventually acknowledge the 'divinity' of Guru Nanak. Walking along the road that forms the circumference of this ancient city, we reached the shop of Abdul Ghaffar Razi, an old friend of Iqbal Qaiser. Ghaffar has written a book on the history of Kanganpur and its surroundings.

A mendicant sitting on the mount of Naulakh Hazari at Shahkot

Gurdwara Rori Sahib at Jhaman

The spot where Nanak and Mardana sat outside the village of Ghavindi

Gurdwara Sacha Sauda

Gurdwara Tambu Sahib where Guru Nanak hid from his father after Sacha Sauda

Gurdwara Janamasthan where Guru Nanak was born

Bhai Lalo di Khoi where once Bhai Lalu lived

Gurdwara Rori Sahib at Eminabad—the site from where Nanak and Mardana were imprisoned by the forces of Babur

Gurdwara Malji Sahib at Kanganpur from where Guru Nanak and Mardana were turned away by the people of this town

Gurdwara Tibba Nanaksar where Nanak met with Sheikh Ibrahim

The shrine of Baba Farid at Pakpattan

Gurdwara Guru Nanak at the village of Makhdoom Pur Pahuran where Guru Nanak is believed to have interacted with the dacoits Sajjan and Gajjan

Gurdwara Bair Sahib in Sialkot

The tomb of Muslim saint Hamza Ghous in Sialkot

Gurdwara Guru Nanak outside Rohtas Fort

Gurdwara Panja Sahib on the festival of Vaisakhi

There was an ancient banyan tree in front of his shop, under which there was a small grave. This grave was protected by a boundary wall and was clearly being used as a shrine. Several loiterers sat on top of the long branches of this sacred tree. 'This must have been a Hindu temple,' I said to Iqbal Qaiser. 'As is the case with several other shrines, it must have been converted into a Muslim shrine after Partition, to accommodate the changing landscape of religiosity.'

'That's not true,' said Ghaffar. I wasn't sure if there was a hint of repressed religious sentiment hidden behind his statement. That was my initial reaction but he was a self-proclaimed socialist who acknowledged eventually that he had kept up certain features of Islamic religiosity to make his left-leaning messages accessible to the local people. 'This was not a Hindu temple. This is an ancient graveyard. In the early days, people used to find human skeletons buried under the tree.' I didn't want to challenge the authority of someone who had researched the history of his region but Iqbal Qaiser did not share my sentiments.

'If there were human skeletons then I am afraid this was not a graveyard. This must have been an ancient mound,' said Iqbal Qaiser.

'Really? You think so?'

I was told later that Iqbal Qaiser helped Ghaffar with his project and therefore was regarded as an authority on the subject of history. 'Where were the different Hindu areas in the city?' asked Iqbal Qaiser.

'The Hindus were everywhere. Even in this area.'

'Since the site of this banyan tree was also a Hindu region, we could say that there could have been a Hindu temple here.'

Ghaffar did not argue back, not because he was convinced but because by now tea had arrived. Looking around sheepishly I picked up the cup of tea and placed it on a table. It was the month of Ramzan and it was forbidden to eat in public and here we were sitting on the road having tea in the middle of the day. 'Don't worry about it. Have it,' said Ghaffar. My eyes tried scanning the expressions of a bearded old man who passed by walking along with his bicycle. He didn't look at us. Was he fasting, I wondered? In a little while, one of the men sitting under the tree lit a cigarette and the rest of the group followed. Seeing them smoke in public, I too relaxed. Such display of non-fasting would be almost impossible in a city like Lahore, where everyone wears their religion on their sleeve, but here in a small town like Kanganpur, it was possible.

'Iqbal Sahib, you should help us get the property of the gurdwara,' said Ghaffar. After finishing tea we had moved to a small room at the back of his shop. A door from here led to the courtyard of his house. This was a room that served as a boundary between his domestic and public space. 'It has been under the control of this inspector for the past few years. Under him the gurdwara has suffered immensely. You must have seen its condition. We want to preserve this shrine.'

'What exactly do you want to do?'

'We want to establish the office of our organisation at the gurdwara. We also want to a set up a small library there and encourage research on Kanganpur.' Ghaffar is a member of a literary organization, which is a collection of local socialist poets. 'This gurdwara is part of our history and we want to preserve this history.'

Ghaffar was probably in earnest about his vision but I grew sceptical of his motives. Like other gurdwaras in Pakistan, this one too had vast property attached to it, which technically came under the Auqaf Department. In reality though, it was under the control of local usurpers. Just the property of the gurdwara itself was lucrative. I wasn't sure if getting the gurdwara freed from one occupier and giving it to another group was a good idea.

'We are discussing whether to forcefully take over the shrine. We'll just sit there with a few men,' he suggested.

'Don't do that. Things would get really messy in that case,' warned Iqbal Qaiser.

'Should we approach officials from the Auqaf Department and tell them about the precarious condition of this shrine?'

'You should write a letter to the Prime Minister of Pakistan. Copy that to the Chief Minister and Chairman, Auqaf Department,' said Iqbal Qaiser. 'In your letter you should say that this gurdwara is part of our village's history and we want to preserve it. For reference you could also send a printout of the page from my book that mentions this gurdwara.'

'I could also send a few pages of my own book,' said Ghaffar. He went into his house and emerged with two copies of his book. The picture of this gurdwara was on the cover.

'Yes, that's a good idea. Once the letters reach the Prime Minister, then members of the Auqaf Department will come to you directly and ask you how to go about the renovation. In the end they will give you the keys of the shrine itself and ask you to look out for its maintenance.' Iqbal Qaiser's idea seemed to excite Ghaffar and the discussion about writing the letter continued for a little while. The more they planned, the less interested I became in their conversation. I slowly immersed myself in my thoughts, where I imagined Nanak and the people of this city.

'Would you like to ask Ghaffar any questions?' Iqbal Qaiser asked me, diverting the topic of discussion. I asked him if he thought Nanak's assessment of the people of this city was a true reflection of the facts.

ੴ

Dejected at the behaviour of the people of Kanganpur, Nanak and Mardana headed east. Mardana was stressed. He was surprised at the treatment meted out to them. He couldn't understand why the villagers had reacted the way they did. He had neither asked anyone for food nor had they yet preached their message. Nanak was calm as usual, as if he knew exactly why the villagers reacted the way they did. Mardana wanted to ask him but he remained quiet. There was an awkward silence between them on account of the encounter.

Sensing Mardana's uneasiness, Nanak said, 'May the village of Kanganpur prosper!'

They continued walking in silence.

ੴ

'There is no doubt that the city of Kanganpur has prospered,' said Ghaffar. 'Most of the locals continue to live within Kanganpur.' During the British era, a railway station was built here, leading to the rise of a thriving market town, which continues to burst with activity. 'However, I won't say that the people of this city are ill-mannered. I believe that Guru Nanak was a bit harsh in his assessment. In fact I feel that it is the people of Manakdeke who are known for their bad manners. As

Nanak predicted, they have scattered everywhere and the village is on the verge of extinction. Wherever they have gone though, they have brought disrepute upon their village. They are known to commit petty crimes like stealing sandals and the shirts of other workers at factories where they work.'

I wasn't willing to accept anything being said by Ghaffar. For me, it was his feelings against the villagers of Manakdeke that were coming out. This was perhaps due to the fact that their minor village was extolled as opposed to this major market town. Then I wondered if maybe my own biases were leading me to form opinions against the people of this city of which Ghaffar was the only representative I had interacted with. Maybe in trying to validate Guru Nanak's analysis, I had already made up my mind.

What would the Sikhs in Kanganpur have thought about the verdict? There are none left to check with. All that remains of this community are abandoned houses and shops which have now been taken over by victims of Partition and the land mafia.

After a little while, we were led towards another gurdwara by a young friend of Akram Rehan, who happened to be a poet. This was a gurdwara that had been raised due to the demands of the local Sikh community, after the population of the city increased. We parked our car in front of a mosque, which was being extended by labourers. I was told by our guide that this mosque belonged to the Ahle-Hadith school of thought, the puritanical sect of Islam similar in ideology to the Wahabis of Saudia Arabia. To counter Iranian Shia influence, the Saudis have pumped money into Pakistan and funded these puritanical schools of thought since the Iranian revolution. It is because of this influx of money that their political strength in recent years has grown, which is reflected in the size of their mosques. 'This used to be a small mosque only a few years ago. Look at its size now,' our guide told us.

We walked into a narrow alley and headed straight towards the gurdwara. The gurdwara now serves as a residence for a Muslim family and there was a lock at the entrance. We were told that the occupiers were not home and no one had any idea when they would be back. Walking back, Iqbal Qaiser whispered into my ear, 'The only difference in recent history is that earlier this street was called Gurdwarewali *Gali* (lane). Now it is called Masjidwali Gali.'

ੴ

The journey from Kanganpur to Manakdeke was short. It took about twenty minutes for Nanak and Mardana to get there. There was a stark difference between Kanganpur and Manakdeke. Kanganpur was protected by a wall and there were several hundred houses within. Some were several storeys high and visible from afar.

The rulers of Kanganpur lived in a fort a few metres away from the city. Being the only protected community in the area, Kanganpur served as the unofficial regional capital. Whenever villagers from other areas were harassed by marauders and looters, they would take refuge behind the walls of Kanganpur. The marauders refrained from attacking Kanganpur because it had a small army of its own and besides, it wasn't easy seizing control of a walled city.

Manakdeke was one of those small villages that were regularly harassed. It was a collection of a handful of houses, surrounded by open fields, a few of which belonged to the landlords of the village while the rest belonged to the aristocracy of Kanganpur.

Nanak and Mardana walked through the streets of this village, followed by a group of naked children. A few ran back to their houses to tell their parents that a couple of jogis had come to their village. Soon the crowd behind Nanak and Mardana increased. Older kids and women walked behind the kids, keeping a respectable distance. No one knew why they were following them but everyone seemed to be doing it and that was reason enough in a place like this.

As soon as Nanak and Mardana stopped at a small mound next to a few houses, the group of women following them gave them fresh water to drink. Children ran to the nearest sweet shop to get them *ladoo* and *gulab jamun*. In a little while almost the entire village surrounded the duo and started asking them questions about their journey and other religious matters.

'You must be tired,' said Ghasita Ram, a Hindu landowner from the village. He was a respected man in the community because of his cordial relationship with everyone. 'Let me arrange for bedding in my house,' he suggested.

The rest of the men too wanted to extend their hospitality to the holy men but they did not, respecting Ghasita's offer. There was an unlimited supply of food for the travellers. Some brought forward *saag* and *makkai ki roti* while others brought dal and roti. Nanak refrained from eating too much but Mardana ate without a break and soon could not move. Both of them then decided to rest for a little while at Ghasita's house.

When it was time to leave Nanak turned towards the villagers and said, 'This is a hospitable village and it was an honour to stay here. I hope that this village never prospers and remains small. May the villagers of Manakdeke scatter from this place to the different regions of the world!'

ੴ

Iqbal Qaiser asked me to stop in front of an unassuming door. There was a small building behind it, made of thin bricks. The village of Manakdeke is still a small village like Nanak hoped. A young boy came out of the door and when we told him that we wanted to see the gurdwara, he invited us in. His family now lives at the place where Nanak is believed to have stayed. After his visit, Nanak's followers constructed a gurdwara at the spot, which now serves as the house of this Mewati family, who moved to this village after Partition.

The gurdwara was a single room with a charpoy in the centre. Next to it was a *tandoor* (a clay oven) where an old woman was tending the fire to prepare roti for lunch. There were other rooms on one side of the gurdwara. These too were being used by the family.

'You have come here earlier as well, haven't you?' asked the woman who was working at the tandoor. 'A Sikh woman and a boy were with you.'

'Yes,' said Iqbal Qaiser.

'Can we offer you some tea or food?' she asked.

'No, thank you,' said Iqbal Qaiser. 'We just wanted to photograph the gurdwara.'

'It is not a gurdwara anymore,' she said. 'We are too poor to take care of this building. Please write to the authorities in the city to renovate this structure. It is now in poor condition and might fall down anytime.'

Our trip to Manakdeke was short. We left after taking a few photographs. On the way back to Lahore I asked Iqbal Qaiser about the Sikh woman and boy the old woman had referred to. 'It is an interesting story. A few years after my book, I was visiting this place when I saw a Sikh woman and her son here. The boy came to me and asked me if I was Iqbal Qaiser. He was carrying my book in his hand and told me that they had come from England. With my book as their guide they were planning to visit the gurdwaras of Pakistan. I then came with them to this gurdwara.'

Confused by Nanak's enigmatic response to the behaviour of the people of Kanganpur and Manakdeke, Mardana asked him why he would wish prosperity for the people of Kanganpur who had been hostile to him and curse the second village, where the villagers had been so kind.

'That is because I don't want the people of Kanganpur to spread to other regions. Wherever they go, they are likely to spread ill-will and hatred. I have prayed for their city to prosper so that they remain within its walls. Whereas I have prayed for the people of Manakdeke to spread to other regions instead of remaining confined to their village, so that wherever they may go they should be able to spread their goodwill.'

'Strange are the ways of the Guru!' said Mardana.

10
Guru Harkrishan

Guru Har Rai was aware of his failing health and knew that he did not have much life left. He also knew that if he died without appointing Harkrishan as his successor, Ram Rai would be successful in appointing himself as the Guru. So about fourteen days before his death, in front of his loyal followers, Guru Har Rai appointed his six-year-old son as the next Guru. Guru Harkrishan became the youngest leader of the Sikh community.

Before his death, Har Rai made the child Guru promise that he would never engage in Mughal politics. It seems that Har Rai had learned from his mistakes. During the internecine war between the Mughal princes, Har Rai had backed the losing horse, Dara Shikoh. Aurangzeb, his chief opponent, emerged victorious and after establishing himself on the throne in Delhi, he summoned Har Rai to explain his association with Dara Shikoh. Guru Har Rai then sent his elder son, Ram Rai, to Delhi.

According to Sikh tradition, Ram Rai succeeded in allaying the fears of the Emperor but in the process went overboard in pleasing Aurangzeb and ended up misinterpreting some of Nanak's philosophy. He did earn the approval of the Emperor but ended up offending his father, who disowned him. On his deathbed, instead of appointing his elder son, Guru Har Rai appointed his younger child as the Guru. Ram Rai, who had his own group of followers, rebelled against his father and decided to challenge the appointment of a child to 'Nanak's pontifical throne'.[48]

The Sikh version of the story puts the blame of Ram Rai's disassociation with the Sikh community on the actions of Ram Rai. However, there is another point of view that explains why Guru Har Rai appointed his younger child as the Guru, even though his elder son was, due to his age, in a better position to handle the affairs of the seat. This version is recorded in *A History of the Sikhs* which states that Ram Rai was the son of a handmaiden and not of a wife of equal stature to Harkrishan's mother.[49] At the time of Harkrishan's ascension it was clear that the institution of Guru had become a Sodhi family dominion and hence if the son of a handmaiden was raised to the status of Guru, it could have tarnished the entire institution.

During the short tenure of Guru Harkrishan, the Sikh community as a whole saw some major setbacks, which explains the immediate steps taken by Guru Tegh Bahadur, when he replaced the child Guru. By the time the mantle of Guruship was bestowed upon Harkrishan, the Sikh community had expanded beyond the confines of the Punjab into places as far as Kabul and Ghaznvi. It was therefore becoming increasingly difficult for the Guru to have some form of central control. To administer the Sikh community, Guru Hargobind had created the concept of the Sangat, which was then put under a *Masand*, who was responsible for maintaining a connection between the Guru and the Sangat.

Sikh historians record that due to the influence of Ram Rai and the threat of the Mughals, many Masands had started paying more attention to their own interests. P. S. Grewal also talks about this in his article 'Nanak's Doctrine and the Feudalization of the Sikh Gurudom', in which he records that reports of corruption by Masands poured in from various parts of the country. Grewal blames unchecked power as the main reason for this sort of corruption. In the same article he points out that the institution of Guruhood at this time had also become feudal in nature, with large tracts of land under its control. This is ironical

---

[48]This term is used in *The History of the Sikh Gurus Retold* by Surjit Singh Gandhi

[49]Cunningham, *A History of the Sikhs*, page 108

because Sikhism is seen as a reaction against the feudal land structure of Punjab by a lot of historians. The way a young child was appointed to lead a religious community of a large size only reinforces this opinion. The Masand system was abolished by Guru Gobind Singh when he established the Khalsa. It is for this reason that devout Sikhs believe he purged Sikhism of corruption.

Ram Rai exploited to the fullest the weaknesses of the rule of Guru Harkrishan. He used his former connections with the Masands to spread rumours that his father had appointed him as his successor. However, this strategy did not yield results and the disgruntled son soon decided to make use of his connections with the Emperor, which had been the initial cause of the estrangement with his father. He made it known to the Emperor that Harkrishan had wrongfully placed himself on the seat of the Guru, whereas his father had appointed him (Ram Rai) as his successor. He also told the Emperor that Sikhs all over the country acknowledged Ram Rai as the true Guru.

After listening to Ram Rai's complaints, Aurangzeb summoned the Guru to Delhi. This put Harkrishan in an awkward position because it meant presenting one's case to the Mughal court and hence associating with the Mughals, something his father had strictly warned him against. On the other hand, the risk of defying the Emperor could result in imprisonment. In this precarious situation the Raja of Jaipur, Mirza Raja Jai Singh, came to the rescue of the Guru and assured him that he would provide protection to the Guru. Raja Jai Singh also offered the hospitality of his house to the Guru.

Marching from Kartarpur and stopping over at various places on his way to meet devotees, the Guru reached Delhi with a handful of his most loyal supporters. His mother, Mata Sulakhni, also accompanied him, to verify, if need be, to the Emperor, that her husband, Har Rai, had bestowed the seat of the Guruship to Harkrishan and not Ram Rai.

Once in Delhi, the Guru was in no hurry to meet the Emperor. He stayed on for weeks, during which he used his time to meet the Sikh Sangat of Delhi. During the Guru's stay in Delhi, cholera broke out in the city. The Guru, along with his devotees, spent time in working with the afflicted people. In the meantime, the Emperor, using his intelligence and observing the growing popularity of the Guru in the city of Delhi, realised that the Sikh community regarded Harkrishan as their Guru and not Ram Rai. He dismissed the petition of Ram Rai by giving him a *jagir* (feudal land grant) where the city of Dehradun was later established. In this way, Emperor Aurangzeb too acknowledged that Guru Harkrishan was the real Guru of the Sikh community.

While the Guru was still in Delhi, chicken-pox broke out and the Guru too was afflicted by it. It was clear to the Guru and his followers that the Guru would not be able to pass this ordeal. One day before the Guru passed away he gathered all his followers and told them that their next Guru would be found in Bakala. In this indirect manner, Harkrishan ended up appointing his great-uncle, Tegh Bahadur, as the next Guru.

11
Two Paisas Worth of Truth

The evening prayer was beginning at the temple of Puran Bhagat. Mardana could hear the faint sounds of Punjabi songs being sung in honour of this ascetic. He was overcome by a rush of nostalgia. As a younger man, before Mardana had devoted his life to the cause of Nanak, he would roam the cities and villages of Punjab, singing folk songs and legends. One of the most popular legends that he used to sing about was that of Puran Bhagat.

Puran Bhagat was the son of the King of Sialkot, Raja Salivahan. As a young child he was thrown into a well on the orders of his father when it was suspected that he had made sexual advances towards his young step-mother, the latest wife of the king. The child was recovered from the well by a group of ascetics and while living with them, he too became an ascetic. Eventually, he confronted his father, the king, and it was due to his blessings that the king was bestowed with another son who eventually became Raja Rasalu, another folk legend that became popular with the Mirasis.

The well of Puran Bhagat was at a little distance from the city of Sialkot. A temple had been raised by the devotees of Puran Bhagat around his well and in this way the legend was provided with a site of worship. This was the most important temple in the ancient city of Sialkot, whose origin was also linked to the story of Raja Salivahan. It is believed that Sialkot was founded by this king, whose son was Puran Bhagat. Every day, hundreds of devotees gathered at the temple of Puran Bhagat to sing songs dedicated to him.

These songs were not only famous around this region but had slowly seeped into the folk religious identity of the rest of the Punjab as well. They were sung as far away as Amritsar and Multan, where local dialects imparted unique flavours to the story.

Mardana had never been to Sialkot prior to this visit. After roaming around the Lahore and Kasur region, Nanak and Mardana decided to visit the city in the foothills of Jammu where this ancient temple was located. Mardana wanted to visit the temple of Puran Bhagat immediately upon arrival, not due to his religious convictions but because of the memory associated with the legend. This was one of the connections that Mardana had with his past life, before he had met Nanak. This reminded him of what he was and what his life could have been, had he not abandoned all for the cause of Nanak. He asked Nanak if he too would want to visit the temple but Nanak refused. After a long walk from Eminabad where they had stopped to meet with Bhai Lalo, Nanak and Mardana had reached Sialkot. Nanak was tired and wanted to rest. He spotted a giant berry tree not far from the city and decided to rest under it.

Had Nanak known that the visit to the temple of Puran Bhagat meant so much to his friend he would have accompanied him but he was unaware of the chords of nostalgia that were being struck in his friend's heart by the sounds of the bhajans and folk songs. He had planned to visit the temple the day after.

Both Nanak and Mardana sat quietly under the tree. There were a few scattered houses and shops around. Nanak sat with his back resting on the tree and his eyes closed. He was meditating, a technique he often used to cope with his tiredness. It also helped him revive the motivation within to travel and discover more.

A woman in her early twenties walked towards the berry tree with her little daughter. Looking at the way she was dressed, one could tell that she was a Hindu woman. '*Namaste Maharaj,*' she said to Nanak and Mardana. After her prayer she drew a small piece of cloth from within her sari and tied it to a branch on the tree. All the while, her little daughter mimicked her mother.

As she circled the tree, chanting Vedic prayers, Nanak and Mardana observed her without comment. On finishing she touched Nanak and Mardana's feet, also asking her daughter to do the same, and was about to walk away when Nanak stopped her and asked her about her whereabouts. She lived in a house nearby and often came to this tree to pray. She told him that a number of people from the community regarded this tree to be sacred, as holy spirits resided in them. She came here regularly to pray for a son.

'That's not true, O holy mother,' said Nanak. 'Spirits and Gods do not reside in rivers or trees. They reside in a devotee's heart. You don't have to walk away from your home and your loved ones to get closer to God. God is where there is love and you have love at home.'

The woman, in a hurry to get back to her house before the evening fell, listened to Nanak patiently. Mardana knew that in this particular case Nanak's sermon was falling on deaf ears; however, Nanak continued. Mardana was getting more and more frustrated as Nanak spoke. He could see the contradiction in his words. He was exhorting the woman to stay at home to find God, whereas he was travelling the world in search of divinity. If God is where there is love then why did Nanak leave his loved ones behind?

When the woman left, Mardana could not help but ask Nanak about his revulsion for ancient customs and traditions. 'Who are we to tell them that what they believe in is false when their ancestors have believed in the same truth for many years? Is it possible, Nanak, that what you have believed to be the truth all this while is actually false?'

'It is, Mardana,' said Nanak. 'I have never said I have the truth. All I have ever said is that one should not believe something to be true just because one's ancestors have always believed it to be true. Instead, one should strive to find one's own path towards the Truth. Everyone's path would be different. For me this is Truth, this life of uncertainty, travel and unrest. But I know that this will not be my path forever. There will come a time when my bones will become weak and tired and then I shall settle. That will then be my path to Truth.'

'But Nanak, if everyone has a right to find their own path to truth then why did you just tell that woman who came here to pray to this very berry tree that it was false to do so?'

'Because there is no striving and pain in her effort to tread the path of Truth. She, like so many others, takes the journey that has been destined for her without questioning. All I want her to do is think, think beyond what she has been taught to think.'

Mardana gave up his effort at dialogue. He once again receded into his melancholy mood. Nanak on the other hand, had glimpsed the confusion that his friend and most loyal companion was going through. That disturbed him and he could no longer meditate as before. After a little while he said, 'Mardana, here take four paisas. Go to the city and buy me two paisas worth of truth and two paisas worth of untruth.'

Mardana did as he was instructed.

He wandered through the streets of Sialkot aimlessly, not sure how to interpret the instructions of his mentor. He knew that if he approached a shopkeeper with the request he would be ridiculed but on the other hand he did not want to disobey Nanak. He had accepted Nanak as his eternal guru a long time ago and vowed to fulfil all his wishes and desires, even though Nanak did not expect such a form of devotion. For Nanak, Mardana was a friend and an equal, never a devotee.

'Sir, can I get truth worth two paisas?' asked Mardana, as he approached a shopkeeper. Handing him four paisas, he continued, 'For the remaining two paisas, please give me untruth.' The shopkeeper looked back at him not knowing if this was some sort of a joke. Looking at Mardana's clothes, which was a white chola, he could tell that he was a religious person, a fakir or a dervish and one could expect all sorts of weird requests from such people. Putting the money in his till, he offered him a few sweets and some salt. 'This sir, is truth,' he said referring to the sweets, 'and this is your untruth.'

'That is a lie,' said Mardana. 'These are mere eatables and hence not truth or untruth. I want my money back.'

Mardana went to a couple of other shopkeepers, some of whom shooed him away from the shop, while others welcomed him, offering him things to eat and drink and then politely saying that they were not sure what to offer to the fakir.

In one street corner, Mardana found a vendor selling dry fruit. His young son sat next to him, while he sat lost in his own world. Mardana had given up hope of buying truth and untruth for his mentor by now and was heading back to the berry tree. The shop was not far from where Nanak was seated. For some inexplicable reason Mardana felt drawn towards the vendor. 'Bless you, little child,' he said as he passed his hand over the little boy. 'Your son is adorable.'

'Namaste Maharaj,' said the vendor. 'May I offer you some dry fruit?'

'No, thank you, kind man,' said Mardana. 'Here take these four paisas and please give me truth worth two paisas and untruth for the remaining two paisas.' The vendor looked at Mardana dumbfounded for a little while and then taking the money he disappeared into the shop. He returned a little while later with a piece of paper in his hand and asked Mardana, 'Kind sir, will you be buying truth and untruth for yourself?'

'No,' replied Mardana with a light laugh. 'I am the companion of a wise man called Nanak, who is sitting under the berry tree not far from here.' The vendor nodded, expressing that he knew where the berry tree was. 'He has asked me to purchase truth and untruth. I have been walking the streets of Sialkot like a madman and nowhere have I found what my master has asked me to look for.'

The vendor handed the piece of paper to Mardana and said, 'Here you go. I have given you truth worth two paisas and untruth worth two paisas. Take this to your master and tell him that there is one vendor in the city of Sialkot who deals in the commodities he is looking for and his name is Maula Karar.'

'Life is false,' was written on one of the chits that was sold to Mardana by Karar, while the other one read, 'Death is truth.'

A glow appeared on Nanak's face as he read what was written on the pieces of paper. He asked Mardana about the vendor who had sold him the paper and then requested him to arrange for Nanak to meet him. After a little while Mardana reappeared with Maula Karar, who walked with a straight back, taking steps which were sure of himself. Nanak noticed that despite his confidence there was humility and wisdom in his eyes. Nanak stood up and greeted his guest.

Nanak and Karar sat under the tree, engaged in conversation, till the evening. Mardana was no longer in a gloomy mood and was rather enjoying the conversation. Nanak questioned Karar about this area and the people here. He asked about the various shrines here and about the importance of each one of them. He was told about the shrine of Hamza Ghous, one of the most popular saints of Sialkot, which was not far from where they were seated. A few kilometres from Sialkot there was another shrine belonging to Mian Mitha, another important Muslim dervish from the region. Nanak asked Karar if he could show Nanak and Mardana these shrines, to which he readily agreed.

The three of them travelled together for the next few days, exploring the region and the religious practices of people living there. They became friends during this period and made plans to travel more once Nanak returned from his trip to Sindh. Karar had enjoyed travelling and exploring these past few days and was eager to accompany these holy men for the rest of their journey.

After their short excursions to the neighbouring shrines they returned once again to Sialkot after a few days. Karar went back home and Nanak continued his journey along with Mardana.

Several years later, after travelling through various new countries and regions, Nanak decided that it was time to revisit his old friends. He first went to Eminabad, where he met Bhai Lalo. Sialkot is not very far from Eminabad and so Nanak decided to also pay a visit to Maula Karar.

Karar was seated in his shop engaged in a discussion with a wholesale vendor who wanted to buy a large order of food from him and sell it in the rest of Punjab. It was the middle of the day and the streets were empty. Karar heard the sound of Nanak's wooden sandals from afar and saw his old friends approaching. He was delighted to see them but then he thought about his promise, which was to travel through Punjab together, a promise that he was no longer interested in fulfilling.

In the years between when they first met and now, Karar's business had thrived. He was now busier than he had ever been and was making a lot of money. His products were travelling to faraway regions. This was due to the fact that a couple of wholesalers were now doing business with him. Karar felt that this was the worst time for him to leave his business. His eldest son was still too young to handle the business on his own, even though he had been trained for several years. Karar thought about his family and came to the conclusion that with him gone, they would have to suffer many financial difficulties.

Sending the wholesaler away for a little while, Karar shut down his shop and went home, which was behind the shop. He told his wife that in a little while two men would appear at the door asking for him. She should tell them that Karar was away on work and would return several days later. His wife also remembered the last time Karar had disappeared for a few days when these two men came. She too did not want Karar to leave again.

When Nanak knocked on the door, Karar's wife emerged and told them what she had been instructed to. She was not good at lying and hesitated as she spoke. Both Nanak and Mardana, who had by now travelled the world, knew that Karar was evading them. They left without telling Karar's wife that they knew that he was hidden in the house all this while.

While his wife was lying to his friend, Karar, afraid of the truth being disclosed, was hiding in the store room, where he used to store food for the household animals. Here in the hay, there was a snake escaping the harsh winter outside. When it felt that its place had been invaded, it bit Karar, who died on the spot.

Just as Nanak and Mardana were about to turn away from the street of Karar's house, they heard the sound of his wife crying out. They returned immediately to find out that Karar was dead. His wife admitted to deceit and asked for Nanak's forgiveness.

'You are a holy man. You knew all this while that we were lying and it is because of this lie that Karar has been killed. Please pray to God that he be returned.' Karar's wife did not know that Nanak could not perform any miracles.

'This is the man, who taught us about truth and falsity, the last time we came,' said Nanak to Mardana, but Karar's wife was also listening. 'Isn't it sad that today he forgot what he said that day?'

After spending a little while with the distraught family and taking part in the final rites, Nanak and Mardana left for their next destination.

'Mardana, I have composed a new poem,' said Nanak. 'I've been meaning to tell you ever since Karar passed away but I thought it would have been inappropriate to recite it sitting at Karar's house.' Then without waiting for Mardana to speak, Nanak recited the poem:

Friendship with a money-monger
Is false and leads to falsehood;
You knew not O Maula,
Where death would overtake you.[50]

ੴ

Iqbal Qaiser and I drove down the newly constructed motorway that connects the Grand Trunk Road with Sialkot. After our visit to Eminabad we were now heading to Sialkot. Nanak too must have followed a similar route.

Sialkot has become one of the most important cities in Pakistan. A number of industries have been set up around this region which is the reason for the rise of this place as an economic centre. So powerful is the business community of this region today that it has financed its own airport, which now handles international flights, responsible for the export of products made in Sialkot. This newly constructed highway has also been financed by the business community, members of which travel frequently between the three important cities of Lahore, Gujranawala and Sialkot. I noticed several factories on both sides of the road.

Besides the industries, I noticed a lot of mounds on both sides of the road. Several of these are probably archaeological ruins, converted into graveyards. It seems like we would never be able to unearth the mysteries buried within.

Iqbal Qaiser and I were talking about different things, politics, history, theatre, music, etc. The conversation shifted to Nanak and Mardana and we discussed the story of their interaction with Maula Karar.

'Iqbal Qaiser, isn't this story similar to what happens to us a lot of times?' I asked him.

'How so?'

Several times in the past few years people have come up to me and told me that they would like to travel with me the next time I visited a remote area. These requests have come from friends, family members and also random acquaintances. Reading the final version in print, the

---

[50]Singh, *Guru Nanak: Founder of Sikhism*, page 444

trip seems fascinating but what a lot of people do not realise is the hard work that goes into it.

For example, on my latest trip to Lahore I ended up covering more than one thousand kilometres, visiting various sites associated with Nanak. One often travels for several hours to a place to just stop there for ten minutes and then head back. However, in an article, the several hours are edited down to a thousand words or so, therefore giving an intensity to the story. By reading these final versions, a lot of people associate romanticism with travel.

In my early days as a travel writer, when I did not know any better, I would invite all such friends who at one point or the other had shown some interest. For most of them, who had made such requests at dinner parties and other social gatherings, travelling on a Sunday, the only holiday in a week was too much to ask. There were a few who travelled, but they returned disappointed by what they saw.

'It is nothing like you described,' is what they have said to me at the end of the trip and then they inevitably backed out of all subsequent trips. In the end, it is once again just me and Iqbal Qaiser who are left.

'You are right,' said Iqbal Qaiser, when I described it to him. 'What a lot of people do not understand is that this kind of work requires passion and devotion. Easy as it may look, it is not easy when it comes down to doing it. I feel like there is a poem of Nanak that sums up what we are trying to say:

> *As hands or feet besmirched with slime,*
> *Water washes white;*
> *As garments dark with grime*
> *Rinsed with soap are made light;*
> *So when sin soils the soul*
> *Prayer alone shall make it whole*
>
> *Words do not the saint or sinner make,*
> *Action alone is written in the book of fate,*
> *What we sow that alone we take;*
> *O Nanak, be saved or forever transmigrate.*[51]

---

[51]Singh, trans. *Hymns of the Gurus*, page 16

Words without actions have no value.'

'I think that's what happened with Maula Karar as well. Earlier, it must have sounded fascinating! Travelling with Sufis all over the country, exploring new cultures and religions, but when it came to actually doing it, it became difficult for him to do so,' he added.

As we reached closer to the city, I noticed that several agricultural fields were flooded, this being the start of the monsoon season. However, this was not the case in Lahore. I explained my observation to Iqbal Qaiser.

'It is because India releases water from its dams when it crosses a certain limit,' he said.

This is a continuous bone of contention between the two countries. During every monsoon, the Indian government releases its extra water, which causes a flood in the border regions of Pakistan. Sialkot is located right on the border. In fact, this is no ordinary border. Here, Pakistan is connected to Jammu and Kashmir, the disputed area and the eternal source of animosity between these two countries. Historically, Sialkot provided Punjab with a connection to Kashmir.

'This also means that historically, the people of this region have been closer to the people now living on the other side of the border, as compared to central Punjab?' I asked Iqbal Qaiser.

'Yes.'

It was then that I started noticing how the facial features of the people here are different from that of people living in Lahore and other regions of Central Punjab. Here, the complexions are fairer and the noses sharper, something of a connection with the mountainous people living on the other side of the border, that Partition could not erase.

Living in the border region, these people are also always under the shadow of a threat. Only a few days after my visit to this region, tension on the LOC (Line of Control) rose and firing began from both sides. It was reported by Pakistani media that shells from the Indian side fell on many villages in the Sialkot district.

'Where is Baba Bair (the shrine of the berry saint)?' asked Iqbal Qaiser of a policeman in a white traffic police uniform, standing on the edge of the road, as a major traffic jam snarled in front of him. He was perhaps planning to resolve the issue once he was done eating his *chali* (corn). He pointed right, away from the ancient city of Sialkot perched on top of a mound on our left hand side.

'Do you know, one can see the mountains of Jammu on a clear day, from the roof tops of the city,' said Iqbal Qaiser. This little piece of trivia excited me, as Jammu was forbidden fruit for us.

Closer to the shrine, an old man sitting on a chair directed us towards the shrine. Driving through the narrow streets of this *mohalla* (locality), which is now known as the mohalla of Baba Bair, we reached the entrance.

'Everybody seemed to know where Baba Bair is but do they also know that it is called Baba Bair because of Guru Nanak?' I noted in my diary, sitting in the car, after I parked it in front of a small shop. The vendor across from us peered from behind his counter and continued observing us in a passive manner till we entered the gurdwara.

There was a board at the entrance of the building which noted that the gurdwara was renovated in 2012 by the Auqaf Department. Inside, the story of the renovation was a little different. New tiles that were meant to be used for the building were placed on one side, rotting away. A few renovations had been done, the floor had recently been completed and the building refurbished, but the gurdwara was far from ready to become functional.

'The government of Pakistan has only recently realised the potential of the revenue they can earn through Sikh pilgrimage. It is because of this that they now welcome the funds of foreign investors to renovate the gurdwara and start the worship anew. Initially, they were reluctant to allow the renovation even if the money was coming from somewhere else. Now they have gotten over their paranoia,' said Iqbal Qaiser.

Before coming to this gurdwara, we had been told that the renovation of the gurdwara had been completed and that it was now functional, by a few Sikhs living in Nankana Sahib. However, it was clear that the situation was quite different.

The gurdwara was an open structure. There was a veranda which was supported by pillars holding the roof up. There was only one room here in the centre of the building where the Guru Granth Sahib was recited. The berry tree was behind the building. A number of men were present within the premises, looking at us suspiciously. There was one group sitting near the entrance that was preparing *bhang* (cannabis); another one in another corner was smoking dope. Under the berry tree where once Nanak and Mardana sat, a few men were busy playing cards, most probably gambling, but no money was visible as gambling is illegal in Pakistan.

The berry tree was a thick tree, bending towards the ground. It looked ancient, if judged by its size. There was a long grave under it, which was covered with a red sheet with Quranic verses on it.

'This grave is new,' said Iqbal Qaiser. I touched the bark of the tree in an attempt to travel through time and relive the moment when Nanak had been here. With my hand on the tree, I noticed a red flag at the entrance that I had missed earlier. It was at this moment that the story of the tree, the grave and Nanak all converged in my mind, like an epiphany.

A young man of about thirty years, with unkempt hair and an untrimmed beard, started shadowing us. He started telling us about the building and that it was a gurdwara which was abandoned in 1947. He was perhaps hoping for a tip. Pointing at the pictures of Hindu deities, he said that they were frescoes. On the tiles on the ground there were names of Sikh devotees who had contributed towards the initial construction of this gurdwara. My self-appointed guide did not fail to mention this point.

Realising that this man was here to stay, I asked him about the occupant of the grave, even though I had figured out what the story was.

'That is the grave of Pir Bairi (the saint of berries),' he said.

'How old is this saint?' I asked him.

'Very old. Do you know that Guru Nanak also came to this saint and stayed with him? Guru Nanak realised that Pir Bairi was a powerful saint.'

This is an apocryphal story. I have seen quite a few shrines around the country to know how to tell a real story from a fabricated one. There could be one of two possibilities in the case of this ancient tree. First, that this tree was already considered sacred in the local folk religion of this region when Nanak came here. Besides berry, kikar, waan, bodh and peepal are some of the trees that have historically been worshipped and are still revered in the Islamic folk religion. The second version of the story could be that this place became sacred after Guru Nanak's visit. As has been seen earlier in the book, Guru Nanak is still regarded as a holy figure in this part of South Asia, particularly by those Muslims who belonged to areas where Nanak visited.

After Partition, even though the gurdwara was abandoned, the place, and particularly the tree, remained sacred because of its association with Guru Nanak. Over the years the association weakened but the tree continued to remain sacred. Eventually, that subconscious bond was broken when the grave of this non-existent saint was constructed here. Iqbal Qaiser told me that the last time he came here for his book, there was no such grave.

Perhaps in reality, the truth lies somewhere in the middle of these two stories. It is possible that the tree was sacred before Nanak came here and continued to remain sacred with Nanak becoming one of the reasons why it was sacred. Iqbal Qaiser too agreed with my analysis. Now this gurdwara has become a shrine to Baba Bair with the red flag at the entrance as his symbol.

On one of the walls of the building I noticed graffiti that read 'Ya Allah' and 'Ya Muhammad'. It is clear that the building had been Islamised. Then I noticed that some of the Gurmukhi text on the building had been wiped clean and instead these two slogans had been scribbled with a piece of coal.

The devotees of this shrine had a strange relationship with this building. On one hand they were subconsciously carrying forward the tradition of Guru Nanak, giving it a contemporary interpretation because of changing political conditions; on the other hand, they were determined to completely erase the legacy of this place.

Not far from this shrine was the house of Maula Karar. After Nanak's visit to this place, it was converted into a gurdwara. It is no longer a gurdwara but an institute for the blind. It was shut as it was a Sunday. I could not help but notice that there was a newly built mosque next to the shrine.

We walked into the deserted school, expecting to be stopped by a guard sooner or later. In the main hall, I glanced into a room where the guard was sleeping on a charpoy, snoring loudly. The building of the school was not part of the original gurdwara. The shrine was an abandoned structure next to the building. Tall grass grew around it. Iqbal Qaiser busied himself photographing the structure from one side whereas I attempted to enter the shrine. Just as I was about to step into the building, a dog from within gave out a warning bark. I ran out, content to simply imagine the state of the structure.

Our trip to this gurdwara was short. We walked out of it, heading towards our next destination, which was not far from here: the shrine of Hamza Ghous.

When Nanak was visiting the city of Sialkot, the city was gripped by fear. A Muslim Sufi by the name of Hamza Ghous had threatened to destroy the entire city. He was sitting in a building not far from where Nanak was sitting and was preparing for the destruction. He was a powerful Sufi and could invite the wrath of God over this city if he so wished. Before locking himself in the room, he had told the people of Sialkot that he would pray for forty days without a break and at the end of that time the city would be destroyed and only then would Hamza Ghous emerge from the building.

When Nanak settled under the berry tree, people realised that another man of God had come to their city, one who could perhaps save them from the powerful Hamza Ghous. They approached him and told him about their situation.

The problems between Hamza Ghous and Sialkot began when a Hindu man from the city approached Hamza Ghous and asked him to bestow him with a son. The saint told him that he would have several sons but on condition that he would give his first born son to Hamza Ghous. In desperation, the Hindu man offered him his first-born son but when the son was born he refused to fulfil his promise and offered him money instead. However, Hamza Ghous would not settle for anything less than a son and concluded that everyone living in the city was a liar and a cheat. Several people tried reasoning with

him but in vain. Hamza Ghous decided that the punishment for such a sinful
city would be destruction at his hands.

On hearing the petition of the city dwellers, Nanak visited the abode of
Hamza Ghous and knocked on the door but the Sufi refused to open it. Nanak
continued doing this for several days in an attempt to dissuade him but there
was no progress. In the meantime, rain started to pelt down hard on the city.
For two days, rainwater flooded the streets of Sialkot and everyone started
believing that the curse of the saint was coming true.

During the rain, thunder struck the dome of the building in which Hamza
Ghous was meditating. In desperation and fear he emerged from his room and
finally gave up his mediation and hence the curse to destroy the city. He saw
Nanak and realised that this was the way of God to humble him and teach him
that there was a Sufi in the city who was even more powerful than he was. In
this way, Baba Guru Nanak saved the people of Sialkot from annihilation.

ੴ

Looking at the shrine of Hamza Ghous, where he is believed to have
meditated for the destruction of the city and was later interned, I could
see what could have given birth to the legend. The architecture of the
shrine clearly demonstrated pre-Mughal features, with a large oval shaped
dome, as opposed to the round dome that became fashionable during
the time of the Mughals. There was a hole on top of this dome from
where the legend of thunder striking the building probably developed.

By focusing on the architecture of the shrine, I had no doubt
that Nanak and Hamza Ghous could not have been contemporaries.
His building looked older than regular fifteenth or sixteenth century
structures, which is when he needed to have been alive if he had ever
met Nanak. The architecture of the shrine resembled the structures of
buildings that were constructed during the Delhi Sultanate period. The
shape of the dome was of key significance here, with its long shape, as
opposed to round, which became fashionable after the Mughals came
to India. The hole on top of a shrine was also not something that was
particular to this shrine. In older shrines, this was a technique adopted
to facilitate the return of the soul to God.

The shrine of Hamza Ghous was located in an old graveyard not far from the berry tree under which Nanak sat. There were several houses between these two places, but at the time that Nanak visited, the building would have been in plain sight from where he was sitting.

While driving to Sialkot, I had been under the impression that the shrine was still popular amongst the people of the city. On the contrary, this was a completely abandoned structure. Just outside the graveyard there was a small shop. While looking for this building, Iqbal Qaiser had gotten out of the car and asked a shopkeeper where the shrine of Hamza Ghous was. Even though his shop was right at the entrance of the graveyard, he had no idea who Hamza Ghous was.

Historical books and online records are also quiet about the identity of the man buried here. The only references are found in Sikh records, in which this Muslim figure is depicted as the antagonist of the story from which Nanak emerges as the hero.

'Why is this?' I asked Iqbal Qaiser, while we were standing in front of his shrine. There was one door by which we could enter but it was locked. The building was in a dilapidated state with several cracks on its side. Perhaps the lock had been placed there by the Auqaf Department to protect people from falling victim to this feeble structure.

I could not understand why, over the years, several such stories had been associated with Nanak, where he humbled Muslim and Hindu ascetics. I put my question to Iqbal Qaiser.

'That is to show that our saint is more powerful than yours,' replied Iqbal Qaiser. Nanak, in my opinion didn't need such pointless stories to establish his credibility as a great personality. His genius lies in the poetic use of words and not in miracles.

ੴ

About thirty kilometres from Sialkot lay the city of Pasrur. Following Nanak's footsteps, this was our next destination. My companion, Iqbal Qaiser, was exhausted by now and wanted to return to Lahore. This had been a long trip but I was eager to visit as many places associated with Nanak as I could in the little span of time that I managed to extract from my full time job as a teacher.

'There is nothing left there,' said Iqbal Qaiser, half-heartedly, knowing full well that I wasn't going there for the building itself but rather to trace the spirit of Nanak.

'Even if the structure has been demolished, I would still want to visit it,' I insisted. Iqbal Qaiser agreed politely and we headed towards our next destination.

The road that connected Sialkot to Pasrur was perhaps one of the worst roads that I have ever travelled on. It was a short distance but given the pitiable state of the infrastructure, it took us well over an hour to reach. There were potholes as large as mini-craters. It was a single lane road shared by all sorts of vehicles and animals.

The legend of Pasrur is similar to that of Sialkot; Guru Nanak humbles an arrogant Muslim Sufi by the name of Mian Mitha. On hearing that Nanak had arrived in his city after defeating the powerful Hamza Ghous, he goes to challenge him and has a discourse with him. This discourse is recorded in the Guru Granth Sahib.

ੴ

On hearing that Nanak had come to Pasrur, Mian Mitha was consumed by jealousy. The story of the humbling of Hamza Ghous had already spread and Mian Mitha was not pleased that a Muslim Saint had been humbled at the hands of an unbeliever. 'I will churn him and take the cream out of the milk within him,' he said to his followers. He then sent one of them to the garden where Nanak was staying and asked him to convey the message to him.

'Tell him that if he comes to me to show off his powers I will squeeze all the juice out of him, as one squeezes a lemon,' said Nanak to Mian Mitha's devotee.

The messenger returned and conveyed Nanak's sentiments to his Master. Hearing this remark, Mian Mitha understood the sagacity of the non-Muslim Saint and set off to meet him without any shoes, a sign of extreme respect. His devotees were flabbergasted by Mian Mitha's sudden change of behaviour and asked why he now wanted to meet the man whom he had earlier wanted to churn.

'If I take the cream out of the milk, there will still be some milk left, but if he squeezes me like a lemon, what will be left in me? On second thoughts, I better not take the risk of such a dangerous confrontation.'

*Even though Mian Mitha had been humbled, there was some pride left
in him. He was followed by his devotees, who respected him. He had to keep
up appearances, so he decided to challenge Nanak on the doctrines of religion.*

*Mian Mitha knew that if he asked Nanak questions about Islamic beliefs,
then being a non-Muslim, he would be at a loss for words and thus Mian
Mitha would be successful in keeping face. However, Nanak was well versed
in Islamic injunctions and when Mian Mitha asked him questions about the
nature of hell and heaven and the punishments that are reserved for non-
believers by God, Nanak answered him in Islamic iconography. Nanak said:*

As sesame is heated and pressed,
or cotton carded by means of a thong,
so shall sinners be punished.
Like paper they shall be beaten with mallets,
and put into presses;
They shall be heated like iron;
they shall burn and cry aloud;
The wretched beings' heads shall be taken up with tongs and placed on
anvils
Nanak, he who meets not the true Guru and obtains not divine knowledge,
shall find no rest in this world or the next.[52]

*During the discourse, Nanak impressed Mian Mitha with his knowledge
about Islam. In fact, so well versed was Nanak that even Mian Mitha's
knowledge was found to be wanting in front of him. As Nanak spoke, Mian
Mitha touched Nanak's feet, kissed them and became his devotee. Towards the
end of the discourse, Nanak uttered the following words:*

The present are favoured; the absent are not.
Faith is a friend, want of faith an infidel;
Pride is ruin, wrath is unlawful;
Concupiscence is Satan, conceit is infidelity;

---

[52]Guru Nanak, translation by Max Arthur MacAuliffe, *The Sikh Religion, Its
Gurus, Sacred Writings and Authors*, Internet archive, 1909, https://archive.org/
stream/thesikhreligion01macauoft/thesikhreligion01macauoft_djvu.txt

The slanderer's face is black.
The man without faith is unclean; he who is tender-hearted is pure.
Knowledge is gentleness. The non-avaricious are holy, the avaricious are
impatient.
The honest man has a bright, the ungrateful man, a yellow face.[53]

ੴ

It was a Sunday evening and the garden where Nanak and Mian Mitha
had their religious discourse was full of young boys and girls playing
different games. The structure which commemorated the spot where
Nanak and Mian Mitha interacted was on one side.

Iqbal Qaiser was right. Hardly anything of the original gurdwara had
been preserved. There was just the floor and towards one end was a niche.

Near this ruined structure was a *jamun* (a purple berry) tree. There
was a group of young girls standing at its base cheering the brave girl
who had dared to climb to the top of this tall tree. Sitting on one of the
high branches, she started hitting the branches with a stick and it started
raining fruit. The other girls standing at the base collected the fruit.

I stood there observing the girls when a goat that had strayed onto
the platform charged towards me with its horns. I caught sight of the
animal just in time and moved away from its path. I stood next to the
floor of the gurdwara for a little while, anticipating the animal's next
move. It stood there patiently. I returned once again to the floor and
once again it charged towards me. It turned out that every time I stepped
on the floor of the shrine, the goat charged towards me. This was the
goat's territory and I was an intruder. Perhaps for a religiously inclined
pilgrim this could be interpreted as a sign of God, where an animal was
guarding the sanctity of a shrine. Clearly the animal had misinterpreted
my intentions.

At the centre of this plot, there was a long recess in the ground,
where an old woman had guided her buffaloes. They were grazing on
the grass that was growing there. Towards the edge of this recess there
were remains of steps that led into this place.

---

[53]Ibid.

'This was the sacred pool attached to this gurdwara,' Iqbal Qaiser told me. I walked towards them as a pilgrim ready to wash away my sins.

After our short trip to this gurdwara, as we headed back to the car, I pointed towards several trees that were spread throughout the garden. These were short trees yet stout and beautiful. I could not tell what their species was. 'These are very old trees,' said Iqbal Qaiser casually. 'They are mentioned in the book called *Tarikh Guru Khalsa* written by Bhai Lakha Singh. This man belonged to Sialkot and the book was written sometime in the nineteenth century. This used to be a beautiful garden.'

12
An Unmarked Grave

I stood at the edge of the mound. It was about twenty metres deep. The city ended here. In front of me was the Gurdwara of Guru Nanak, famously known as Chota Nankana. There was a pool of dirty water next to it. This had once been the moat around the fort of Deepalpur. Buffaloes were swimming in the dirty pool, as the herdsman, a young boy of eighteen, lay on the ground next to it, singing songs. I walked along the edge and saw below me the ancient gateway into the city that once used to be shut at night, but now was just like any other thoroughfare.

Iqbal Qaiser returned after a little while and told me that the young boy Usman could not allow us to see the temple from inside as womenfolk were around. This was the temple of Deepal, the ancient Hindu temple of this city after whose namesake the city was named.

According to the legend, Deepal was a Hindu sadhu who had acquired spiritual power because of his devotion to God. His head was completely shaved with only a lock of hair remaining on the back, typical of Hindu Brahmins. One day when he was at home, the same building in which Usman and his migrant family from Hissar now lived, he teased his mother. In frustration his mother cursed him to get buried in the ground, a diatribe meant to be semi-humorous. However, Deepal took the curse to heart and decided to bury himself in the ground. His mother only realised what was happening when Deepal's entire body had been buried and only that one lock of hair was left aboveground. She rushed towards it and held it. The body stopped sinking further. Eventually, the lock of hair converted to stone while the house of Deepal became a major Hindu shrine.

Usman, who was following Iqbal Qaiser, came and stood next to us. This was a magnificent building, a broad double storey house decorated with traditional patterns of wood and brick work. It was in a rundown state though and one could imagine how splendid it must have looked when this was a sacred place.

Facing the temple was another double-storeyed building, much bigger than the temple. These were the residential quarters built by devotees of the temple for pilgrims who gathered here throughout the year and specifically for the annual festival of the temple, which was a big affair. On top of this residential building, the names of devotees who had provided money for the construction of the buildings were inscribed in Devanagari script. There was a vacant lot between these buildings where the festival used to be organised. On one side of the plot was an abandoned well. A few houses had been built in the surrounding spaces by newcomers. Their architecture stood in sharp contrast to the intricate architectural patterns of the temple and the accompanying caravanserai.

'Kindly forgive me,' said Usman. 'I would have happily shown you the temple but I cannot today as our womenfolk are inside.'

'That's alright,' said Iqbal Qaiser. 'Son, I came here a few years ago and photographed the temple. I believe it was your father that I met. At that time I saw an object inside the temple that was covered with a silver utensil. It was like a lock of hair but made out of stone.'

'Yes. It is still there. It is in our living room. We cover it with a utensil so that it doesn't get destroyed. Sometimes Hindus and Sikhs come to us from India and we show them the lock. They offer their prayers in front of it. Some even bow down to it.'

We walked the narrow streets of this ancient city, which was once on an important route connecting the cities of Delhi and Multan. In the thirteenth century, during the Delhi Sultanate, for a brief period, Deepalpur also served as the capital of Punjab. Looking at our cameras and notebooks, a middle-aged man called Arshad, along with two other men, decided to accompany us. 'I too am from the media,' he said. 'I am based in Dubai and have come to visit Pakistan on vacation. I run a hotel there which I rent to people working for the Geo and ARY channels (two prominent Pakistani news channels).'

We exited from the southern gate of the city and headed towards Chota Nanakana. Arshad knocked on the door and a child stepped out. 'These are my guests from Lahore and they want to see the gurdwara from inside. They will just take a few photos and leave.'

'Who is it?' asked a voice from within the house. It was that of an old woman, sounding irritated.

'*Ammaji*, I am Arshad. I live in the market area. I have a few friends over from Lahore who want to photograph the gurdwara from inside. Please allow them to do it.'

'What will they get out of photographing this place? It is destroyed now. Come in, anyway.'

We walked into the courtyard. There was a charpoy in the centre, on which the old woman who spoke to us was sitting. She must have been in her early seventies. Her hair was dyed red with henna and there was a black *paranda*[54] in her hair. There were two other young girls in the house whom I guessed to be her daughters-in-law because of the strict manner in which the old woman was speaking to them.

The gurdwara was in front of us. It was a white structure and the borders were decorated with blue patterns. Within those blue patterns, animals and floral patterns were painted in white. It was a double storied building.

The rooms on the ground floor had been converted into residential rooms while those on the upper floor had been razed, leaving only the façade. There were small arches and piers decorating the face of the building. Nothing of the original shrine remained on the inside.

'When I moved here, the gurdwara was in much better condition,' she said. She too happened to be from Hissar and had moved into the shrine along with her family after Partition. 'I remember there used to be a mud grave behind the building. In the earlier days, we used to take care of the grave. We would clean it and put a cloth over it. My father planted a tree next to it but over time the grave has vanished.'

---

[54]A decorative braid, tied to the hair by South Asian women

Iqbal Qaiser and I returned from the gurdwara disappointed at its dismal condition. 'If they were taking care of the grave, they could have also looked after the gurdwara,' said Iqbal Qaiser.

'You know how Pakistani religiosity works. There has to be a Muslim symbol for any place to remain sacred. Whose grave was it by the way?'

A small lantern shone at the top of the building. A few men and women scrambled around it, perhaps in search of something. And then in a little while the sun completely set and darkness spread its cloak. The light of the lantern shone brighter as the sounds of a bhajan emerged from the temple.

'Master, let's go and take part in their bhajan,' suggested Mardana to Nanak. 'I am sure they will have langar for us.'

'You have now been travelling with me for years and yet you are not familiar with my ways. You know that I would never go into to the city. I don't have anything against that temple. If it was located in some wilderness, we could have spent the night there but not when it is located at the edge of such a big city,' replied Nanak.

They circled around the city, walking next to the moat. The gates of the city had now been closed for the night and Mardana was sure that they would have to spend the night in the jungle. They were so close to a city and yet in the wilderness. One could hear the howls of the jackals and the squeals of other animals, yet Nanak continued to walk.

Like Saidpur, Deepalpur too was an ancient city and one of the biggest in Punjab. The entire city was perched on top of a mound and there was a protective wall around it. Deepalpur had grown in importance because it was on the route from Multan to Delhi. No one knew when this city was formed and by whom, but there was a folk legend that there was a temple of Deepal here and the origin of this city was related to the temple which was thousands of years old. The temple that Mardana and Nanak were looking at was that temple.

On regular days Nanak usually stopped at sunset and enjoyed hearing the sounds of the birds returning to their homes. Mardana knew that every evening, watching the birds go by, Nanak thought of his home, his mother and his sister. Now that they were heading home after their journey to the East and South, this longing seemed to increase.

Often, when Nanak and Mardana were alone, Nanak talked about his mission to walk all over the world. Nanak would say that he wanted to shatter the boundaries raised by religious divisions. He would often narrate the poetry of Bhagat Kabir and Baba Farid which talked of similar things. Often in the night when Mardana pretended to be asleep, Nanak would talk to the imaginary Bhagat Kabir and Farid. He would call them by their first names. He would tell them about his frustrations with the idiocy of the world. Then he would recite to them their own poetry, sometimes offering his own explanations. Ever since they had entered Punjab, the frequency of Nanak's imaginary conversations had increased.

It was on nights like these that Mardana would worry about his friend. He would jump to the conclusion that Nanak was behaving the way he was because of exhaustion and homesickness. They had been away from home for thirteen years now.

Tonight, Nanak pressed on with no signs of stopping. It was as if he was searching for something. Mardana wanted to ask him but he had become accustomed to his friend's moods by now and knew better than to interrupt. Nanak would stop immediately if Mardana expressed the slightest sign of discomfort but then he would spend the entire night in agony, as if something important had been taken away from him. Therefore, Mardana wanted Nanak to stop of his own accord.

Following an abandoned trail in the jungle, covered in undergrowth, which indicated that it wasn't used much, Nanak and Mardana found themselves in front of a wooden hut. There was no sign of activity there. Nanak and Mardana stood at the entrance for a little while. Deciding that it was empty, Mardana was about to barge in when Nanak stopped him. 'What if someone is sleeping inside? We should be polite enough to knock first, just in case.'

They knocked twice but there was no reply. On the third knock the door opened and a shadow peeked out from the darkness. They could not see anything but the yellow eyes that stared back at them.

'You must be a hermit, living so far away from the city,' asked Nanak.

'Master, you are misinformed,' said the shadow in a shaky voice. There was a sudden flutter of the eyes as if Nanak's question had shaken him. 'My name is Nuri and I am a leper. I am not living here out of choice. I have been chased out of the city. My own sons have abandoned me. This humble house that you see, is one I have constructed myself. It provides me shelter from the extremes of the weather. This is the only place in the world where no one despises me.'

Nuri then opened the door and Nanak and Mardana were able to see his crippled body. There was hardly any skin on him, just bones. His eyes seemed to pop out of their sockets and he could barely stand on his feet.

Mardana's initial reaction was to move away from the haunting figure. He took a step back but Nanak took a step forward and holding Nuri, helped him sit on the ground. Nuri was so surprised by the action of this stranger at his door that he allowed his body to respond to his kindness. Mardana feared that Nanak would also contract leprosy now, but remained quiet.

Nanak and Mardana stayed with Nuri the leper for two days. Every day, Nanak would wake up early and prepare breakfast for the three of them and serve them. He would then complete other chores around the house, which would usually be collecting wood from the jungle and cooking. In the evening, after having their supper they would sing *kirtan* (devotional songs).

Nuri was so surprised by the acts of kindness by this stranger, when his own kin had abandoned him that he would cry all day while Nanak served him. Often, he would want to express his gratitude to Nanak but every time he tried, tears welled up in his eyes and he would end up crying more. After two days, Nanak and Mardana left Nuri in his hut and headed for Pakpattan to meet his friend Sheikh Ibrahim. After Nanak's departure, Nuri would sing the poems of Nanak in remembrance of his friend. After his death a few years later, he was buried in his hut by his sons.

13
Guru Har Rai

After his defeat at the hands of his brother Aurangzeb, Dara Shikoh decided to head west to Lahore and continue his fight against his younger brother from there. However, by this time, the tide of the war had turned against the eldest prince and it seemed like he was mentally prepared for an impending defeat. At this moment it is assumed that he was giving his followers and allies false hope and perhaps planning to flee before his brother captured him.

It was in this condition that Dara Shikoh stopped over at Goindwal, where the fort of Guru Har Rai had been constructed only a few years ago. The fort had a spacious stable, a tank and residences for his warriors. Following the tradition of his grandfather Hargobind, Har Rai too kept horses and a force of twenty-two hundred fighters. The Guru was escorted by an armed guard wherever he travelled.

Dara Shikoh and Guru Har Rai had become friends much before the internecine war broke out between the Mughal princes. While Emperor Shahjahan was still secure on the Mughal throne, his eldest son and crown prince, Dara Shikoh, fell seriously ill and no doctor was able to cure him. Hearing about the news of the prince, Guru Har Rai sent him some medicine that cured him. Both the Emperor and the prince acknowledged the wisdom of the Guru, even though the Emperor had earlier been directly in conflict with the former Guru, Guru Hargobind. After this event Dara Shikoh regularly visited Guru Har Rai and some

Sikh sources claim that he became a devotee of the Guru, even though he was fifteen years older than him.

In his pitiable situation, the prince relied on his friend and asked him for blessings as well as military support against his brother. Not only did Guru Har Rai bless Dara Shikoh but he also promised him that once he reached Lahore, Har Rai too would follow him and fight alongside the prince. At this point there are several versions of the story. One version says that the day after Dara Shikoh left for Lahore, the forces of Aurangzeb reached via the Beas, a place near where the Guru was staying. Using his forces the Guru prevented Aurangzeb's army from disembarking. This version is rubbished by other claims, which state that Aurangzeb followed the trail of his brother almost a month after he fled to Lahore.[55]

As promised, the Guru, along with his forces, reached Lahore to assist Dara Shikoh. In Lahore, Guru Har Rai observed that the forces of Dara Shikoh were slackening and Dara himself, aware of his approaching defeat, had planned to flee to Multan from Lahore, from where he planned to head further west to Kandahar. Guru Har Rai met Dara Shikoh in Lahore and then returned to Kartarpur after looking at the condition of the prince.

When Aurangzeb took over the throne of Delhi and established his position, he summoned Guru Har Rai to Delhi asking him to explain his role during the war between the two princes. Guru Har Rai wrote back to the Emperor with a petition to be exempted from a visit to Delhi, saying that he was a religious leader and had nothing to do with the imperial court. He also said that he would instead be sending his son Ram Rai to Delhi who would be his representative there. It is recorded that Ram Rai had a detailed conversation with the Emperor spending much time discussing the religious philosophy of Sikhism. The Emperor had been under the impression that Sikhism was anti-Islam but through his conversation with Ram Rai this impression was dispelled. All was going well in court according to Sikh tradition when a Hindu minister, with

---

[55]Prithi Pal Singh, *The History of Sikh Gurus* (New Delhi: Lotus, 2006), pages 105–106

the intention of creating a controversy, quoted a poem of Nanak which had the potential to be misinterpreted by the Emperor and perceived as un-Islamic. The poem was:

> *The clay of a Muslim's grave*
> *Falls into the hands of the potter*
> *Pots and bricks out of it he makes*
> *In the fire burns the poor clay*
> *As it burns it weeps and wails*
> *Shedding tears of cinder at its fate*
> *Says Nanak, God and Creator*
> *Who is the Cause of all causes*
> *Knows where departs and what befalls*
> *The soul of man hereafter.*[56]

Ram Rai realized that the poem could potentially offend Muslims. Muslims believe that the graves of the deceased should not be tampered with in any way. Nanak, in this poem, implies a disfigurement of the grave when he says, 'The clay of a Muslim's grave… Falls into the hands of the potter,' from which he makes pots and bricks. This could be viewed as a desecration of the grave and hence offensive to Muslims. Ram Rai knew that his position in the court of the 'pious' Aurangzeb was already in a vulnerable position, given his father's links with Dara Shikoh. Therefore, to avoid the censure of the King, Ram Rai felt it necessary to change the wording of the poem.

In the original poem, 'Muslim' was 'Mussalman'. Instead of using the word 'Mussalman', Ram Rai used the word 'Beiman' without altering the rhythm of the verse. 'Beiman' is someone who is dishonest. Hence the first verse of the poem became, 'The clay of a dishonest man's grave… Falls into the hands of the potter.' By changing one word, Ram Rai avoided the possible displeasure of the King. Altering the grave of a dishonest man is not as sacrilegious an act as altering the grave of a Muslim, one of the faithful. The Emperor was satisfied and Ram Rai remained in Aurangzeb's good books. However, news of this misquotation by his

---

[56]Gandhi, *History of the Sikh Gurus Retold*, page 583

son reached the ears of Har Rai through Sikh devotees in Delhi. Guru Har Rai fumed at the actions of his son and disowned him. He also declared that any Sikh who associated with Ram Rai would also be excommunicated from Sikhism.

Ram Rai tried seeking forgiveness from his father through various mediums but Har Rai was in no mood to forgive him for the sacrilegious act of manipulating the *Shabd*. The Shabd had still not become the Eternal Guru. This was done by Guru Gobind Singh but the significance of Shabd, or the divine word, was still immense at this time. A month after disowning Ram Rai, Guru Har Rai appointed Harkrishan as the next Guru.

14
Not Hindu Enough

Sea water splashed the side of the ship, jumping up into the unguarded eyes of the sailor. He had been standing there for several hours trying to discern in the horizon the temple he had heard about while he was at Muscat.

This trading vessel originated from Arabia and had stopped at Muscat on the way, where a few local sailors had told them about this ancient temple on the coast of a village called Kolachi. They were told this temple was dedicated to the sea god and it was his desire that all trading vessels passing from the Arabian Sea offer tribute at this shrine. As a word of caution it was added that those who failed to pray at this shrine of Varuna drowned. The captain of this ship (called a *dhow*) was a superstitious man and had taken the prophecy a bit too seriously. He had appointed a young sailor, who was on his maiden journey, to look out for this temple off the coast of Makran.

The crew was told that as soon as the mountains of Makran submerged into the sea, this small shrine would appear on the coast. Its sign was that there would be several lamps lit at its entrance and that it was located in a part of the coast where there were lots of cliffs. The young sailor had been standing on the side of the vessel for hours now, but in vain. Far away in the haze he could see land but no lamps. He was afraid that he had missed the lamps and had hence invited the wrath of the captain. Most of the occupants of the dhow were Muslims. Only the accountant of the owner and the captain was a Jew, and the sailor who had been asked to look out for the shrine was a Coptic Christian.

The story of the sea god was a popular story amongst the sailors of Muscat and Arabia, who often travelled across the Arabian Sea. Those ships that were lost to the violent storms of the monsoon were explained to have been drowned by the curse of Varuna. Everybody listened to the stories with immense interest but no one took them seriously. For the rational-minded Muslims, these were legends of pagans that had nothing to do with the truth. It is for this reason that most vessels bypassed the coast of Kolachi and travelled furthered to their destinations in eastern and southern India.

The shrine of Varuna outside this village was well known to the local Hindus of this region, who often visited it but outside of this region it was hardly known. The shrine of Somnath in Gujarat further east was much more popular and most sailors chose that place to pray for their safe journey. It is for this reason that Gujarat had developed into an economically powerful region while Kolachi remained a small village.

To his relief, the sailor saw a few small fishermen's boats not far from his ship. The fishermen told the sailors that Varuna's shrine was not far from there and that they would have to travel on the smaller boats to get there as their large ship would not be able to manoeuvre around the rocky port.

The captain and a few senior sailors disembarked and left to see the temple of Varuna. The captain carried a few gold coins with him that he was going to offer to the sea god for a safe journey, leaving behind the sailor who had laboured for hours to look for the temple.

ੴ

I saw my friend Humayun Memon and his colleague Vijesh Ramparshad Reel disappear into the sea of people. It was a Friday and the *khutba* (sermon) of the muezzin was blasting from the loudspeakers of the neighbouring mosque. I was stranded in the parking lot of Park Towers, the first shopping mall of the megapolis of Karachi. Standing next to me was my friend Sadia Khatri along with a few of her friends.

Earlier in the morning, I had gone to Humayun's office where he worked as a photographer and picked up Vijesh, a Hindu boy who worked with him. Vijesh was trying to get us into this temple, Shri Ratneswar Mahadev Temple, which was at Clifton, the most expensive part of Karachi.

'Do you know how old this temple is?' I asked Vijesh while we were driving towards it. After a few minutes of silence he replied, 'Very old. At least one hundred and fifty years.' I smiled and told him that this temple had to be at least five hundred years old because Guru Nanak is said to have visited this shrine. Vijesh looked back at me blankly and then said, 'Yes. That is possible,' making a quick jump by several centuries.

Since this was my first visit to the city of Karachi in many years, I had also invited another friend, Sadia Khatri, who too like Humayun, had an interest in such travels. She had arrived with two other friends and looking at the number of visitors, Vijesh was worried that he might not be able to get everyone into the temple. 'Worse comes to worst, I'll visit the temple alone,' I assured him.

We stood there for quite a long time with no news of Humayun or Vijesh. The guard standing at the entrance of this shopping mall looked at us suspiciously. In a city torn by conflict, security guards and law enforcement authorities are quick to react to any irregular activity.

I tried calling Humayun but his phone was busy. After a little while he called back and said that the authorities at the temple would not allow us to see the temple. I told him that I was coming over to the other side of the road and would talk to the authorities myself.

Putting my phone in my pocket, well aware of the street crime rate in Karachi, I crossed the road and met Humayun on the other side. He took me to the entrance of the temple. Here, a few Hindu men were sitting selling sweets and flowers, used as offerings at the temple. Vijesh was still inside the temple, which was under the ground. A staircase led to it. A man emerged from the stairs carrying a few sweets which he placed carefully on the ground as food for the ants. Quickly, they attacked the food given to them.

In front of me was a manicured garden, beyond which lay the Arabian Sea. 'This is reclaimed land,' said Humayun pointing towards the garden.

'At one point the sea must have come all the way to the temple, which is located inside a cave,' he added. A large part of Clifton is constructed on reclaimed land.

'Sorry Haroon, they will not allow anyone to see the temple,' said Vijesh, clearly distressed at the rejection. It seemed as if it was a personal failure for him. 'Can't I talk to the pandit myself?' I asked.

'I said that to him,' said Vijesh, 'but he is not willing to come upstairs even for a chat. They are being rather difficult about it.'

I had flown down to Karachi after spending several thousand rupees on airfare and cutting my vacation in half to visit this temple in Clifton, which had once been a famous temple dedicated to the sea god, and here I was standing on its threshold, unable to go inside. I was not willing to give up without trying. I called up my contacts in Lahore, trying to find the person in charge of the administration of this temple. After a few phone calls, I found the number of Raj Kumar, the only person who could give me permission to visit the temple. He was in charge of administration at the temple. I was confident that once I got to talk to him I would be able to convince him to allow me to see the temple for a few minutes. 'The person you are trying to contact is currently unavailable,' said the computer-recorded voice of a woman on the other side of the phone.

'Sorry, Haroon,' said Vijesh. 'I feel so bad I cannot help you. You know I asked the pandit and he said that Guru Nanak had never visited this temple. This is a purely Hindu temple dedicated to the worship of Shiva.'

Despite what the pandit was saying, I was sure that this was the temple that Guru Nanak visited in Karachi. In Iqbal Qaiser's *Historical Sikh Shrines of Pakistan*, this temple at Clifton was identified as the temple which Nanak had visited on his tour of Sindh. Iqbal Qaiser was as credible a source on Guru Nanak and Sikhism as it could get, as far as I was concerned.

We stood aimlessly at the entrance of the temple, hoping to get through to Raj Kumar. I tried his phone several times but it was switched off. A few Hindu women emerged from the temple, wearing saris. Before departing they stood in front of the staircase and offered one last prayer to the Hindu deities inside. A man who was probably a guard here asked us to move away from the entrance of the temple. We decided to head to our next destination and keep trying Raj Kumar's number, and if possible, come back in the evening.

ੴ

The temple of Varuna was located within a cave in these cliffs on the shore. Water from the sea reached right up to these caves during high tide. Stone steps led up to the temple from the sea, while there was another set of stairs for devotees arriving by land.

Within the cave were two rooms. In one of them there were several lamps placed on niches between the rocks. The pandit of this temple urged the captain to do the same. He told him that each of these lamps had been lit for a particular ship that had set sail in the sea. Some of them had been lit by the sailors themselves, while others had been lit by their loved ones. Taking an unlit lamp, the captain lit a flame for the well-being of his own ship and crew. He then placed it in an empty niche.

Since this was a pagan shrine, the captain had expected to find an idol here but there was none. He posed this question to the pandit who explained that the sea god Varuna resides in the waves and winds of the ocean. He lives underwater with the fish and occasionally manifests himself by riding on a giant fish. Several centuries ago, he had meditated within these caves and harnessed the powers of the ocean. This is not just a shrine but his actual home. 'He comes even today,' said the pandit to the captain. 'But one needs to be a pure-hearted soul to see him.'

The pandit told the captain that several holy men came to this temple, to meditate in the room where Varuna meditated, in order to harness his mystical powers. Out of the millions who had tried doing this, only a handful had succeeded, the pandit said. 'There are holy men meditating as we speak.'

The captain expressed a desire to see the room where the holy men were meditating but the pandit told him that it was impossible to go there because that might disturb their peace and in their wrath they might curse the ship. The captain, however, was determined to see the meditation room and if possible get blessings from the holy men. The captain who had earlier been so superstitious about his journey was now much more confident, after lighting the lamp. He was sure that now nothing could sink his ship even if a holy man cursed him. He placed a gold coin in the pandit's hand and insisted that he wanted to see the meditation room. He assured him that he would do so quietly.

The pandit and the captain sneaked into the room where the holy men were sitting on the floor, lost in their meditation. Some were sitting in acrobatic yogic positions while others were sitting in comfort. There were a few who were standing with their hands raised vertically, while one leg was resting on the knee of the other leg. This was hardly a quiet room. The roar of the sea splashing against the rocky shore echoed in this small hall. None of the occupants noticed the intruder except one. He was sitting in one of the corners in a saffron chola. He had a long beard which was greying and there were dark circles under his eyes. He had long hair which was covered by a saffron turban.

The old man looked straight at the sailor without expressing any emotion. The captain felt the stare of the holy man pierce him as if he was looking at someone beyond him. It seemed as if the holy man was still in a daze from his meditation, even though his eyes were open. The captain attempted to walk out of the room but the old man gestured at him to stop and headed towards him.

Sitting on top of the cliff, the captain and the holy man engaged each other in conversation. The sea was in front of them, trying desperately to climb up the cliff. Not far from there was a Muslim shrine which was known as the shrine of Abdullah Shah Ghazi. It was a modest building with a little courtyard where langar was served to devotees. This too was on the edge of the cliff. The village of Kolachi was further west from there, along the shore.

The old man told the captain that his name was Nanak and that he belonged to Punjab. He told him about his journeys and purpose in life. The stories of Nanak's travels had an immense impact on the captain. It was hard for him to believe that one man could walk the many miles on foot that Nanak had traversed. Nanak explained to him that he was far from being a holy man and that it is just a misconception that people had about him. He was an ordinary devotee much like the captain, in search of religiosity. The purpose of his life, Nanak said, was not to spread his message but to understand the message of different religious and spiritual traditions.

The discourse with Nanak touched a chord within the captain. He felt that Nanak was a manifestation of all his aspirations. He sat there for hours talking to Nanak, asking him about his various adventures. He also shared stories of his own adventures, for the captain too was widely travelled.

'Baba Nanak, how do I become your follower?' asked the captain. 'What is the religion I should follow to become your devotee?' For the first time during their conversation, Nanak asked the captain what his religion was. Nanak had assumed that he was a Muslim but he still wanted to be sure. Nanak was rather surprised when he was told that the captain was a Jew.

'You are my follower if you are willing to learn all your life. You have to remain a student forever like me. Learn from not only scholars and holy men but also from those whom you chose to ignore—servants, women, children, animals, plants, the sea, the land and the sky. Keep an open mind and never become too rigid in your beliefs. Dogma is the end of inquiry and hence the death of enlightenment. Have faith. Have faith, not only in your own goodness but also in that of others. Have faith in people even when you know they are deceiving you. Have faith that things will always work out for the good. Have faith that the sea will not betray your trust and will not swallow you even if you have not offered your prayers to the sea god. Have faith that the sea god is not a monster who will, like a jealous woman, take his revenge upon you if you don't present him gifts. Above all, have faith in divinity. You don't have to belong to a particular creed or religion to become such a believer. If you are a Muslim, then become a good Muslim of such repute that no one can say you have brought disrepute to the religion of Islam. If you are a Christian, then become a true disciple of Christ and if you are a Jew, then follow the message of Moses to the core.'

The captain was moved to tears while listening to Guru Nanak's sermon. He thought about all the people he had wronged in his lifetime. He thought about the young Coptic Christian in the ship who had spent several hours exhausting his eyes searching for this shrine and how he had looked sadly towards the captain when he disembarked for the temple without taking him along. He realised that his hatred for all the people who had wronged him over the years was also unnecessary. He knew now that all of them had their own baggage that they carried and their immediate reaction was not a result of just one event but an entire historical process. The captain kissed the hands of his new master and wept loudly, allowing the sound to drown in the roar of the sea. Nanak stared into the fading sun beyond the horizon. The anchored ship of the captain shone in the sunlight.

ੴ

Dejected after the aborted visit to the temple at Clifton, Humayun decided to show me other Hindu temples around the city. To be honest, I wasn't very keen to visit them. I was focused on shrines that Nanak had visited.

There was one more shrine in Karachi which was associated with Guru Nanak that I had to see. In Iqbal Qaiser's book, this shrine was said to be located on the Justice Kayani Road near Saddar. When I showed Humayun the picture of the shrine in the book, he told me that this was now the office of the National Academy of Performing Arts (NAPA). To update Iqbal Qaiser on my journey down south, I called him up.

I told him what had happened at Clifton and also narrated to him the pandit's story that Guru Nanak had never visited this place. 'Let them say what they want to say. There is a political issue behind them saying that,' he said. Karachi is a deeply contested political city. Upon landing, the first thing I noticed was the series of flags of different political parties on the street lamps. There was also graffiti on the wall, representing the points of view of various religious sects. One could tell that political tensions ran high in the air. It is also perhaps in this context that the different groups of Hindus and Sikhs within the city interact.

'I'll explain to you the problem when you come to Lahore,' said Iqbal Qaiser. 'I can show you the reference in *Mahant Kosh*. It clearly states that the Hindu temple at Clifton is the Hindu temple that Guru Nanak visited.'

I told him that now we were heading towards the gurdwara on the Justice Kayani Road. Iqbal Qaiser warned me that the corresponding picture of the shrine in his book was actually not the right picture. His book was published before the era of computerised printing, which is why there were a few pictorial mistakes. Suddenly, from knowing exactly where the shrine of Nanak was situated, we were lost in this city of about twenty million people.

'Near Justice Kayani Road, there is an area known as Ram Bagh. It is a well-known locality. The gurdwara is there,' said Iqbal Qaiser.

'What is the name of the temple it is located in?'

'The gurdwara has its own name. Gurdwara Pehli Patshah.'

Sadia's friends called up someone he knew who belonged to that area. He was told that Ram Bagh was no longer called Ram Bagh but Aram Bagh. The addition of an 'A' neutralised its religious connotation.

'My friend has told me that there used to be a gurdwara there but it doesn't exist anymore,' said Ali, Sadia's friend.

'That's alright. I just need to see the space,' I said.

'I guess we'll just go there and ask around,' said Humayun.

We drove from the newer part of Karachi to the older part, with its narrow streets and colonial buildings. Old rusty structures with long colonnades lined both sides of the road. This part of the city could easily be conflated with the colonial part of Bombay or Colombo.

Humayun parked the car in front of a colonial tower and led us towards a Hindu temple that he had visited at the time of Holi last year. The plan was to check out this temple before we attempted to locate the gurdwara.

We walked through an arch and the temple was on our right. The name of the temple was noted at the entrance: Shri Swami Narayan Mandir. The temple had a tall, cone-shaped structure placed on top of a small platform. The shrine itself was a courtyard from where columns were sprouting to support the cone shaped structure on the top. The cone of the temple was beautifully decorated. On the summit was a picture of a Hindu deity carved on the structure. It wasn't one from the Hindu trinity. Outside the arch there were vendors selling religious paraphernalia in their makeshift shops. There was a small building next to the temple while on the other side was another platform covered with a canopy and a carpet on the floor. A few Hindu children were standing there making fun of us.

Behind the temple, I noticed cardboard cuttings of Hindu deities, including those of Ram, Krishna and Shiva. These were perhaps cut-outs for Diwali, which must be a huge affair here. There was also some beautiful artwork under the roof of the main temple. Pictures of Krishna with his maidens were painted in bright colours. The main door of the temple was locked and there was a peacock guarding the entrance.

Right at that time, an old man with a dark complexion and hunched back walked in carrying bags. I stopped him and introduced myself, and followed up by asking questions about the temple. 'This temple is one hundred and fifty years old,' he said. Hundred and fifty seemed to be the standard age of all temples here. 'If you want more information you should ask the administration of the temple. I'll take you there.'

Saying this he started walking away while I walked briskly behind trying to keep pace with him.

'Are all these Hindu households?' I asked, pointing at quarters that were constructed behind the temple. A charpoy had been spread there in the middle of the courtyard, where a man was lying, while two young women, both of them wearing saris, were sitting.

'Yes. Most of them.'

As soon as he said that I noticed a man with a long beard and skull cap walk out of one of the buildings along with his wife who was wearing a *burqa*. This was a Muslim family.

We walked around a compartment where a few healthy cows were eating hay. They were probably used in religious ceremonies. It was clear to me that the conditions and the customs of the Hindu community here in Karachi were starkly different from those that I was used to in Lahore. The temple was much more elaborately decorated and the community seemed to be much larger.

The old man led me into another tall building where he introduced me to an officer and walked off. The officer, who was a middle aged man with a fat belly, looked at me as if I was a menace to his work. I showed him my press card and started asking him about the temple.

'I don't know exactly how old this temple is but it is an old one. It existed before Partition.'

He told me that several of Guru Nanak's followers also come to this temple, along with a few other devotees. I asked him if there was a picture of Guru Nanak at the temple, similar to the Hindu temples in Punjab. 'Yes, there is,' he said. 'In fact, there is a separate building that is reserved for the followers of Guru Nanak. It is a gurdwara and is referred to as Pehli Patshah. It is right next to the temple.'

This was the gurdwara I was looking for.

'It is recorded in the Sikh tradition that Nanak visited this region and visited these two temples, is that right?' I asked the man.

'No, that is not true at all. Nanak never visited this temple. He remained in Punjab.'

Clearly this guy had no idea about Nanak's travels.

I walked back to the temple and once again noticed the newly constructed building right next to it. In my haste I had missed the Khalsa symbol made on its window and also the saffron Nishan Sahib, the symbol of the Sikh community, posted on top. I called up Iqbal Qaiser and asked him if this was indeed the gurdwara that was constructed to commemorate the visit of Guru Nanak to this temple. 'Yes,' he said.

Along with the temple at Clifton, this too must have been a historical Hindu temple at the time and Nanak while visiting this area must have visited this place as well. Standing here, I wondered how different this place must have been at that time.

ੴ

Humayun wanted to show me Port Grand, the latest addition to Karachi's food scene. Near the port a new food street had been constructed above the sea with the latest restaurants. It was also convenient that there was another Hindu temple there. We decided to head in that direction to see the temple and also have lunch.

After giving the car to the valet we walked out of the gate of the Port Grand and headed to a small street next to it where the temple was situated. Right on top of the temple, within the complex of Port Grand was a newly constructed mosque for tourists.

There were two entrances to the temple. The first one read 'Ghat for women', while the other one was for men. Outside the entrance of the men's section was an old woman sitting on a charpoy with a younger man. The woman was wearing a colourful sari. 'Can we go inside?' asked Sadia. 'Yes,' she said.

We walked in the door. There was a small temple next to the entrance. Inside were a few people collecting material for food on one side of the room. This probably was an offering from a rich Hindu. They seemed unperturbed by our presence. Right in front of us was the sea and ahead of that was a mangrove forest. A young boy lying on his back on top of a small boat was floating in the sea. There were stairs leading into the water, which was blackened by all the industrial waste that is disposed into the sea. Several small boats were tied next to the stairs. This was a fishermen's community. The bridge of Port Grand too was in front of us, beyond which lay the port. On one side there were numerous pigeons fluttering on the floor, pecking at the rice that was offered to them.

Around us were a couple of other rooms, all of which were reserved for different deities. Sadia was busy photographing the temple when one of the men standing there told her sternly to stop photographing. I noticed a mural on the wall behind him, with a male deity sitting on top of a giant fish. Layers of water had been depicted underneath the fish. This was the famous Hindu deity also revered in certain Muslim traditions—Jhule Lal.

Given the backdrop of Port Grand, the temple was in a sad state. It was hardly noticeable in this posh area, where the gentry of the city descend every evening. Karachi is a politically contested area, but in essence it belongs to such fisherfolk communities who lived here before Kolachi became Karachi. Today, they are the most neglected community of the city. This entire area is known as the area of Mai Kolachi.

'Why is it called Mai Kolachi?' I asked Humayun.

'According to the legend there was an old woman in history who was known as Mai Kolachi. Mai means an old woman. Her son was killed by a fish. It is said that she tore apart the belly of the fish and retrieved her son. It is because of her bravery that this area came to be known as Mai Kolachi.'

It seemed to be as if these Hindu fisherfolk are now the only connection that the city of Karachi has with the village of Kolachi, the village that Nanak once visited.

ੴ

The edge of the boat narrowly missed the heads of two women who were sitting on the other boat. Both of them were wearing black burqas. These women continued yelling at the captain as he ignored them and manoeuvred the boat out of the mess of the several boats around us.

'Do you understand their language?' I asked Humayun, who was sitting next to me on the boat. 'Yes. I can make sense of it. But their Sindhi is different from ours.' Humayun belongs to Thatta on his paternal side and Shikarpur on his maternal side. 'This language that these women are speaking is a combination of Sindhi and Makrani.'

The port of Karachi, the symbol of the origin of this grand city is a modest structure, a minor tower rising from the middle of a single-storey building. A clock is placed within the tower. The port symbolizes colonial rule. At the time of Partition, Karachi was a minor port city with peaceful beaches. There were a few British clubs here, along with bungalows. The rest of the community comprised the indigenous fisherfolk, who are now a minority in their own land.

Partition changed the landscape of this city. Millions of migrants who had arrived from India were herded together to this port city, and within no time, Karachi emerged as the largest city of Pakistan and one of the biggest in the world. It has been growing exponentially ever since.

A little girl sitting across from me dipped her hand into a bag that her mother was holding. She picked up a little piece of dough and making a round ball out of it threw it into the water. I figured that she probably did that to attract the small fish swimming near the surface of the water, but no fish appeared. The piece of dough disappeared into the depths of this green water, while plastic bottles and bags that other travellers had thrown over the years floated on the surface. The girl and the woman continued throwing dough into the water but in vain.

Out in the sea, away from the port, the boat gained speed. A group of sea gulls started to follow us. They dived towards the sea to catch the dough being thrown into the water. Some of them caught the dough in the air while others dipped their beaks into the water. Most of them missed their catch.

As we moved further away from the port I could see giant ships anchored near the shore with several containers each. Behind them were the cranes of the port that removed the containers from the ship.

We were on our way to the small island of Manora not far from Karachi. This island has been connected with the mainland recently but travel by boat is still the preferred way of getting here. While in Karachi I was informed by a local Sikh that there was a gurdwara on the island called the Guru Nanak Gurdwara. When I asked him if it was possible that Guru Nanak had visited that place, he said that it was not a possibility. Like the Hindus that I had encountered here, he also refused to entertain the idea that Nanak had ever visited the southern coast. Humayun and I were now on this boat to see that gurdwara. There was also an abandoned Hindu temple here which was on our list of things to see.

Boats travel to and fro between Karachi and Manora every half an hour. I looked at the crowd of people to see if they were all tourists like us or also residents. Most of them came across as tourists but there were some residents from the island who needed to travel to Karachi for supplies.

The tyres attached to the edge of the boat bumped into the pillars supporting the port at Manora. We got out of the boat and headed towards the island. There was a gate next to the port which said that everyone entering Manora needed to pay twenty rupees, except for residents.

Humayun led the way while I walked not far behind. I had imagined this to be an isolated place but there were several restaurants and shops here. A few of the buildings were abandoned but a majority of them were occupied. A large portion of the island is under the control of the Navy, which monitors the sea regularly to ward off infiltration from India. There were Navy guards and check posts at regular intervals scattered all over the island.

While walking on the pavement, I peeped into one of the houses and saw a huge banyan tree behind it, on which was a plaque which read, 'Gurdwara Guru Nanak and the Temple of Valmiki'. Taking my shoes off next to the tree, I entered the shrine. There were two rooms here, one of which was dedicated to Guru Nanak while the other was dedicated to the Hindu deity Valmiki. I entered the room of Guru Nanak. Guru Granth Sahib was placed in front of me, covered in a red cloth. On the walls were posters of the Gurdwara Panja Sahib and also one of Guru Nanak, Mardana and Wali Gandhari, in which Guru Nanak is stopping with his hand, a rock hurled towards him from the top of a mountain where the Muslim saint was.

As I walked out of the gurdwara, I noticed a short dark old man wearing only a lungi and vest emerging from one of the rooms. After noticing us he went and wore his pyjama and shirt and greeted us. He had a long beard and a turban similar to the Sikhs of Punjab.

'Are you from Manora?' I asked him.

'Our family has been living here since before Partition. We originally belonged to Amritsar,' he said.

'Do you think Nanak ever visited this place?' I asked him.

'Absolutely not. He was from Punjab, Nankana Sahib.'

The name of this man was Jeeta Singh and our conversation took place in Punjabi, an aberration in Karachi. Jeeta Singh told me that every November when the festival of Guru Nanak is celebrated at Nankana Sahib he too arranges a small festival at this temple. Several Hindus and Sikhs from Karachi and other areas come here at that time. He tells me that there is another gurdwara here, also known as the Gurdwara of Guru Nanak and it is not too far from the Hindu temple. After taking down the directions to that temple and the shrine, we headed off.

It was a picturesque beach, with golden sand and shiny blue water. Far away, near the horizon, the sun was preparing to dip into the water and its reflection burned the sea. Behind us, towards the Western side, emerging from the mist was the Makran mountain range, the boundary line between Sindh and Baluchistan. In front of us was the skyline of polluted Karachi.

My feet sank into the sand. This was a popular tourist destination.

Several families and couples were walking on the beach hand in hand, or playing games. Navy patrols patrolled the road at regular intervals.

The Hindu temple was hard to miss. It was a tall conical structure constructed right on the beach. During the summers the waters probably came all the way to the base of the temple. I didn't know how old this temple was but I allowed my imagination to provide it with its historical context. Perhaps this was originally constructed by the indigenous community of this area many centuries ago and renovated several times over the years.

The way into the temple was cordoned off so we climbed the fence that was protecting it and entered. On top of the cone was the face of a Hindu deity whom I could not associate with any of the gods in the Hindu pantheon. This too must have been part of the local culture. The room was locked. The floor was constructed out of tiles which were also placed on the adjoining walls. There were figures of Hindu deities on these tiles, pictures of Krishna and Radha and Ram and Sita. All the faces had been wiped clean owing to the Islamic sensibilities of the newer communities settled here.

Is it possible that Nanak ever travelled to this island? It is recorded in Sikh heritage that he came to the village of Kolachi and then visited the temple of a sea god for which he had to take a boat and travel to an island neighbouring Kolachi. Later Sikh writers have asserted that this was the temple at Clifton. However, that temple was on the mainland, so Nanak travelling there on a boat makes no sense. On the other hand he would have needed to travel on a boat to come to the island of Manora. We will never know for sure if Nanak ever reached here.

A cool breeze was flowing from the sea. Humayun was busy photographing this beautiful temple, while I was immersed in my thoughts. Sitting here I thought about what Jeeta Singh had said. He had said that Nanak had never left Nankana Sahib, the place of his birth. Was he talking about himself or Nanak? Nanak in this case was a reflection of his own self. We are all like that. We project ourselves onto others. For the later Gurus, Nanak was a reflection of themselves. This was the case with me as well. My interpretation of Nanak is also a reflection of my own self. Sitting at the temple, I realised that my depiction of Nanak in

this book is not an accurate version of Nanak. This is nothing but what
I want Nanak to be like. In reality, Nanak must have been different from
my understanding of him.

We walked onto a road facing the temple and saw another gurdwara
in front of us. It was a small single storey structure painted orange, while
the Khalsa flag stood next to it. The Khalsa symbol was embossed on the
windows of the gurdwara. After asking around we found the caretaker
of the temple, who was a practising Sikh with a turban and a long beard.
His name was Rajesh. He agreed to show us the shrine from the inside.

It was a recently renovated structure with the Granth Sahib in the
centre. There were pictures of Guru Gobind Singh and the Golden
Temple on the walls. This shrine which was originally constructed
to honour the memory of Guru Nanak had now been completely
incorporated into the beliefs of the Khalsa. The distinctions between the
teachings of the other Gurus and that of Guru Nanak have now become
blurred for his followers.

Earlier there were communities who refused to incorporate
themselves into the Khalsa of Guru Gobind. They referred to themselves
as the followers of Guru Nanak. They still exist in Sindh and in Khyber
Pakhtunkhwa. Baptised Sikhs look down upon them. But here at the
shrine, looking at how Rajesh had transformed this shrine from that
of Guru Nanak to a shrine of the Khalsa, I could see that slowly these
independent followers of Nanak were now merging into the larger
groups of Sikhs.

Rajesh's family once belonged to that sect of Hindus. Today, they
refer to themselves as Sikhs. Is this because of the distinct boundary
lines that are now solidifying between different religious communities:
Hindus, Muslims, Sikhs and Christians? Does that mean that Nanak's
legacy in its true essence is also slowly disappearing?

15
Guru Hargobind

On the 24 July 1606, after Guru Arjan had already appointed Guru Hargobind as his spiritual successor, Guru Hargobind decided to give darshan to his followers. The throne of the Guru, the *Akal Takht*, translated as the Eternal Throne, had also been prepared by then. On this auspicious day the Guru dressed himself as a royal, wearing *churidar pyjama*, a saffron gown and a beautiful turban with an aigrette fixed on it. There was a precious necklace around his neck, while two swords were hanging to his left and right.[57]

These swords signified the new interpretation the Guru had given to the Sikh religion. When Hargobind was to be appointed as the new Guru of the Sikh community after the assassination of his father, he refused to take up the religious symbols of Guruhood that were borne by the Gurus before him. Instead he picked up the turban with an aigrette and placed two swords upon himself. On the day of his anointment he is reported to have said, 'My rosary shall be the sword belt and on my turban, I shall wear the emblem of royalty.'[58]

The Guru introduced the concept of *miri-piri* into the Sikh religion, which was symbolised by the two swords he chose to wear. One sword symbolised 'miri' which meant temporal power while the other, the Guru said, represented 'piri,' which was spiritual prowess.

---

[57]Gandhi, *History of the Sikh Gurus Retold*, page 481

[58]Ibid., page 475

Hargobind deliberately wanted to be seen as regal. It is for this reason that along with the construction of the Akal Takht he also started hoisting a saffron flag facing it. This was to eventually become Nishan Sahib, the symbol of the Khalsa. He also kept with himself a large drum called the *nagar*, which at that time was used by a ruler to summon his subjects. As a symbol of his new status the Guru also kept a hawk as a pet.

P. S. Grewal points out in his article 'Nanak's Doctrine and Feudalization of Sikh Gurudom' that the militarisation of the Sikh community had started during the period of the fifth Sikh Guru, Guru Arjan, but it was during the time of Guru Hargobind that it gained impetus. Initially, the Guru raised fifty-two bodyguards who would accompany him wherever he went. Along with this he started working on raising an army who were given the title of *Sant Sipahi* or saint soldiers. There were five hundred soldiers to begin with. They were not paid a salary but were exempt from paying the required tribute to the Guru.

Mohsin Fani, a Persian historian from the seventeenth century, who had a friendly relationship with the Guru, says that the number of Sant Sipahi was seven hundred cavaliers and sixty artillery men.[59] In addition to this the Guru also retained Afghan mercenaries whom Cunningham identifies as criminal elements.[60] An *akhara* (training hall) was constructed facing the Akal Takht where the soldiers practised wrestling and engaged in other physical exercises. Sant Sipahi were also instructed in the various arts of warfare. In 1660, the Guru ordered the construction of a fort wall around the city of Amritsar.

War songs too became a regular feature of the reign of the sixth Guru, who was, according to Sikh theology, the fifth incarnation of Nanak. These were sung by a special group of people called *dhadhi* on an instrument known as the *dhadh*. These songs of epic battles were known as *var*.

---

[59]Ibid., page 483

[60]P. S. Grewal, *Nanak's Doctrine and the Feudalization of the Sikh Gurudom, Social Scientist* 11.5 (1983): 25. JSTOR. Web. 20 Aug. 2014. <http://www.jstor.org/stable/10.2307/3517100?ref=no-x-route:699f2def62feec6c81235b0 a59d51197>

Through his Masands the Guru had given instructions to his devotees that they should offer him arms and horses instead of money as a tribute, which the Guru was expected to receive ever since Guru Arjan passed the rule of *Dasawandh* (one-tenth). On the day the Guru sat on the throne of Akal Takht, giving his subjects a chance for darshan, his devotees presented the Guru with the gifts that he had asked for. The militarisation of the Sikh community began with the rise of Hargobind to the pontifical throne of Sikhism and hence started a new chapter in Sikh history.

There is no doubt that Guru Hargobind had a deep impact on the philosophy of the Sikh religion. His sword was a cherished possession for his son, Guru Tegh Bahadur, when he rose to the pontifical throne. This sword was then passed on to Guru Gobind Singh who in many ways can be seen as the true descendant of Guru Hargobind. Looking at the histories of these two Gurus, Hargobind and Gobind Singh, it is not difficult to identify the similarities in their approach. Like Guru Hargobind, Guru Gobind too loved war epics, used to hunt regularly and took an active part in military exercises.

Many critics of the Guru have identified the militaristic features of the reign of the Guru as being a departure from the teachings of the early Gurus. It has been stated that the religion founded by Nanak was peaceful and gentle, whereas Guru Hargobind added the fervour of warfare into it. It is argued that the Guru was too drawn to the glamour of politics and arms which took him away from the religious leadership which was originally what the seat of the Guru was meant to exemplify. The critics point out that unlike the previous Gurus, Hargobind did not even compose a single hymn, in support of this argument.

Coming from Nanak and passing through Angad Dev, Amar Das, Ram Das and then Arjan, it is not difficult to see that the institution of Guruhood changed drastically under the leadership of Guru Hargobind and hence brought about the change in the religious outlook of the Sikh community. However, it would be unfair to criticize this change without taking into account the context in which the Guru accepted the leadership of the Sikh community.

Guruhood was bestowed upon Hargobind when his father, Guru Arjan, was summoned to Lahore by Emperor Jahangir to explain his role during the rebellion of Prince Khusro against his father. Guru Arjan knew that he might not return from his trial and hence before his departure he appointed Hargobind as the sixth Guru. Guru Arjan was subsequently martyred, throwing the Sikh community into disarray. Guru Hargobind was appointed the leader of the Sikh community at a time when they were suffering from an existential crisis. Their Guru had just been assassinated by the Mughal Emperor and there was no way for them to fight back.

There were different opinions as to what was to be the next step of the Sikh Guru. One suggestion was that the Sikh community should completely disavow any form of interference in politics and become a purely religious group, while there was another swell of support for revenge. It was in such an environment that Guru Hargobind decided to militarise the Sikh community. It was argued that it was un-Sikh like to bear oppression. Guru Hargobind made it the duty of a Sikh to fight oppression and be unafraid to die in the process if need be, following the example of Guru Arjan.

The martyrdom of Guru Arjan provided the Sikh community with a cohesive motivation which united them against the tyranny of the Mughal Emperor Jahangir. In the interpretation of religious history, Jahangir became the oppressor while Guru Arjan and Guru Hargobind the victims, similar to the situation in the case of Aurangzeb and Guru Tegh Bahadur and Guru Gobind Singh.

The reality, however, is much more complex. Whereas the oppression of Jahangir served as an excuse for the militarisation of the Sikh community, Hargobind eventually managed to reconcile his differences with Emperor Jahangir. In fact, some claims have asserted that Hargobind joined his employment, serving him in the Punjab. The Sikh version of the story states that this is because Jahangir eventually became much more religiously tolerant towards non-Muslims, which might well be the case, but is quiet about the politics of the Guru. Hargobind and Jahangir eventually established a cordial relationship and the former is said to have assisted the Emperor to overcome Tara Chand of Nalagarh who had been rebelling against the Emperor for a long time.[61] It is hard to ignore the political motives of the Guru in forming a friendship with the 'tyrant' Emperor who had been responsible for the assassination of his father.

During the period of Emperor Jahangir, Guru Hargobind was incarcerated in Gwalior jail on the orders of the Emperor. Several explanations are put forward to explain the imprisonment of the Guru, one of which is that the Guru had retained the money that was given to him by the Court to be disbursed to his troops.[62] Once again, this is an indication of employment of the Guru by the Mughal Emperor. The Sikh version of the story is that the Emperor felt threatened by the growing militarisation of the Guru. It is believed that the Guru was released after the Muslim saint Mian Mir, who was also a friend of Guru Arjan, interceded on behalf of Guru Hargobind.[63] It is believed that the relationship between the Guru and the Emperor improved after the former was released from jail.

The relationship between the Sikhs and the Mughals deteriorated rapidly after the ascension of Jahangir's son Shahjahan to the throne. Sikh sources claim that to appease the religiously orthodox segment of his court, the Emperor, like Jahangir of the early days, also showed intolerance towards non-Muslims. Three battles were fought between the Mughal forces and those of the Gurus and all of them were won by the Sikhs. These were the battles of Amritsar, Lahira and Kartarpur. After the final battle, Guru Hargobind decided to settle at Kartarpur, which is explained as the reason for peace between the Mughals and the Sikhs. Kartarpur is located in a somewhat desolate place and is not as accessible as Amritsar. All these victories under the leadership of Guru Hargobind provided a morale boost to the weak Sikh community, who started viewing themselves as a divinely favoured community.

Guru Hargobind remains one of the most controversial Sikh Gurus. It was his policy of militarisation that gave a new face to the peaceful religious community of Guru Nanak. He laid the foundations of the contemporary face of Sikhism.

---

[61]Gandhi, *History of the Sikh Gurus Retold*, page 506

[62]Ibid., page 500

[63]Ibid., page 505

16
The Shiva of My Imagination

The chill pierced the bare feet of the pilgrims and sent them jumping on the marble floor. It was a cold February night and it had been raining all day. It was the annual festival of Shivratri at the holiest of holy temples in Punjab—Katas Raj. Situated on the slope of the mountain, this complex was a collection of temples located around a sacred pond. This pool which was constructed in the shape of an eye was created when Lord Shiva shed a tear after his wife Sati passed away, or so the story goes. His tear, in a beautiful emerald shade, could wash away the gravest of sins. Pilgrims from hundreds of kilometres away came here to purify their lives.

One of the temples constructed at the edge of the pool was dedicated to Lord Shiva. This was the most important temple here. There were temples dedicated to the goddesses Kali and Durga here as well but after the pond the focal point of the complex remained the temple dedicated to Shiva. It is believed that these temples were constructed by the Pandava brothers when they were sent on a thirteen year exile after their cousins, the Kauravas took over the throne. In the *Mahabharata* these temples are mentioned as sacred spaces that could uplift the soul of a devotee.

Standing on the edge, Mardana observed the proceedings at the temple below him. At the shrine of Shiva, devotees were bathing the idol with milk, while others stood behind, singing his praises. Some lit lamps and placed them in the pond. They were then taken away by a small stream which emerged from the pond and disappeared into the mountains across the road. Across the road there was also a small cave where a few yogis, the devotees of Lord Shiva, sat in meditative postures. Mardana could see a trail of pilgrims ascending to the top of the mountain where there were other temples and peaceful places to meditate.

It was a quiet night, except for the sounds of the bhajans that were coming from the temple. The rain had ceased and in a full moon all the clouds had disappeared while bright stars emerged from their hiding places. It was one of the most beautiful night skies Mardana had ever seen. He thought about his time in Sri Lanka, where together Nanak and he had climbed Adam's peak. There too, the sky was as clear as it was here. Mardana wanted to share his observation with his best friend but he was busy. Nanak was sitting with the devotees who were gathered at the temple of Shiva.

Being residents of Punjab, both Nanak and Mardana had heard about this temple which was about fifty kos from Talwindi. Among the several yogis that Nanak met on the outskirts of Talwindi, several had spent a large portion of their lives here or were en route to here. While he was still a youngster at Talwindi, he had made plans to visit the temple but difficulties in his personal life had prevented that. Now that Nanak had travelled East and South and was now heading north to the Himalayas, he decided to stop at this temple.

Sitting inside the temple amongst the devotees, Nanak looked up at his friend who was sitting on top of the adjacent mountain. He felt bad for him. Nanak did not want to abandon him but he had to, because being a Muslim, Mardana would not have been allowed inside such a sacred Hindu space. If it was about his personal convictions then Nanak too would have boycotted any place that did not allow his friend, but here, his aim was to end the exploitation of religion by priests and pandits. He wanted to show the people that there is a direct path to God, one that doesn't travel through temples and shrines. He needed to show them that these rituals and rites have nothing to do with spirituality. For this he had to mingle with these people, at their shrines, during their rituals. There were several religious reformers who criticised such practices while sitting in their isolated jungles, but not many took the bold step of actually travelling to such places and criticising them from within.

This of course had its own challenges. Being surrounded by thousands of devotees while telling them that what they were doing was wrong, was likely to put the critic in danger. Nanak though was not afraid to call a spade a spade. He went to Benaras and told the pandits there their rituals would not help them attain salvation. He travelled to Tilla Jogian and told the ascetics there that they needed to engage with the world to save it from evil. Every time he did that, he put himself and Mardana in a dangerous position. Nanak knew well enough that people got easily charged up, rallying around religion, especially when it gave them a sense of security. However, luckily or through divine intervention, he had stayed clear of any mortal threat.

Often, Mardana had told him to tone down his rhetoric and to become a little less confrontational. On such occasions Nanak would listen and then smile politely as if implying that he understood what was being said and would heed the advice. But then when it mattered, Nanak would completely disregard these words of caution. Mardana knew that it was not by divine intervention that they had avoided physical harm but rather by the magic of Nanak's words. Nanak had a way with words and would often engage his enemy in a conversation out of which no one had yet been able to untangle himself. Such was the web that Nanak cast with his words. In fact, Mardana believed that the more people there were when Nanak was challenging a religious dogma, the better it was, because if Nanak's words were not having any impact on the person arguing with him, then the magic would at least influence someone from the audience, who would prevent any attempt by the mob to harm the saint. Confident of Nanak's poetic language, Mardana shut his eyes and lay down on the grass, inhaling the fresh air of the mountains.

He thought about his home, from where they had just returned after a long trip to the East and South. On the way to Talwindi, Mardana had made up his mind that he would no longer travel with Nanak. Years of separation from family and a life of being constantly on the road had taken its toll and he thought that he would need years to recuperate from the exhaustion of the journey. However, he had underestimated the air of his village. Within days, all the tiredness disappeared from his body and he felt like a young man again. A few months after their arrival at Talwindi when Nanak asked him if he would be willing to travel north with him, Mardana was surprised at his immediate 'yes'. Only for a little while did he regret his decision, when both of them were once again walking away from the familiar streets of Talwindi, heading towards the cold North. Their friends and families had gathered at the edge of the town to see them off. Mardana was moved by the tears of his son. He felt bad for him as he was growing up without a father. Nanak's wife Sulakhni was also there along with her two sons Sri Chand and Lachman Das. Looking at their forlorn faces, Mardana knew that as much as the world acknowledged the sagacity and wisdom of their father, these two boys would never be able to understand the motives behind their father leaving them at such a tender age.

Throughout the journey, Mardana often brought up the topic of his family members and how much he missed them. He was surprised that Nanak did not talk about his family even once. He was surprised to find that a man who loved the world so much was so quiet about his own family. He had planned to ask Nanak several times but he could never bring himself to ask him about the pain he felt of being separated from his own family. He wanted to ask him if Nanak's divine mission was unfair on his family but he never could.

Lost in his thoughts, Mardana shut his eyes and listened to the wind blowing. He was lying under a young peepal tree whose leaves danced to celebrate the end of the rain. All the sounds from the temple receded to the periphery and only that of the breeze flowing through the grass and leaves remained. It was then that he realised that however much he longed for his home, within him was the soul of a wanderer, which was also the case with Nanak.

A sudden noise from the temple disturbed Mardana's tranquillity. He could hear a lot of people speaking together. The activities around the temple had stopped and everyone it seemed was stunned by a certain event. In the darkness of the night Mardana could not see anything but could very well imagine what could have caused this uproar at such a gathering. Amused at the behaviour of his friend he once again lay down on the grass and attempted to block off all sound.

ੴ

Nanak sat patiently in one corner of the temple, while the pandit poured litres of milk over the *shiv ling*. Sitting in the corner, he looked like any ordinary sadhu in his saffron garb. The difference was that while the rest of the sadhus were immersed in the spirituality of the occasion, praying under their breath as the pandit worshipped the shiv ling, Nanak viewed the practice with scepticism. He noticed a small passageway way from which the milk flowed out of the temple and mixed in the stream that disappeared under the mountains. He found the practice to be atrocious, especially when there were so many hungry people to feed. There were dozens of beggars lined up outside the temple who looked as if they had not eaten for days. Instead of being poured on a rock, why couldn't this milk be presented to these poor people outside, as a gift from God, he wondered?

As the offering of milk to the deity concluded, everyone stood up and the pandit began leading the communal prayer. People turned to see who this disrespectful man was who kept sitting while everyone stood up around him. A sadhu standing next to Nanak nudged him with his leg and when Nanak looked at him he directed him with his eyes to stand up. Nanak ignored him and continued looking straight at the shiv ling. Because of Nanak's audacious behaviour there was unrest in the prayer. No one could concentrate on singing praises to the god, when this man was being so disrespectful right under their noses. The pandit too by now had noticed Nanak from the corner of his eyes. However, since it was considered inauspicious to leave a prayer in the middle, he continued with his recitation, planning to rebuke the recalcitrant sadhu later.

Perhaps to add fuel to the fire, Nanak got up and left the temple during the middle of the prayer, an act which sent shock waves down the spines of all the devotees. Hurriedly finishing the *aarti*, the priest rushed outside to find this blasphemous sadhu. Several holy men had been to this temple before him and a lot of them had acted strangely but no one had ever been rude to the gods.

'Hey you,' shouted the priest, locating Nanak sitting with his feet dangling in the holy pond not far from the temple of Shiva. 'How dare you behave in this manner?' he roared. 'You have not only brought a curse upon yourself but also on all of us that have gathered here. You have spoiled our aarti for us. Do you know how sacred this temple and our traditions are? How dare you continue sitting during the aarti and then walk out as if this were a trivial affair? What kind of a sadhu are you? Do you not know how to behave when an aarti is being performed?'

'I very well know how to behave during an aarti. While you were singing in front of that stone, I was praying to the Eternal God. I was performing an aarti for him,' said Nanak.

'Jogi, are you calling the shiv ling a stone? Don't you know that Shiva has the power to destroy the world with a single dance? Do you not believe in the power of our Lord Shiva?'

The priest's words had the desired impact. These words were not uttered for Nanak but for the pilgrims who were slowly gathering around these two individuals, listening in on the conversation. The priest knew that by raising such questions he could incite the crowd which would then turn hostile towards Nanak. After the priest completed the sentence, he looked around to the people, seeking support from them, which he was getting. An offended look had emerged in people's eyes. They were now waiting to listen to Nanak's reply and were sure that he would not be able to emerge victorious from such a rhetorical question. The priest too believed that he had trapped Nanak.

Nanak knew that he would have to choose his words carefully. He was after all standing in one of the most sacred temples dedicated to Shiva, and his followers were passionate and believed in destruction for the right causes. If Nanak did not utter the right words, his life could be in danger.

However, as much as he wanted to calm himself down and answer the question in a polite and harmless manner, he could not help but to feel angry. Nanak did not have much tolerance for the exploitation of innocent people in the name of religion. He also could not stand such conversations, which were not about learning more about the unknown but about impressing one's knowledge upon the other. He knew that the priest was doing exactly that by raising his voice while asking the last question.

'Listen, priest,' replied Nanak, this time with some anger in his voice. 'I believe in Shiva. He is as much my guru as he is yours. But my Shiva is not the Shiva of the Hindu trinity which you and other exploiters of religion, who fool innocent people like the ones around us, use for occult powers. My Shiva doesn't assist a wrongdoer, no matter how hard that person strives. My Shiva is the Supreme Creator and His blessings are unshakeable. His law is unchallengeable.'

The priest was at a loss for words. He did not expect this sort of a comeback. Adept in the use of words and sentence construction, the priest had never met anyone who could disentangle the web cast by his words so quickly.

'What aarti were you performing inside the temple, sitting on the floor, while all of us were standing in the court of Shiva, wise man?' asked the pandit.

'I, at that time, was in the court of the Lord of the Universe, my friend. I was accompanied by the entire sky, all its stars and even the moon, while your mind and heart was turned against it all. I was praying to the Supreme Lord while you were standing dumbfounded in front of this stone. While your mind lingered greedily on the offerings before the idol, which I hope you enjoy eating, my mind was fixed on the eternal presence of the Lord. While your mind was disturbed by the noise of the bells, I was enchanted by the music of the universe and the fragrance of His presence in nature.'

The priest realised that Nanak had had gotten the better of him in this conversation. He knew that this holy man was likely to have an answer for anything that he could throw his way. He was still hopeful though that the people would turn against Nanak as he had earlier planned. He knew that Nanak was saying controversial things but there was a conviction in his voice that had an impact upon the hearts of the people gathered around him. The priest could see the faces of the people turn soft. He hoped that in the conversation Nanak would say something unguarded, which he could then turn against him. This was not about Shiva or aarti anymore. This was personal.

'And may we hear your aarti and see it performed before the Lord of the Universe?' he asked.

'Your religion might not allow that,' replied Nanak. 'For that you might have to give up your sacred vows temporarily. My message is not for those who are not willing to tread a difficult path. It requires coming to terms with uncertainty. It requires risking losing your religion.'

'O manipulator of words, we will not be impressed by your shallow words. So stop trying to impress this audience. Say simply whatever you want to say.'

'What I mean to say O wise man is that for me to sing my aarti I would require the company of my companion, whose presence you will not be able to tolerate in your sacred temple,' said Nanak.

'And why is that?' roared the priest.

'Because he was born in the house of a Muslim Mirasi family. Would you be able to carry the burden of his family's sins?'

The crowd gasped at Nanak's words. Murmurs emerged from different corners of the crowd. 'A Muslim, a Muslim' was on everyone's lips. The priest was caught in his own trap. He had challenged Nanak and now did not want to back down. That would be admitting defeat. But on the other hand he could never allow the footsteps of a Muslim to fall on this sacred space.

'Where is your despicable friend?' asked the priest in a pensive manner.

'He is sitting right there,' said Nanak, pointing towards a lone tree on the mountain facing the temple.

'Well, he cannot come here but we can go to him. We will not get too close to him because I don't feel like taking another dip in the holy pond on this cold evening. But we will listen to your aarti so that you are left with no excuse.'

Sitting under the tree, with Mardana at his side, playing the rubab, Nanak started to sing. The crowd stood at a little distance from them, to avoid Nanak's Muslim companion. At the head of the crowd stood the pandit with his hands folded across his chest. He stared at Nanak with piercing eyes. Nanak sang the following poem:

In the salver of the firmament,
The sun and the moon shine as lamps;

The stars are like pearls for offering;
The fragrance of the sandal trees is incense,
The breeze blows as Thy royal fan;
The forest offers their flowers to Thee, O Eternal Light.

Thousands are Thine eyes,
And yet Thou hast no eyes,
Thousands are Thy forms,
And yet Thou hast no form,
Thousands are Thy feet,
And yet Thou hast no nose.
This wondrous play bewitches me.
In every heart is the same Light;
It is the Light of God,
Which illumines every soul,
And gives light and fire to everyone.
Through the Guru's Word,
This Light is revealed within the soul.
What pleaseth the Lord,
Is the best Arati: worship with lamp.

O Lord, my mind yearns for Thy lotus feet,
As the honey-bee for the nectar of the flowers.
Day and night, Lord, I am athirst for Thee,
Give to Nanak Thy water of mercy:
He is like the Sarang: the hawk-cuckoo;
That drinks only heavenly rain drops;
And let me repose in the light of Thy Name.[64]

The pandit was moved by the melodious voice and words of Nanak; however, he was too arrogant to admit defeat. The pilgrims who in following the pandit had kept their distance from Nanak and Mardana were now leaving the pandit behind and heading towards the duo. They urged them to sing more songs. The pandit quietly disappeared into the

---

[64]Singh, *Guru Nanak: Founder of Sikhism*, pages 228–229

night, returning to the temple of Shiva; to pray alone this time—for the magic of this strange jogi to wane from the minds of the people he had just influenced.

ੴ

What should have been a minor detour turned out to be a disaster. My wife Anam and I were driving back to Islamabad after a weekend in Lahore and I had decided that on the way I would stop at Katas Raj to see Nanak's Gurdwara.

I had been to Katas Raj several times but never had I seen the building which was associated with Guru Nanak. A few years ago when I came here to document the festival of Maha Shivratri, I asked the local guide about the gurdwara. He told me that there was no such building here. He insisted that he had been working here for over a decade and if there was a gurdwara, he would have known. I was sure that the gurdwara existed because historical records clearly state Nanak visited this sacred site and Iqbal Qaiser too had seen and photographed the place for his book. Anam on the other hand had never been to Katas Raj and was excited about the prospect of finally being able to visit the place she had heard so much about.

The sacred complex of Katas Raj is only a few kilometres from the exit of Kallar Kahar on the Motorway. On my last trip there this journey took us about fifteen minutes; however, this time we had been on the road for more than an hour and the complex was nowhere in sight. The National Highway Authority had recently decided to expand this single lane road, which is why it was dug up and was hardly usable when we found ourselves on that road on this unplanned tour. There are several cement factories dotting this area and therefore the political lobbying to expand this road had been intense.

The road dragged on for a long time. The sun slowly started to sink in the sky. Even though this road is reasonably safe and I have travelled here well after midnight, I still began to get worried. On the left hand side of the road I noticed a small road side café where Iqbal Qaiser and I had once stopped for lunch. I knew that the temple was not far now.

Placed comfortably within the embrace of the mountains, the temples of Katas Raj appeared on the right side of the road. I had seen these buildings way too many times to be fascinated by them anymore but Anam was delighted. There on our right was the haveli of Hari Singh Nalwa and behind that were the Kashmiri temples dedicated to Shiva built in the seventh and eighth century. Hidden behind them was a half excavated *stupa* (mound-like or hemispherical structure) at least four thousand years old and next to the stupa was the temple dedicated to Ram. The sacred pond, believed to be the tear of Lord Shiva was at the base of these buildings. Across the road were the offices of the Archaeology Department and nearby was a small hotel.

I had no idea where the Gurdwara of Nanak was. I was sure that I had explored all the buildings around the complex and the gurdwara had to be within one of these structures. I parked my car in the parking lot and started to climb the stairs that led to the temple of Ram.

Below us the pond of Shiva which had recently been renovated was brimming with water. There was no garbage floating on the water like the last time. Several groups of boys had gathered around the pond and were diving into the water from the rooftops of the buildings around it. These were all Muslim boys and hence the pond and the complex were not sacred to them.

Recently the water level of this sacred pool had started to fall. This was because the cement factories around this area were sucking the groundwater in this region. Cement being a water-intensive industry is an environmental hazard. But writers and journalists started writing about the disappearing pond here, as a result of which the government woke from its slumber and came to protect this temple. The water level has now been restored.

I approached a tourist guide standing on the stairs and asked him if he knew where the gurdwara was, even though I was sure that he would not be able to help me out. 'There is no gurdwara here,' he insisted, while I kept arguing that there is one.

'I think it is within that building,' I said, pointing towards a grand structure that was the temple of Ram.

'There is no gurdwara there. That is a Hindu temple.'

'But that is also a gurdwara.'

'No.'

I was lost without my mentor, Iqbal Qaiser, who would have taken me straight to the gurdwara. I called him on his cell phone and asked him the exact location of the shrine.

'It is next to the fort,' he said. There was only one fort here, built by Hari Singh Nalwa. The temple of Ram was in front of that fort. Iqbal Qaiser confirmed my conviction that the shrine was within the temple. I asked Iqbal Qaiser to explain the exact location to the guide. The guide listened to him patiently and after the call told me that he now knew where the gurdwara was.

'Is it within the temple of Ram?' I asked with an air of confidence. 'No,' he said. I was embarrassed. I had been insisting all this while that the gurdwara was within the temple and that the guide did not know anything.

We walked away from the pool, away from the group of boys having a good time. The gurdwara was at a little distance from the complex. It was not renovated as the rest of the complex was. I am not sure if the department concerned with the renovation of the structure even knew about the significance of the building. Even the path leading to the gurdwara had been neglected. We climbed the stairs leading into the gurdwara and entered the main room where once the Guru Granth Sahib must have been recited. It was a big building, with several pillars that once supported a roof on top. The roof was now gone. On one side there was a staircase leading nowhere. Before Partition, this must have been an impressive structure. It was bigger than I had expected it to be. Perhaps there must have been few frescoes on the walls as well.

'We never knew what this building was,' said the guide, while we were walking out of the gurdwara.

'Now you know,' I said. 'You can tell all the tourists that this is the Gurdwara of Guru Nanak.'

A few years ago, Iqbal Qaiser and I were driving back from Pattoki after one of our research trips. This was years before I started working on Guru

Nanak. At that time Iqbal Qaiser and I were travelling every weekend, spending the entire day with each other, for one of my projects on the Multan road. As usual, Iqbal Qaiser and I were engaged in a discussion, talking about everything under the sky.

'Iqbal Sahib, in all of your travels what has been the most difficult journey you have ever undertaken?' I asked.

He sat silently for a little while, thinking, and then said, 'I think it has to be the trip I made to Nanak's Gurdwara in Jhelum. This is next to Rohtas Fort.'

Rohtas Fort is a popular fort located on the Grand Trunk road constructed by the Afghan King Sher Shah after he defeated the Mughal Emperor Humayun.

'I was accompanied by a friend called Ilyas Ghuman. This was in the month of June,' Iqbal Qaiser continued. 'We got off on the main road and then took a rickshaw to the fort. I thought that the gurdwara was located within the fort. We climbed one of its walls and saw that the gurdwara was in front of us, just under the shadow of the wall of the fort. The problem was that there was no way to get there. We climbed down the wall and started walking towards the gurdwara. From the top it had looked as if the gurdwara was only a few steps away but when we started walking we realised that the shrine looked closer than it actually was. There were shrubs around us with thorns. Throughout the journey we were picking out thorns from our clothes and feet. We walked for hours in the scorching heat of June. We were parched. It felt as if we were going to die.'

'Finally, after hours, we reached our destination. We fell on the steps of the gurdwara and passed out. An old man who was working there came to us and without asking any questions brought us an entire pot of water. We gulped it down and came back to our senses. When we were able to talk he asked us how we had managed to come via the route of the fort. He told us that there was a simpler route from the road which we had missed. He told us that we were lucky to have made it alive from there. There was quicksand and even wild animals on the way. To top that, there were dacoits who had taken refuge in the forest around that region who do not allow anyone to pass through alive.'

When I finally got to see the gurdwara next to Rohtas, I did so without Iqbal Qaiser. Jhelum is about a hundred kilometres from Islamabad. So once again, this is a place that is closer to my new home as opposed to my old home. When Nanak decided to head north into the mountains of the Himalayas he visited Jhelum along with Katas Raj and Hassan Abdal.

On another occasion, when Anam and I were returning from Lahore, we decided that we would stop at Rohtas for a little while. I had already seen the fort once but I wanted to show it to Anam. I had forgotten all about the gurdwara and the story that Iqbal Qaiser had told me while I was en route to this fort.

Just at a little distance from the fort, I noticed a building with a dome on top on our right. There was no doubt that this was a Sikh gurdwara. A black corrosive powder had collected on the walls of the building. This was an abandoned structure. Looking at the building I was reminded of Iqbal Qaiser's story, which I told Anam. 'Let's visit it,' she said with enthusiasm. Anam has a sense of adventure that I sometimes find hard to match.

We quickly walked through the remains of the fort, which included a *baoli* (step well) and a couple of abandoned Hindu temples. This was not the kind of fort that was found in Lahore, where only royalty stayed. This was a protective fort as well as a royal fort. There was a palace within it. There was also a small village within the fort. The fact that the village was located within the protection of the thick walls of the fort as opposed to being outside reinforced the notion that this was not a safe location. The sun had disappeared beyond the horizon and a sharp blue was now spreading through the sky.

After the trip to the fort we drove on a small road that connected the main road to the shrine. This is the road that Iqbal Qaiser had missed. Facing the shrine in an open field was a grave next to which was an *alm* (a pole, usually the shape of a hand at the top, with a black flag. It is the symbol of Shiaism in South Asia), a sign that this was a Shia shrine. The grave was covered by a couple of berry trees. There were a few lamps placed next to the grave with oil in them. This meant that devotees still come to the shrine.

We walked into the gurdwara which was a three storey building. It was a beautiful structure located on top of a small mound. Behind it was a forest on the edge of which was the fort. Iqbal Qaiser and his friend must have come from there. Anam and I climbed to the top of the shrine and walked around the dome. It was a beautiful sight. There was nothing else on the horizon besides the fort.

While we were standing on top of the shrine I saw a motorcycle driving on the mud road that we had just used to get to the gurdwara. There were two men sitting on it, both of them wearing black shalwar kameez. I hoped that these two men would eventually change their direction and head away from us but I was hoping against all possibilities. There was no other route that these men could take. I wasn't scared for my own safety but for Anam's. I was also worried about the car.

These two men drove straight into the open plot facing the gurdwara, passing our car and parked at the base. They then started catering to the Shia shrine. Anam and I decided that we should head off given the scary story that we had heard about this place.

'Where are you from?' asked one of the men in the black shalwar kameez as we were walking past him. 'And what are you doing here?' he continued. I gave him a brief introduction about myself. He then said that we should head out of this place as soon as possible since it was getting dark and this place was not safe. Without asking any further questions we walked back to the car and drove away as fast as we could.

While we were still in that locality, heading down to the Grand Trunk Road, Anam surfed the internet on her Blackberry to find news about this place. 'Two tourists beheaded' was the first link that popped up.

Later, when I met Iqbal Qaiser, I shared my story with him. 'Standing at that place made me realise how extraordinary Nanak's journey was,' I said to him. 'These two men were travelling without a vehicle. When Nanak stayed at this place, there was no Rohtas fort, so this must have been a desolate space. There must have been many more wild animals here at that time. And yet these men sat here for days, braving not only the climate but also quicksand, animals and hostile humans. This journey is really not for the faint-hearted.'

'Yes, that is correct,' said Iqbal Qaiser, 'but you also need to take into account another thing. You had possessions while you were there—your phone, car, money, etc. that you were worried about. Nanak travelled without any material possessions, which meant that the fear of loss was not there. When you have nothing to lose, there is no fear.'

'I understand that, Iqbal Sahib, but what about wild animals? They can still attack you. I am sure at night when Nanak and Mardana used to light a fire, these animals must have been attracted towards them.'

'Animals are more scared of humans than humans are of animals. Humans are the worst kind of animals. Nothing is worse than humans. Remember that.'

17
Guru Arjan

'In Goindwal which is on the river Beas, there was a Hindu named Arjan, in the garments of saint-hood and sanctity—so much so, that he had captivated many of the simple-hearted of the Hindus and even the ignorant and foolish followers with his ways and manners, and they loudly sounded the drums of his holiness. They called him Guru and from all sides stupid people crowded to worship and manifest complete faith in him. For three or four generations they had kept this shop warm. Many times it occurred to me to put a stop to this vain affair or to bring him to the assembly of the people of Islam.[65]

'At last, when Khusro passed along this road, this insignificant fellow (Guru Arjan) proposed to wait upon him. Khusro happened to halt at a place where he was and he came out and did homage to him. He behaved to Khusro in certain special ways, and made on his fore-head a finger-mark in saffron which the Indians call Qashqa and is considered propitious. When this came to my ears and I fully knew his heresies I ordered that he should be brought to my presence and having handed over his houses, dwelling places and children to Murtaza Khan and having confiscated his property, I ordered that he should be dealt with the penal Laws of Yasa.[66]

For five days the Guru was tortured. The Laws of Yasa did not only prescribe death, it also ordered torture before capital punishment. In the

---

[65]Gandhi, *History of the Sikh Gurus Retold*, pages 414–415

[66]Ibid., page 415

walled city of Lahore there is a place near the Rang Mahal known as
Lal Khoi, or the Red Well. It is believed that Arjan was kept in a room
next to this well, which was the haveli of the Mughal Diwan of Lahore
at the time. Guru Arjan was tortured there.

In the burning heat of summer, boiling sand was poured on top of his
head, while he was immersed in a cauldron with a fire under it. After five
days of torture the body of the Guru gave up and he passed away near
the bank of the river. His body was then thrown into the river.[67] Next to
Lahore Fort there is a small yellow structure which is now referred to as
the samadhi of Guru Arjan. It is believed that the Guru lost his life there.

The Sikh version of the story, emerging out of a religious ethos is a
little more elaborate. It recalls that the Guru bore his punishment with
patience. During his torture, it is believed that his friend, the Muslim
saint of Lahore, Mian Mir, came to him and asked for permission to
bury alive his oppressors. The Guru refused. On the fifth day, the Guru
expressed the desire to take a dip in the waters of the Ravi. He was given
permission. After taking a dip the Guru did not emerge from the water.
The Sikhs believe that the Guru had performed a miracle and passed
onto the other world.

There are two reasons which explain why Guru Arjan was assassinated
by the Mughal Emperor. The traditional Sikh version of the story is that
Arjan was martyred due to the connivance of a Hindu Khatri called
Chandu Lal who was appointed as the Diwan of Lahore by the Mughal
authorities. Chandu Lal asked for Hargobind's hand for his daughter in
marriage. Guru Arjan refused, saying that his was a spiritual journey and
he did not want to be associated with the political aristocracy. Taking
the rejection personally, Chandu Lal began conspiring against the Guru
along with the Guru's disgruntled brother Prithi Chand. It was his
influence over the Mughal court that eventually led to the assassination
of the Guru.

Prithi Chand was the eldest brother of the Guru, who had turned
against his brother and father when Guru Ram Das appointed Arjan
over him as the subsequent Guru. Things fell apart between father and

---

[67]Ibid.

son when Arjan was sent to Lahore by Ram Das to attend his nephew's wedding.[68] After the wedding Arjan wrote to Guru Ram Das several times, seeking permission to return home but all those letters fell into the hands of Prithi Chand, who hid them. He was making sure that Arjan was removed from the picture and had no chance of inheriting the Guruship.

By the time of Guru Ram Das the institution of Guruhood had acquired considerable power and wealth unlike the time of any previous Guru. Guru Ram Das had a jagir where he laid the foundation of the city of Ramdaspur, which eventually became Amritsar, one of the holiest cities for the Sikh community. Guru Ram Das was also responsible for the establishment of the Masand system, which brought power and wealth to the Guru, as the deputies of the Guru spread to various parts of the country.

Keeping in mind the development of the institution of Guruhood, one can imagine the enthusiasm of Prithi Chand to inherit not only his father's property but also his legacy, which at this time had started bringing in rich rewards.

Arjan continued writing to his father from Lahore, asking for permission to come back to his family but all of his letters fell into Prithi Chand's hands. When Guru Ram Das finally discovered his eldest son's deception he called Arjan back and disowned Prithi Chand. A few days later he appointed Arjan as the next Guru.

Conniving with rebel Masands, Prithi Chand looked for help from Mughal officials to inherit his father's property. According to Sikh sources (which are biased against him) Prithi Chand also used his connections with the Mughals and complained to the Mughal Emperor Akbar about his younger brother, Guru Arjan. After Guru Arjan completed the compilation of the *Adi Granth*, it was due to the connivance of Prithi Chand that he was summoned to court to explain the anti-Muslim and anti-Hindu content of the book as stated by the rebel brother. Arjan sent one of the senior members of the community, Bhai Gurdas, to court, who after reciting from the Granth clarified the misunderstanding. The

---

[68]Singh, *The History of Sikh Gurus*, pages 57–58

Sikhs believe that when the 'tolerant' Akbar was replaced by the 'narrow minded' Jahangir, the influence of Prithi Chand and his ally Chandu Lal penetrated the thick walls of the Mughal court, which resulted in the execution of the Guru.

Mughal sources, however, and particularly the *Tuzk-e-Jahangiri*, the autobiography of Emperor Jahangir, are glaringly silent about the role of Chandu Lal. His name is not mentioned anywhere. Jahangir, on the other hand, clearly states that Arjan was punished because of his sympathies for his rebel son Khusro.

The Mughal Emperor Akbar ruled for a long period of time (1556–1605). During the later part of his rule when he was busy in the southern part of the peninsula, his son Salim, the future Jahangir, rebelled against his father and took control of the northern part of India. Eventually, Akbar succeeded in quelling the rebellion and forgave his son naming Jahangir as his successor before his death. However, there are a few sources which point out that though Akbar named Jahangir as his successor, the differences between father and son after the rebellion were permanent. There was a segment of the Mughal court that favoured the succession of Jahangir's son Khusro and lobbied for him. This never happened but during this period Khusro gained considerable power with the support of powerful nobles.

When Jahangir became the Emperor he was aware of the growing influence of his son and also wary of the consequences it could have. He therefore confined his son to the fort of Agra and barred him from leaving it. However, only five months after the ascension of the Emperor, Khusro rebelled against his father and moved towards Lahore. His rebellion was quickly quashed by the Emperor and he was blinded, making him illegible to ever become Emperor. All his supporters were killed gruesomely and their bodies were left hanging out in the open for days, as a lesson to others. From the text mentioned above it is clear that Guru Arjan too was crushed in the fight between the Mughal 'elephants', not very different from how Guru Har Rai, Harkrishan and Tegh Bahadur were dragged into Mughal politics.

The assassination of Guru Arjan was the Karbala of Sikh history. It had a huge impact on the psyche of the Sikh community and precipitated the development of the Khalsa. It is using this incident and the imminent threat from the Mughals that Hargobind justified his militarisation of the Sikhs, a legacy that was completed by Guru Gobind Singh.

Guru Arjan's death marks the end of an era in the history of the institution of the Guruhood. He was the last Guru in the line of the Gurus who focused solely on spiritual matters. He wrote profusely and has the highest number of hymns in the Guru Granth Sahib, numbering 2218. The second highest number is that of Guru Nanak at 974.[69] All the Gurus before Guru Arjan also composed hymns. This tradition was broken by his son and then the two subsequent Gurus. Guru Tegh Bahadur treaded the middle path between spiritual and religious matters. The fact that Tegh Bahadur was initially bypassed by his nephew, Har Rai, must have played an important role in establishing his spiritual nature. Had he too succeeded the pontifical throne of Guruhood at a young age, his personality would have perhaps developed in a different manner.

One of the biggest achievements of Guru Arjan during his Guruhood was the compilation of the Sikh holy book, the Adi Granth. The compilation of this book played a significant role in the development of a separate Sikh identity. Before the compilation of the Adi Granth, the verses of the previous Guru were either found in the oral tradition or in scattered collections. Guru Arjan brought them all together. It is also recorded that one of the reasons why Guru Arjan started the work of compilation was that there were rumours that Meherban, the son of Prithi Chand, who was now head of a separate sect, was compiling his own version of the Granth, which was to have the poetry of all the previous Gurus along with his own. The Sikhs claim that this was his way of stealing the legacy of all the Gurus from the rightful descendant, Arjan. In order to prevent this development, Guru Arjan had to work on his own version of the Granth.

Another legacy of the Guruship of Arjan that eventually found its way into the Khalsa of Guru Gobind Singh is the system of *Daswandh*. This was a system by which all the followers of the Guru were exhorted

---

[69]Nikky-Guninder Kaur Singh, *Sikhism: An Introduction* (London: I.B. Tauris, 2011), page 33

to give one-tenth of their earnings to the Guru through the Masand appointed by the Guru. Even today, Sikhs are required to present one-tenth of their income for sewa (service), a tradition that was started by Guru Arjan. Whereas on one hand this system secured the economic base of the Sikh community, it also brought wealth and power to the seat of the Guru and his appointed Masands. Various stories of the corruption of the Masands are recorded in Sikh history. The system of Masands was abolished by Guru Gobind Singh.

Finally, Guru Arjan is also credited with the completion of the Amrit Sar, the tank of nectar that was started by his father at Ramdaspur. After the completion of the tank, the Harmandir Sahib was constructed there and hence the first structure of the glorious Golden Temple was raised around it, which developed into the city of Amritsar.

18
The Legend

The streets of Hassan Abdal had never looked so deserted. Naju the fakir turned left from the street of the temple into the street of the Imambargah. In between lay the old main bazaar, once the pride of the city. On a regular day this place would have been flooded with people, some negotiating prices, others simply loitering around, drawn by the charm of this bazaar. Traders from far away brought their wares here. This was the connecting town between Punjab and the Khyber. But today, all the shops were shut.

For the arriving Sikh forces this was a hollow victory. They had marched into a town abandoned by its citizens, left unprotected for pillage. Despite such loot available, the Sikh force marched with discipline. The sounds of their boots echoed through the streets. Their order was now to see if there were any citizens left in the city. Most of the Sikh soldiers who had arrived from the Punjab were surprised at the ease with which they had managed to take over the town. In their imagination Hassan Abdal had always been a part of the ferocious West inhabited by the wild tribesmen. For almost a thousand years now invaders had crossed into the Punjab from the West. Therefore in the eyes of the Punjabi the West was a fearful place where giants resided. What these soldiers did not know that the tribal west was still a long distance away from here. This was only the start of the Khyber.

When it was first made public that an army would be marching towards the Khyber from Lahore, a lot of soldiers attempted to opt out. A few pretended to be sick while others said that they had family issues. Initially, the senior officers of the Khalsa army did not realise what was happening. They allowed a few soldiers to opt out of the mission, but later when the news spreading through the ranks reached the ears of the officers, they banned soldiers from taking leave for any reason whatsoever.

Soon it was made public that Hari Singh Nalwa would be in command. He was the valiant commander-in-chief of the army who had distinguished himself during the campaigns in Kasur, Sialkot and Multan. Under him the frontiers of the Khalsa Empire had expanded. In his campaigns he had earned a reputation for himself. He was known as a fearless commander and a merciless ruler. He was the kind of commander who believed that oppression was the best way of controlling a population. The forces of the Khalsa felt comfortable under him.

Hari Singh Nalwa was yet to enter the city. He was camped out in the outskirts, on the Grand Trunk Road, waiting for news to arrive from Hassan Abdal. He did not know that the city was unprotected. Sitting in his camp he wondered why there was so much silence. The city of Hassan Abdal was on a small mountain and so it was higher than where Hari Singh was sitting. He was waiting for screams and the smoke from the burning houses to rise from the horizon but this conquest appeared awkwardly quiet. He dispatched one of his lieutenants, a Muslim man, to check on the progress. Hari Singh was not known for his patience.

Meanwhile, in the city, Naju had found refuge in the shrine of a minor Muslim saint not far from the main bazaar. This was a small shrine, one of many which existed in the multireligious city of Hassan Abdal. It was a small structure with a single room, where the grave of the saint was situated. The main building was painted in white, while the dome on top was green. On a regular day the building played host to several devotees. They would not only be Muslims but also Hindus and a few Sikhs. Finding the shrine empty, Naju decided to light an incense-stick, which he found next to the grave. Next to it there was a lamp, which he lit as well.

He sat quietly in a corner, reflecting on what was happening to his beloved city. He had spent his entire life of forty years here. Ever since he remembered, he would roam the streets. He was an orphan. As a child he would play with other children of his age but one day he came across a group of fakirs singing and dancing in the streets. They were singing the songs of Sufi saints. Naju was mesmerised and ever since that day stuck to that group.

As a grown man Naju decided to live an independent life, without associating with any group. Carrying an *ektara* (a one-string musical instrument) in his hand, he would walk around the narrow streets of Hassan Abdal singing songs that he had learned as a child. He was a well-liked figure in the community. He was a friend to everyone and still had no friends. He liked it this way.

On the eve of the Sikh invasion, when the augury of approaching death and destruction arrived in the form of the news of Hari Singh Nalwa's approach, all the residents of this small town decided to leave this city and move to the town of Attock, not far from there. While people were rushing about their homes, packing their belongings, loading their mules and preparing to leave, Naju was singing songs of patience and love. 'He has gone crazy,' said the people of the town. 'You should leave too, Naju. Hari Singh Nalwa will not spare you. He is no friend to Muslims,' he was warned.

'All my life I have been asserting that I am a Muslim but my Muslim friends never allowed me to be one. Today thanks to Hari Singh Nalwa, I have finally become one, why should I then choose to reject this honour?' said Naju and continued to sing.

The Sikh forces found Naju sitting at the shrine and immediately took him into custody. He was the first living soul they had come across all day. These soldiers had come here to fight and were emotionally charged up. Now they were planning to take out their entire wrath on this Muslim dervish.

But before they could do that Hari Singh Nalwa's messenger arrived, asking for updates of the conquest. The soldiers were afraid of Hari Singh's anger and did not want to tell him that the locals had run away before the conquest. They knew that in that case Hari Singh might kill the messenger who brought this inauspicious news to him. So they decided to present Naju to the commander so that any anger that Hari Singh had would be directed towards him.

The poor fakir in tattered clothes was ushered into the royal tent. In this elaborate setting, the condition of the fakir appeared even worse than it was. He was wearing a patched-up green chola. On the other hand the camp had all the luxuries of a palace. There was an elaborate carpet on the floor and the furniture was made of intricately carved wood. Hari Singh Nalwa sat opposite the standing fakir. He was wearing a silk gown and there were several pearl necklaces around his neck. His beard was long and his expression stern. There was a turban on his head which matched the purple silk gown that he was wearing. The feather of a female peacock was attached to the front of the turban, white in colour. There was a small pearl necklace around the turban as well, which supported a Khalsa symbol in front.

For the first time, Naju regretted his decision to not abandon the city. He missed the people who had left. When they were there he had kept a distance from them on purpose with the belief that he was harnessing his spiritual skills. Standing here, facing death, he realised that he had been deluding himself. His spirituality was a garb only for the outside, not an ornament that was to be protected within one's soul. He realised that he had lived a life of lies, feeding off people, tricking them into believing that he was somehow closer to God than the rest of them. Living such a life he had also sold the lie to himself but today all those delusions had melted away.

He fell at Hari Singh's feet and started to cry. Hari Singh's lieutenants and other officers laughed at the pitiable state of this Muslim fakir. 'Why did you not run away when you had the chance?' asked the commander. '*Malik*, I should have,' cried the fakir. 'But I could not leave behind the most precious thing I had and there was no way that I could carry it with me.'

'What could a man like you have?' asked Hari Singh.

'I'll show it to you, sir and I know you won't be disappointed but for that I would need the help of your valiant soldiers to carry it here.'

Hari Singh wondered if he should pay heed to the fakir. He doubted there was anything the fakir had that could interest him but he allowed him to show him what he had. In making that decision he had also made up his mind that when the fakir returned he would have him killed after toying with him for a little while. Hari Singh wanted to set an example at the beginning of his invasion of the Khyber. He was aware of the reputation of the tribal people of this region. He wanted to tell them that now it was the time of Punjab to create havoc in the Khyber. He felt the anger of a thousand years running through his veins.

Walking out of the camp, Naju was sure that he would need a miracle to get out of this situation, a miracle of Nanak to be exact. While standing facing his death he had devised a plan. A month or so before the attack on Hassan Abdal, Naju while walking around the streets, had found himself in front of the shop of a Muslim mason called Kamma, who was working on a piece of rock. The mason was an expert sculptor and had been responsible for creating numerous carvings in the temples of Hassan Abdal.

Many Muslims told Kamma that his work was un-Islamic and that on the Day of Judgement God would ask him to put life into his creation but Kamma never took their advice seriously. His family had been in the masonry profession for several generations. They had been a Hindu family earlier. To avoid the *jaziya* tax that the Mughal Emperor Aurangzeb had reinitiated during his reign, his grandfather had converted to Islam.

Kamma, unlike other Muslims who were embarrassed of their Hindu past, was proud of his heritage. For him, the work of sculpturing was not just a profession but an act of devotion that he did to maintain a link with his Hindu heritage. As a Muslim he was disallowed from visiting Hindu temples, so he felt that he was present there through his structures. This was his spiritual connection.

Naju was a regular visitor to Kamma's shop. Here he was assured of food and shelter for as long as he wanted. Kamma on the other hand, considered Naju to be a man of God and regarded serving him to be akin to serving God. Within the Islamic tradition he was a devotee of the Sufi tradition, as opposed to organised religion. Every Thursday he visited the Sufi shrines of the city, distributing sweetmeats and food to the holy men there. Naju was one of the beneficiaries.

That day when Naju visited Kamma's shop, he found him working on a piece of rock. He had placed his hand in the centre of the rock and he was tracing his hand's outline on it. After the delineation he carved

the rock in such a way that the mark of his hand was left on the rock.
'Is that for a particular shrine?' Naju asked him.

'No,' replied Kamma. 'There is not much work nowadays and I was
bored, so I decided to amuse myself with this. Things have been slow
ever since the news of an imminent Sikh attack.'

The truth was that what Kamma was trying to pass off as a trivial
piece of carving was in fact something close to him. Kamma had been
married for several years now but in all of these years he had not been
blessed with a child. He was afraid that after him there would be no
one to keep his legacy alive. His hand print was like a signature that he
was leaving for posterity.

Standing in front of Hari Singh, Naju remembered this rock and
devised a strategy. He led the four soldiers who were accompanying him
to Kamma's shop. After breaking the locks they found the rock in one
corner of the shop. Three soldiers carried the rock back to the camp of
the commander, while Naju walked along.

'O kind ruler, thank you for trusting me. I assure you that you will
not be disappointed. I present to you a gift that you will highly cherish.
This rock carries the hand print of your Guru Nanak,' said Naju, pointing
to the hand mark of Kamma. 'Do you know that your first Guru also
came to Hassan Abdal and spent a few days here? This is recorded in
the Janamsakhis of Bhai Bala.'

Hari Singh was surprised at the fakir's knowledge of this. He turned
to his Granthi who was also present at the camp and asked him if this
was true. The Granthi nodded his head and elaborated that on the
1st of Vaisakh, Nanak had visited Hassan Abdal as is recorded in the
Janamsakhis of Bala.

'How do you know all this information about our Guru?' asked Hari
Singh. 'You are a Muslim.'

'I am a fakir of Nanak. I am his devotee. I may be a Muslim but I
also believe in the teachings of Guru Nanak. For years this rock has been
in my family. When Nanak visited this place my ancestors met him and
took this rock from him, which has his hand print. For generations this
rock has been with us. It is our sacred connection with Guru Nanak.
We have been taking good care of it. During Mughal times we hid it

because we knew that those fanatic Muslims would have destroyed it had they discovered it.'

'Yes, those brute Turks had no respect for anyone's religion,' fumed Hari Singh.

'Today I present this rock to you, my King, for you are the saviour of this city,' said Naju.

The fakir had everyone spellbound. He had sold the story that the hand print on the rock belonged to Guru Nanak.

As a roaming dervish Naju had heard that Guru Nanak had once visited this place. There was a peepal tree on the outskirts of the city, where, according to local tradition, Guru Nanak was said to have stayed for a few days. Naju had never paid any attention to the story before this. He did not even know who Guru Nanak was; he just had a vague idea that the Sikhs of Punjab considered him to be their Prophet. Today as he stood in front of Hari Singh, all those folk stories that had receded to his subconscious came forward on their own. They then fed on the fancy of this Muslim fakir's imagination and took on a life of their own, developing into religious truths.

Hari Singh and the others were convinced that this hand print belonged to Guru Nanak. Hari Singh was the first one to place his hand on the mark. He then excitedly turned towards his audience and said, 'Look. Look at this miracle. See how the hand of Nanak fits my hand perfectly.' He kissed the rock and took out a few gold coins from his purse and placed them on the rock. After bowing before the rock he moved away and allowed others to do the same.

Even while it was at the camp, the rock turned into a shrine. The entire army of Muslims, Hindus and Sikhs gathered in front of the rock and made offerings. Kirtan singers who were present within the camp were asked to sing songs that were written and composed by Guru Nanak. The conquest had become a pilgrimage. Prayers continued late into the night.

In the morning, Hari Singh ordered Naju to take him to the spot where Nanak had stayed. Walking around the city the fakir took them to a spot only a little outside the city where there was a peepal tree. Facing the tree was a mountain. Next to it was a flowing stream. It was a picturesque location. Standing there Hari Singh could also see the Mughal gardens that had been constructed by Emperor Jahangir. He ordered the rock to be placed there, under the tree, and for a shrine to be built to commemorate the spot where Nanak and Mardana had rested.

'Naju, it was a miracle of the Guru that we met you,' said Hari Singh. 'Had you also left the city like the other residents, we would never have discovered the rock of Nanak and this shrine would never have been constructed. The entire Sikh community owes you immensely. I believe that God himself had kept you back to take care of this rock and inform us about it.' Naju stood silently listening to this praise. He wore an expression of piousness. 'You told me that the story of this rock is associated with the story of a Muslim shrine nearby. Where exactly is it? Take us there.'

Anam, Iqbal Qaiser and I started to climb the steep stairs which seemed to be leading us into a housing settlement. I stopped to marvel at the beauty of the sight. This was a beautiful climb, with houses flanking the stairs that take one up the mountain. There was a small stall selling religious paraphernalia, which included not only pieces of cloth with Quranic inscriptions but also alm and other material that one associates with Shia Islam.

'Is the shrine a Shia shrine or a Sunni shrine?' I asked Iqbal Qaiser. This was a relevant question. Only a few days ago, on the tenth day of Muharram, when Shia processions are taken out all over the world, riots had erupted in the garrison city of Rawalpindi. A state of curfew had been imposed for two days. Rawalpindi happens to be the twin city of Islamabad, the federal capital of the country. The Shia-Sunni divide has increased in the last two decades, particularly in the urban areas of Pakistan. It was in this backdrop that I wanted to find out about the shrine we were attempting to get to at the top of the mountain.

'I don't know,' said Iqbal Qaiser.

Perhaps the premise of the question was wrong to begin with. The distinction between Shia and Sunni did not really apply in the conventional sense at such Sufi shrines. Here the boundaries between the different sects of Islam are blurred. Before Partition this must have been true for Hindus, Muslims and Sikhs as well. As we ascended the mountain the path emerged out of the houses and started treading a vacant mountain. We could see the shrine of Wali Qandhari at the top. Below was the shrine of Panja Sahib dedicated to Guru Nanak. In pre-Partition days Muslims must have visited the shrine of Nanak while Sikhs and Hindus would have had no qualms about visiting the Muslim shrine on top of this mountain, which happened to be the tallest peak in the region.

There were several other pilgrims climbing with us. Most of them were school and college students, bunking classes to visit the Sufi shrine. This was not merely for religious reasons but also for social ones. Most of them carried their mobile phones, out of which the sounds of devotional music emerged. I noticed a discarded newspaper on the way with a picture of Jinnah. How much was he responsible for such sharp distinctions between different religious groups and sects? Partition after all aggravated the problem. But then was Jinnah solely responsible for Partition? One needs to also take into account the role of the British in stratifying a society on the basis of different religious groups that eventually led to such distinct religious identities.

Walking up this steep slope with my wife by my side and Iqbal Qaiser a few steps behind us, I tried imagining what the situation of religious divisions must have been at the time of Nanak. Nationalist historians on the side of Pakistan point out that a religious divide existed throughout history, while those on the Indian side point out that it was actually the British who exacerbated the problem. But then if one focuses on Nanak's struggle, his entire movement was for the blurring of the religious divide. This means that different religious identities must have been present even in his time and must have been quite a social problem, for him to talk about it so much.

There were several devotees who were now coming down the mountain. These too were mostly young men. I noticed a few carrying their slippers in their hands, with the intention of making this pilgrimage difficult for themselves.

'They've made the path much easier now,' said Iqbal Qaiser, as he caught up with us while we stopped to take a short break. We were severely out of breath after climbing for about thirty minutes. 'Earlier, the way used to go around the mountain and there were no stairs like there are now. On several occasions one had to lie down on the ground and crawl up under a huge rock that was in the way.'

Iqbal Qaiser's remark made me realise the similarities of this Muslim pilgrimage to that of several Hindu ones to the shrines of deities on the top of mountains. In all religious traditions, mountain tops have had particular spiritual significance. Prophet Muhammad (PBUH) used to climb to the cave of Hira for a spiritual retreat and it was there that the Quran was first revealed to him. Prophet Moses talked to God on top of Mount Sinai. One of the most important sermons of Jesus Christ was also on top of a mount. This goes back to the concept that one is closer to God when one is at a higher point. Several Hindu jogis and Muslim Sufis have also found refuge on top of a mountain away from civilization.

Sitting here on this mountain, I felt a strange sensation of power. The entire world was in front of me, busy in its activities, which seemed so trivial from up here. Perhaps the concept of observing the world from the top is not about getting closer to God but rather getting closer to being like God.

There was a small clearing almost halfway up the mountain. Here there were shops and restaurants for pilgrims. Several pilgrims were climbing with soft drinks and other snacks that they would eat once they reached the top of the mount.

This was a particularly rocky mountain with a few lone trees on the way. On the branches of these trees devotees had tied small pieces of colourful cloths as supplication. 'Allah O Akbar' was written on several barren rocks on the way. This perhaps was done to establish that this space was now Muslim. I find this phenomenon to be more prevalent in places where there is a contested history, like in Sialkot, where there used to be a major Sikh shrine. The Gurdwara of Panja Sahib is in the plain below us. During the occasion of Baisakhi when thousands of pilgrims descend upon this shrine, several also travel up to this Muslim shrine. This message is for them.

At the top of the mountain we were greeted by a wooden frame that marks the entrance to the sacred space. The modest shrine of Wali Qandhari was surrounded by a protective wall outside where there were a few more shops selling religious items. It took us about ninety minutes to get here. We rested for several minutes before continuing on into the shrine. Most of the shopkeepers imagined us to be Indian pilgrims because of the way we were dressed. All of us were wearing jeans, while the other pilgrims were wearing shalwar kameez. The shopkeepers tried luring us into buying ethnic items since they thought we were foreigners.

There was a strong commercial enterprise in the vicinity of the shrine. An old man who was sitting in front of the building quickly gathered the shoes of the pilgrims, when they took them off before entering. He then charged them money to take care of the shoes. Next to him a dervish was sitting on a stall selling sacred water that he kept in earthen pots to the pilgrims.

Before the invention of pumps, devotees considered it their religious duty to carry water pots to the top of mountains when visiting a shrine. This was because there was no other mechanism for bringing water up there. The water would then be served to thirsty pilgrims as a religious service. After the invention of pumps there was no need for this religious activity but several devotees continue to do it as the remnant of a tradition. Since this water is brought as a gift by the devotee to the saint, it is considered blessed. In these days of pumps, the dervish here sold the water back to the pilgrims in the name of religious duty.

I walked into an empty lot next to the shrine. I saw a few dervishes smoking hashish while hiding behind a grove of trees. On top of the mountain, secluded from the world, I could understand why junkies would start living here and become dervish.[70] There was a small courtyard facing the shrine. Inside the shrine the grave of the saint was missing. There was a green box in the middle which read that it has been placed there by the Auqaf Department and that devotees should put their offerings and money in it.

On one of the walls I noticed that all the festival dates of this shrine

---

[70]Dervish are Sufi ascetics

had been put up. It recorded Baisakhi as well. This coincides with the festival at the shrine of Guru Nanak at the bottom of the mountain. This is because the story of these two shrines is linked.

After about fifteen minutes, we decided to head back to the city of Hassan Abdal. However, before we started to climb down we stopped next to the wooden frame at the entrance for a few minutes and tried to make sense of the story that linked this shrine to that of Guru Nanak at the bottom. The grand Gurdwara of Panja Sahib could be seen in front of us.

'Even if a rock was thrown from here, how could it possibly reach the gurdwara?' said Iqbal Qaiser. 'There are several hurdles on the way.'

'What I don't get is that if a rock was thrown, why couldn't Nanak simply move away from its trajectory? Why did he need to stop it with his hand? It was a small rock, anyway.' I added.

Standing next to us, Anam was a bit confused. She didn't know what the story of Nanak, Wali Qandhari and the rock was. Finally, after Iqbal Qaiser and I were done with our analysis, she asked us, 'How is this shrine connected to Guru Nanak?'

ੴ

According to Sikh tradition, Nanak arrived here along with Mardana on the first of Baisakh. It is because of this that every year the festival of Baisakhi is celebrated at the Gurdwara Panja Sahib where pilgrims from all over the world gather. So they came and sat under a peepal tree which is where the gurdwara now stands. Mardana then felt thirsty. There was no stream of water here like there is now. Well at least, there wasn't, according to Sikh literature.

Now Guru Nanak using his miraculous powers realised that there was a lake of fresh water on top of a mount and that there was a hermit living there by the name of Wali Qandhari. He asked Mardana to go up the mountain and get water from there.

Mardana climbed the steep mountain and reached the top where he saw exactly what Nanak had predicted. There was a hermit sitting next to a pool of water. Mardana asked for water and thinking that he was a tired traveller, the hermit agreed to give him water. Just when Mardana was about to drink, the hermit asked him who was he and where he was from. Mardana told him that he was a devotee of Guru Nanak, a saint who was close to God. Wali Qandhari felt jealous of Guru Nanak and said that if this man Guru Nanak was such a big saint then he should arrange for water for his devotee himself. In this way Mardana was sent down the mountain without having quenched his thirst.

At the base, Mardana told Nanak what had transpired. 'Go back and ask for water once again,' said Nanak. Huffing and puffing Mardana climbed the mountain again and did as he was told. The Wali refused again.

When Mardana reached Nanak he was told that he should go back once again and ask for the water in the name of God. When the Wali refused and Mardana narrated the story to Nanak, he said, 'Now that you have asked for the water thrice in the name of God and he has refused, I will provide you with water.' Saying this, he removed a stone from the ground and water started to gush out of that spot.

Nanak had performed a miracle. All the water that was earlier with the Wali disappeared as it came flowing down the mountain. This angered Wali Qandhari and in his wrath he hurled a rock at Nanak and Mardana, which Nanak stopped with his hand. The print of that hand remained on the rock that Nanak stopped.

This is yet another story in which Nanak is depicted as competing with a Muslim saint, where Nanak overcomes him with his powers. This is used to drive home the claim that 'our' saint is stronger than 'your' saint. You should read Salman Rashid's book The Salt Range and the Potohar Plateau. *In that book he argues that this pool of water next to the gurdwara has been here for thousands of years and that it was considered sacred even in the Buddhist era. The Chinese traveller Hiuen Tsang, in the 7th century CE, is reported to have travelled here and observed that this was a sacred lake.*

According to this testimony the lake has been considered sacred for thousands of years. It was believed that people's diseases would be cured after taking a dip in it. After a gurdwara was built here during the tenure of Maharaja Ranjit Singh, this sacred pool of water remained sacred but was given a different iconography this time, based on the miracles of Guru Nanak. One also sees this happening in several Muslim shrines where Hindu temples have been converted into Muslim shrines after Partition.

ੴ

The pilgrim ahead of me was an old man in his sixties. His long grey hair flowed out of his saffron headscarf. He was heavily built and wearing nothing but a lungi. He placed his hand at the hand mark believed to be that of Nanak. As is the specialty of this rock, his hand too fit the hand of Nanak perfectly. Miracle! Then he placed a ten rupee note on top of the rock and kissed it. He then took some water from the pool around the rock and poured it on the rock and then cleaned it with his hands. There was a line of devotees behind him, all of whom were urging him to move on. He was taking too much time. He moved on and now it was my turn.

Before I could place my hand on the handprint and also become engaged in this miracle, mysterious hands emerged from the windows flanking the rock. I tried to see where they were coming from but I could not because of the darkness inside. Women were shouting behind these dark spaces. There was an urgency in trying to touch this holy rock and seek its blessing. These women too placed money on top of the rock after seeking the blessings of the rock by touching it.

In time, I placed my hand on the handprint of Nanak, at that moment genuinely believing in the story that this was Nanak's hand. I knew that it wasn't. I knew this was a fictitious story dreamed up by a man called Naju the fakir to save his life, while the handprint was chiselled by a man called Kamma. But such is the power of imagination in religion that I forgot all my rationality and believed that I was touching Nanak's hand. That was the closest I have ever felt to Nanak.

The gurdwara that was built here by Maharaja Ranjit Singh in the nineteenth century was behind me, while the shrine of Wali Qandhari on top of the mountain was right in front. This was the occasion of Baisakhi and the festival was only beginning. There were thousands of Sikh pilgrims around me, all here to commemorate the formation of the Khalsa.

19
Guru Ram Das

When Guru Amar Das's wife recommended the young man Jetha for marriage with their younger daughter Bibi Bhani, one of the first questions the Guru asked Jetha was about his caste. P. S. Grewal in his article 'Nanak's Doctrine and the Feudalization of the Sikh Gurudom' suggests that the Guru was relieved when he heard that the man to be married to his daughter was a Sodhi Khatri, an ancient caste of kings.[71] Amar Das himself belonged to the Khatri Bhalla caste, a high caste on its own, according to the societal norms of the time. The marriage took place and in this way Jetha, the future Guru Ram Das, was initiated into the family of the Guru.

At the time Guru Amar Das was based at Goindwal, which was also where Jetha lived, serving the Guru and the Sikh community. Jetha's parents had died at a young age, because of which he was raised by his grandmother. As a young child he sold boiled grain and wheat in the village of Basarke near Amritsar where he was first spotted by Amar Das, who at that time was not yet a Guru but a devotee of Guru Angad Dev, the successor of Guru Nanak. Amar Das had a deep impact on the young boy who soon after followed him to Khadur, where Amar Das lived, serving Guru Angad Dev. Jetha too spent his time looking after the langar at the darbar of the Guru and serving the Sikh community.

---

[71]Grewal, Nanak's Doctrine, page 29

Soon after when the mantle of Guruhood was passed onto Amar Das, he moved to Goindwal and Jetha followed him.

At Goindwal, Jetha served his father-in-law with devotion. His family members would often complain about his servile attitude towards his in-laws but he never heeded their complaints. His wife, Bibi Bhani too served her father and the Guru with immense devotion. In the Sikh tradition, an important incident is attributed to her. Once when Guru Amar Das was performing his ablutions sitting on a stool, one of the legs of the stool broke. Immediately Bibi Bhani put her own foot under the stool to prevent the Guru from falling. Her father noticed that it was his daughter's leg that was protecting him from falling when he saw her blood mixing in the water. Impressed by the dedication of his daughter, he asked her what she wished from her father. What Bibi Bhani asked for changed the course of Sikh history. She requested for the institution of Guruhood to become hereditary.[72] The Guru warned her of the consequences, telling her that this promise would bring much pain and suffering. The Sikh tradition notes that he was referring to the assassination of Guru Arjan, the incarceration of Guru Hargobind, the martyrdom of Guru Tegh Bahadur and that of Guru Teg Bahadur's grandsons (Guru Gobind Singh's sons), all of whom were the descendants of Guru Amar Das.

Prior to Guru Amar Das the institution of Guruhood had bypassed the progeny of former Gurus and was bestowed upon the most devoted student. Guru Nanak preferred Angad Dev over his son Sri Chand, while Angad Dev preferred Amar Das over his son Dasu. This was to change with the appointment of Guru Ram Das, the son-in-law of Guru Amar Das. After Ram Das, the succession of Guruhood became a family affair in which the son of the Guru was preferred over others. Ram Das appointed his son, Arjan. Arjan appointed his son, Hargobind. Hargobind appointed his grandson, Har Rai. Har Rai appointed his son, Harkrishan. Harkrishan appointed his granduncle, Tegh Bahadur, the son of Hargobind. Tegh Bahadur appointed his son, Gobind Rai (later Gobind Singh). Gobind Singh decreed that the Adi Granth would be

---

[72]Singh, *The History of Sikh Gurus*, page 50

the Eternal Guru as opposed to appointing an appointing an individual, after he saw the death of all of his sons during his lifetime. (While the Guruship remained within the family, the eldest son was sometimes bypassed as in the case of Guru Arjan and Guru Harkrishan, who were younger sons.)

Guru Ram Das became the first Sodhi Guru. By the time the mantle of Guruhood reached Gobind Singh it was understood that the institution of Guruhood would only be passed onto someone from the Sodhi caste. Gobind Singh wrote various verses extolling the merits of his caste and its ancient history. At the time of appointing a successor to the institution of Guruhood it is believed that Guru Amar Das put his two sons-in-law and his two sons through a few tests to prove to everyone that his choice of Ram Das was the right one. All Sikhs accepted the choice made by Guru Amar Das, except his eldest son Mohan. Keeping in mind his opposition, Ram Das moved to Ramdaspur, a small town that he had founded on the land that was gifted to his wife by the Mughal Emperor Akbar when he met Guru Amar Das. Here the Guru started the construction of the Amrit Sar. In order to fund the construction of the tank, the Guru introduced the system of Masand.

At the time of appointing the next Guru after Ram Das, a conflict arose between the Guru's two sons, Prithi Chand and Arjan. Sikh tradition finds the root of the conflict to be Arjan's trip to Lahore and the machinations of Prithi Chand; however, one also needs to bear in mind the issue of property here. When the mantle of Guruhood was being passed to Arjan, Ram Das' immense property, which was essentially the entire city of Ramdaspur and the area around it, was also being passed onto him. Immediately after the appointment of Arjan, Prithi Chand approached Mughal authorities to get him his rightful share in the property of his father and hence began the tumultuous relationship between the Mughals and the Sikhs.

Therefore, while analysing the appointment of Guru Ram Das as the next Guru of the Sikh community one also needs to be bear in mind that with this event also begins the process of feudalisation of the Guruhood. All subsequent Gurus after Ram Das were huge landowners.

Ram Das also encouraged horse trading from which he earned a profit.[73] In the words of P. S. Grewal, Gurudom became a 'feudal authority and privilege,'[74] which explains the hereditary form it took.

---

[73]Grewal, Nanak's Doctrine, page 23

[74]Ibid, page 26

20
Religio-commercialisation

The boundary between Sindh and Punjab becomes a blur as we drive through Bahawalpur, heading towards our destination at Uch Sharif. According to Sikh tradition, Nanak was invited here by the saint Syed Jalaludin Surkh Posh Bokhari when he met him in Kandahar, on the way back from Haj.

This is where the cultures of Punjab and Sindh merge. Some of the roadside hotels are called Punjab Hotel, while others are Sindh Hotel. The language here, referred to as Siraiki, is also an amalgamation of the two languages. I cannot understand a word of it, even though I consider myself a Punjabi.

'Their Siraiki is different from that in Multan,' I said to Iqbal Qaiser. 'The Siraiki spoken in Multan is closer to Punjabi, while here it is more like Sindhi.' Iqbal Qaiser seemed to have no difficultly in communicating in this language as he asked for directions from the people on the way.

We drove through the town of Uch Sharif and headed towards the shrine of Hazrat Makhdoom Syed Hamid Ganj Bakhsh Gilani. We were ascending a mound and the streets around us were getting narrower. This was the older part of the city. There were massive havelis around us, those of the current caretakers of the shrine, the Gilanis and the Makhdooms. We parked in front of one such haveli and headed towards the shrine.

Passing through a small gateway, another old structure that had remained intact, we entered a small market, the likes of which are found next to all Sufi shrines and temples. Religious paraphernalia was being sold: sacred thread, pictures of saints, religious books on Shiaism and devotional songs. There were posters of Lal Shahbaz Qalandar, Baba Farid, Pir Jalaludin and Bahauddin Zakariya. I looked at them hoping to see a poster of Guru Nanak too. He is after all as important a saint as any of these people, but there was none. It is strange that once Nanak had been invited to visit this place at the behest of the saint himself but today there is no trace of his heritage. To accept Guru Nanak as one of their own would be too much to ask in these days of heightened religiosity.

The southern region of Punjab, where Uch Sharif lies, has more traces of religious and cultural syncretism compared to the northern and central region, where there is a greater prevalence of education and hence religious intolerance.

There is a misconception that lack of education breeds religious intolerance and that education exorcises all such demons. In fact the case in Pakistan seems to be the opposite. This is because education here is closely connected with the nationalistic agenda. One of the stated purposes of education in Pakistan is to promote nationalism among children. It is for this reason that the mainstream education here is diluted by nationalistic propaganda and hence, by association, religious propaganda. One would find references to 'Pakistani' and 'Islamic' heroes like Muhammad Ali Jinnah, Allama Iqbal, Sir Syed Ahmad Khan, Muhammad Bin Qasim, Mahmud Ghaznvi and Ahmad Shah Abdali in curriculums as unrelated as those of Chemistry, Geography and Urdu. It is then easy to understand why such an educational process breeds chauvinistic nationalistic traits. With a strong sense of nationalism comes a strong sense of 'otherization', a demonization of those who are not part of us—'us' being Pakistani, Muslim, and in particular Sunni Muslim.

With education there is also a tendency to look down upon religious practices like visiting Sufi shrines and bowing down in front of a grave or a living saint. Such superstitious tendencies within Islam are no longer acceptable to the educated elite and middle class, who seem to prefer an individualistic and literalistic interpretation of Islam. The mixing of Hindu practices with Sufi Islam is no longer acceptable to the educated class, as it searches for a purer version of religion. Hence over the years

Sufi shrines have lost their significance amongst the educated class and urban centres and remain attractive only to the rural and 'uneducated' who can still tolerate religious syncretism along with the dilution of identity in accepting a Hindu past.

The shrine is situated next to a fifteenth century structure, where the grave of Moosa Pak Shaheed once existed. It's unclear who he was. According to a board next to the structure, put up by the Department of Archaeology, his body was later shifted to Multan. The building was octagonal, constructed in typical Multani fashion with blue tiles. In a dilapidated condition now, it must have been a beautiful building once.

It turns out that we were visiting the shrine at the time of the urs celebration which explained the rush in the market and the throngs of visitors, pushing us aside to pass through. There was a metal detector gate at the entrance, next to which a bored policeman sat. Shrines of Sufi saints, where devotees offer chadars and revere the graves, often bowing in front of them, are considered un-Islamic by the puritanical sects of Islam. In recent years as a wave of Islamic purism has spread over Pakistan due to the influence of the Taliban, such shrines have come under attack. There have been attacks on many such shrines, including Data Ganj Baksh in Lahore, Baba Farid's at Pakpattan and Abdullah Shah Ghazi's in Karachi.

Inside, Iqbal Qaiser busied himself photographing the shrine while I sat in one corner observing people and making notes in my diary. Nanak visited Uch Sharif on his way to Sindh, towards the end of his travels, after he had already visited the East, South, North and West. He had now settled at Kartarpur in Punjab and would travel occasionally to neighbouring areas. The visit to Uch Sharif was after he had settled down.

Sitting here, I wondered if Nanak understood the language spoken around him, with which I was struggling, while he was here. But then there is a difference in the way he travelled and the way we travel. For him, the transitions of language and culture must have been a gradual process, allowing him time to acquaint himself with new words and rules of grammar. In these days of modern travel, that is not possible. In Nanak's poetry we notice that Nanak incorporated several words which were not part of the Punjabi of the time. As he travelled, he picked up words from different regions and we can see an influence of that in his poetry. This helped develop the Punjabi language, which is why Nanak's contribution as a poet to Punjabi is immense.

I entered the shrine where the graves of all the saints were located. A man standing next to the grave of the saint asked me to put in some money into a green box next to it, which would then go to the caretakers of the shrine, helping them expand their houses and buy bigger cars. I ignored him and moved on. This was a small graveyard within a large room. Generations of saints from a single family were buried here. Those who dominate this city, economically, politically and socially, feeding off the charity of devotees, will also be buried here after they die. At one end of the room, there was a grave which was covered by a *purdah* (veil or screen).

'Whose grave is that?' I asked the man who had asked me to put my contribution into the green box. 'That is a female relative of the saint,' he told me. That explained the veil. 'If you give me fifty rupees, I can show you all the graves,' he offered.

I am the product of a post-9/11 world. My understanding of politics, religion and culture has all been shaped by this event. Therefore my perception of Islam is also in a way a direct product of this world. In fact, I am not the only one who has had to grapple with this new version of Islam. This phenomenon affects my entire generation. Being neutral was no longer possible as was stated by George Bush immediately after the attacks. Over the years I have seen my friends and colleagues neatly choose either of two sides. They were binary opposites and the difference between them was stark, yet to me they appear as two sides of the same coin. One side was that of the Islamic fundamentalist, those who were Taliban apologists and critical of the 'secularisation' of Pakistan. For them everything that is part of the world is either Islamic or un-Islamic. All around me I saw members of my generation tilt towards that position.

And then there was the other extreme. For them, anyone religious was a lesser being, a symbol of a partially evolved human. Anything that came out of the mouth of the 'religio-fundoo' was not worth listening to and hence had to be shunned. There could be no debate or discussion with the other side. For them there was only one hope for Pakistan—to become less religious.

I was inclined towards the second side. But over the years I had become disillusioned with them as well. They were as intolerant as the former and as closed to new ideas. I realised that there were several traditions within Islam that weren't necessarily violent but rather syncretic. I discovered that Islam too had a glorious past of intellectual freedom and creativity, when it had been acceptable for a scholar to raise any kind of question. This was the past of Rumi, Umer Khayyam, Ibn-e-Arabi and Ibn-e-Rushd.

I also felt particularly sympathetic towards the shrine culture, an important aspect of Islam in South Asia. This for me represented religious syncretism and a greater tolerance towards the 'other'. I felt as if in this growing environment of religious fundamentalism, this version of Islam could pave the way for the middle way. Yet sitting at this shrine and looking at how innocent people are robbed of their hard-earned money I felt derision towards the shrine culture like I had never felt before.

In his poetry Nanak spoke vehemently against religious exploitation of this kind. For example, he says:

His goodness cannot be priced or traded,
Nor His worshippers valued, nor their store;
Priceless too are dealers in the market sacred
With love and peace evermore.[75]

This could well be a criticism of the commercialisation of religion which was running rampant in this shrine. We find in his poems a disdain for priests and Sufi pirs who manipulate the people for their own economic benefit. Throughout Nanak's philosophy one finds a strong concept of individualism, of discovering the self. Nanak talks about removing intermediaries and establishing a direct connect with God.

As much as I felt disgusted by religious exploitation I could not bring myself to hate it as much as Nanak did. Thinking as an anthropologist, I believe that such rituals and religious shrines play an important role in a society, giving a source of identity to a community. I also do not believe in the concept of a right path towards the divine. I believe that everyone

---

[75]Singh, trans. *Hymns of the Gurus*, page 20

finds their own, depending on their conditions. If coming to a shrine and touching the chadar covering the grave of a saint meant proximity to God for someone, then that is the right way. Nanak too believed in allowing everyone to follow their own path towards the divine, but he would have perhaps disagreed with my tolerance towards such shrines.

'Let's visit the shrine of Bibi Jiwindi,' said Iqbal Qaiser. We walked through the market, heading towards this group of thirteenth and fourteenth century shrines. After a little while we found ourselves in an open field with a few houses in front of us.

'This place has changed since the last time I came here,' said Iqbal Qaiser. 'One could see the shrines from here.' He asked a man standing nearby about the shrines who told us that we would have to take a car to reach them.

We drove around the city. These shrines were on the outskirts, situated on top of a mound, which was being used as a graveyard. Half the structures of the shrine had been razed and were protected by iron rods. Whatever remained though was beautiful, made out of glazed Multani tiles, coloured in blue and white. There was a white dome on top, which shone in the sun like a broken eggshell.

'There was a huge flood here in the sixteenth century and these buildings were destroyed at that time,' said Iqbal Qaiser. River Sutlej, the lost river of Pakistan, used to flow from here before it was lost forever after the Indus Water Treaty was signed between India and Pakistan in 1960. After the Indus Water Treaty, the rivers of Punjab were divided into two parts—three Western rivers—Indus, Jhelum and Chenab, and three Eastern rivers—Ravi, Sutlej and Beas. India was given full rights over using the waters of the Eastern rivers for its agricultural needs before these rivers entered Pakistani territory, while Pakistan was given rights over the Western rivers. Over the years, as India constructed dams and reservoirs over their rivers, the flow of these waters started diminishing. Now the mighty Ravi of history flows like a stream near Lahore, while the other two rivers have completely disappeared. Only occasionally during the monsoons when there is an overflow does some water from the Sutlej flow into Pakistan, flooding the region around Kasur. Otherwise, throughout the year, it is a dry bank. Nanak must have seen these buildings intact with a mighty river flowing next to it. How beautiful they must have been!

The shrine of Pir Jalaludin Bokhari was also situated on this mound. It was protected by a thick wall with barbed wire on top, which was constructed recently to protect it from terrorist attacks. Almost all the visitors here, who numbered in the hundreds, were heading towards this shrine.

We too ascended the stairs and entered the complex. There was an old Banyan tree in the centre. Behind us was a banner on the wall which depicted Pir Jalaludin, Bahauddin Zakariya, Baba Farid and Lal Shahbaz Qalandar. Once again there was no Nanak.

It was strange for me that all these saints were depicted on one banner as if they represented a continuous strand of religious tradition. The truth is that all of them belonged to different schools of thought. For example, Bahauddin Zakariya who is now considered the patron saint of Multan rose to importance because of his association with the rulers in Delhi. He had a madrassa in Multan, where he is now buried. Here he would teach the children of the local Nawab and other important officials. It was an elite school of its era.

On the other hand, Baba Farid moved from Delhi to Pakpattan because he did not want to associate with the rulers there. His madrassa was similar to poorly funded public schools, where the students could not even afford a proper meal.

On closer observation one can pick up these differences between the saints in their pictures. Bahaudin Zakariya is dressed like a rich man, with pearls around his neck and a fancy gown, while Baba Farid is depicted in a simple white dress with a green shawl on his shoulders. In contrast to both of them, Baba Lal Shahbaz Qalandar belonged to the school of thought of Malamti Sufis, who do not believe in any form of organised religion and consider themselves to be beyond the pale of any religious law. Both Bahaudin and Farid would have had serious differences with Lal Shahbaz Qalandar of Sehwan Sharif.

I was walking alone in the courtyard, trying to notice everything I could, when the voice of a man asked me, 'Where are you from, son?'

'Lahore,' I said, even though I now live in Islamabad.

'Are you alone?'

'No. I have a friend along.'

'Call him as well. I want to show you something.'

'I don't think he will be interested. Why don't you show it to me instead?'

He took me inside the mosque, which was next to the shrine, within the same compound. This too was a historical building, as was apparent from its architecture. It must have been constructed around the same time as the shrine. There were several men seated here. Women it seemed were not allowed as they looked on from the boundary. There were a few rooms on one side.

'These are three rooms,' he said. 'In each one of these the three saints have meditated: Baba Farid, Bahaudin Zakariya and Lal Shahbaz Qalandar. I'll show them to you in a little while.'

I was not interested as I was sure that this was an apocryphal story. He took me to one end of the mosque and picked up a green shawl with Quranic verses on it. He placed it around my neck and then offered me some water. 'This will ensure that all your wishes come true.'

I knew what was going to come next. He would ask for a donation and I was in no mood to part with any money. I took off the shawl politely, handed it to him and walked off. He was perhaps in too much of a shock to say anything.

Taking my shoes off, I walked into the shrine of Pir Jalaludin Bokhari. Women were not allowed here either. It was a dark room, with beautiful wooden pillars holding up the roof. The pillars were intricately carved with floral designs, while the roof was decorated with colourful patterns.

There were several graves here, of people who must have paid hefty amounts of money to get buried next to the saint. The grave of the saint was on a raised platform and enclosed in glass. Several people were standing next to it, touching the glass for blessings. I walked around the grave and found myself face to face with another man with a green box. 'Where are you from?' he asked me. 'Never mind,' I said and continued walking. The rest of the devotees were not as rude as me and offered their donations to the saint.

Ayesha Siddiqa is a Pakistani author who wrote *Military Incorporated*, a courageous book that looks at the political and economic influence of the institution of the Army in Pakistan. She belongs to Bahawalpur, which is only about seventy kilometres from here. I have had the opportunity to interact with her a couple of times in conferences and workshops. As a political scientist she is interested in studying the influence of puritanical Islamic organizations on Pakistani society. She points out that for the past few years, organisations like Jamat-ud-Dawa and Laskhar-e-Jhangvi, who associate with the Ahl-e-Hadith school of thought and don't shy away from using violence, have seeped into the social fabric of southern Punjab, a region that has historically rejected such strands of Islam and adopted a syncretistic version of religion. Such Sufi shrines are a symbol of that strand of Islam. However, according to her, this is changing as such organisations are opening seminaries in these rural areas and attracting unemployed youth towards them.

In a recent paper by Dr. Tahir Kamran, titled 'Evolution and Impact of "Deobandi" Islam in the Punjab' he also records a similar phenomenon. In the paper, the historian has explained that such organisations are becoming particularly popular with the youth of the region because they offer an explanation for their current oppression. The first step of their modus operandi is to target such shrines and their guardians, who have become immensely rich feeding off the oppressed classes. Dr. Tahir Kamran notes that in the absence of any Marxist or Liberal ideology, the ideologies of these religious extremist organisations become the only option for frustrated youth.

This phenomenon is best seen in Swat, where the Taliban took over in 2009 and established their writ. More than religious salvation the Taliban ideology presented the oppressed with a path to a political revolution by revolting against the rulers of that region. Initially, the cadres who were attracted to their movement were those who belonged to the lower echelons of society.

Standing at this shrine and observing such blatant religious oppression, it became clear to me why such extremist organisations were becoming popular in this region. I thought about Nanak's opposition to such practices once again and could not help but trace similarities between his revulsion for such practices and those of these proscribed organisations. Both wanted to liberate the oppressed who are being rendered helpless by this feudal culture.

We walked out of the shrine and climbed the steep mound, along with a few other pilgrims. There were several graves on the mound, which were covered arbitrarily with the blue and white Multani tiles that had been recovered from these historical shrines.

The first shrine that we came across was that of Baha-ul-Halim and its date of construction was noted as the fourteenth century. According to the board of the Archaeology Department, Baha-ul-Halim was a literary figure and a teacher at the madrassa that used to run at the shrine of Jalaludin Surkh Posh Bokhari. This meant that this building was here when Nanak visited this place sometime in the late fifteenth century. It was now half broken and supported by iron rods.

The tomb next to this structure was that of Nauria and its date was noted as the fifteenth century. Nauria is believed to be the architect of the two adjoining buildings here, which he raised before his death. His final resting place was later constructed following the same architectural tradition.

The last shrine on this mound was that of Bibi Jiwindi and it is arguably the most important of these three buildings. According to the board here, this tomb was built in 1494, so almost around the time that Nanak came here and it belonged to the great granddaughter of Syed Jalaludin Bokhari.

This came as a shock to me. I had hereto assumed that Syed Jalaludin and Nanak were contemporaries, but if the shrine of his great granddaughter was constructed at the time that Nanak was alive then Jalaludin must have lived much earlier.

'It is possible that Bibi Jiwindi died during the lifetime of Jalaludin Bokhari,' said Iqbal Qaiser, when I posed the question. He did not want to dismiss the Sikh version of the story immediately, but I had realised that the tale of Nanak and Jalaludin meeting was a later fabrication. Nanak must have come here and perhaps interacted with the descendants of the saint but not Jalaludin. When I checked the dates later I found out that Jalaludin had lived in the thirteen century and died before the end of the century.

A similar story of Nanak meeting Bahaudin Zakariya is also found in Nanak's hagiography. Once again one can dismiss this claim, if one compares the time periods. Bahaudin too belonged to the thirteenth century, almost a hundred years before Nanak.

'Do you want to see the well of Nanak?' said Iqbal Qaiser as we descended the mound. 'There is nothing left there anyway.'

Iqbal Qaiser had already prepared me for this. He had told me that the last traces of Nanak's legacy here had almost been destroyed and therefore if that was what I was looking for then there was no point travelling so far. But it was not Nanak's legacy encapsulated in a building that I was interested in. I wanted to see everything Nanak saw. I wanted to travel in his footsteps. I wanted to find any trace of Nanak's memory at the shrine.

The well of Nanak was hidden within the field, shielded by a grove of trees. It was abandoned and juice tetrapaks and wrappers were floating in the black water. Next to it was a small mound which was covered in grass. 'This was the Gurdwara of Nanak,' said Iqbal Qaiser.

Now nothing remained.

Did Nanak sit at this exact spot at a little distance from the shrine of Jalaludin Surkh Posh Bokhari? Did he go inside? If he did, did he interact with the pilgrims or caretakers, or did he, like me, observe everything without talking to anyone, and once out, compose his beautiful verses?

'Iqbal Sahib, how can I ever find out the real story of Nanak? We know that he came to all these places but how can we find out what really happened? The only evidence we have is found within the Sikh religion and they are full of stories of miracles,' I asked, as we drove back to Lahore in the night.

'It is a difficult thing to do,' he said. 'The best thing you can do is read what Nanak wrote at these places and try to get into his mind.'

ੴ

Not far from where Nanak was sitting, there was a jogi wearing only a lungi with white matted hair falling on both sides of his head and a long white beard, beating his hemp with a mortar, preparing it for bhang. Other groups of pilgrims were gathered around him watching the preparations anxiously. Near the entrance of the shrine, where the devotees ascended the stairs after taking off their shoes, there was a man selling *bhangwale pakore* (fritters with the addition of cannabis). There was a crowd of people around him as well.

Looking at the preparation of bhang, one of the main attractions of a festival like this, a jogi carrying an ektara started walking towards the crowd singing a song in praise of the intoxicant.

Offer me as well this little green bite of love
that binds with the heart
Offer me as well this little green bite of love
This leaf of insight.

Nanak was repulsed by what he saw. He knew more than the Muslims in front of him that this was not what Islam taught. In Makkah, when he was there for the Hajj, he had interacted with various Islamic scholars and all of them had pointed out that intoxicants of any kind were forbidden in Islam. In Baghdad where he had stayed for a little while on his way back from the Hajj, scholars had reiterated the same thing.

Having travelled widely, Nanak had come to the conclusion that there was no single form of Islam being practised in the world. In Bengal for example, he had noticed that along with offering their prayers, the Muslims also venerated Devi Durga in their songs. In South India, he had noticed that Muslims still practised a rigid caste hierarchy, similar to the Hindus of that region. So those Muslims whose families had been Brahmins before conversion still thought of themselves as high caste, whereas those whose families formerly belonged to the lower castes were excluded from certain social circles. In Arabia, he had seen a new form of Islam, alien to the traditions of South Asia. Here he noticed how local Muslims would sometimes sleep in the Kaaba, using the holy Book as their head support. Also Arab Muslims never offered prayers, like Indian Muslims did after offering *namaz*. In Baghdad where there was a strong influence of Shiaism, Nanak had noticed various paintings of the Prophet and his son-in-law, Ali.

Then of course was the Islam of the dervish, a different brand of religion even within the South Asian tradition. They smoked hashish, consumed bhang, fornicated and sometimes even roamed around naked. Nanak was particularly averse to such manifestations of religiosity, which was prominent in Hindus as well as Muslims. He usually came across them at Muslim shrines. He noticed a few at the shrine of Baba Farid when he visited it for the first time. After becoming aware of Farid's philosophy through his poetry, he realised how far away these dervish were from the message of the saint they were singing praises of.

Having spent twenty-four years of his life travelling, Nanak had finally settled down at a place called Kartarpur on the banks of the Ravi. Here he had started working on a piece of land that was given to him by one of his devotees. He was joined by his parents and also his wife and children and slowly the community around Nanak started growing as more of his devotees started moving to Kartarpur. Using Kartarpur as his base, Nanak now started travelling to nearby regions. Uch Sharif was one of the most famous Muslim shrines in Southern Punjab and Nanak had arrived here only a day ago, travelling from Kartarpur. The difference was that Nanak was no longer accompanied by his lifelong companion, Bhai Mardana. Mardana had passed away in Baghdad while they were on the way back from the Hajj. Nanak did not have a fixed companion anymore like in his earlier travels. In his shorter trips he was accompanied by different younger companions. This time, he was accompanied by the son of his best friend, who also happened to be a master rubab player.

At the shrine of Jalaludin Bokhari at Uch Sharif, Nanak saw an overwhelming number of dervish and ascetics, who roamed around the shrine, pretending to be religious scholars and made fools of innocent devotees. Some were selling beads, while others sold leaves of trees which they passed off as sacred entities with magical properties. A few pretended to practise black magic while others even sold prayers.

Nanak wanted to scream to the world that is not the true religion of Islam. He wanted to tell them about the message of Farid, which for Nanak captured the true essence of religion. He went to the shrine and sat under the shadow of the banyan tree which was in the centre of the courtyard. To the ordinary folk, he was another dervish or jogi. A few

came, touched his feet, asked for blessings and moved on. Other placed
food items next to him and moved on. Nanak sat silently, observing the
religious practices of the people. 'Mardana, play Raag Ashta Padya,' he
said. Nanak had forgotten that it was not Mardana that was with him
but his son, who, without correcting the Guru, did as instructed.

Nanak sang the following lines:

To the opium addict there is nothing like opium.
To the fish water is everything.
Those imbued with the Name of their Lord
Find every prospect pleasing.

May every moment of my life be a sacrifice to Thy Name, O my Master!

My Master is like a tree that beareth fruit
The Name of the fruit is nectar
Those who drink its juice are truly fulfilled
May my life be sacrificed to them!

Thou livest among all creatures
Yet I see Thee not;
How can the thirsty their thirst slake,
If a wall separates them from the like?

Nanak is Thy tradesman;

Thou art my Master and my good.
My mind would rid itself of delusion
If to Thee I addressed my prayers
And to Thee my petition.[76]

---

[76]Singh, trans. *Hymns of the Gurus*, pages 114–115

21
Guru Amar Das

When Guru Angad Dev told Amar Das that he had chosen him to be the next Guru, he asked Amar Das to go away from Khadur where the Guru was living and stay at Goindwal instead, for a little while. For the last few years, Amar Das made Goindwal his home. He would come to Khadur in the mornings, where he would serve the Guru and his family like a servant and then return to Goindwal in the evening. The Guru told him that when the time was right for the formal initiation of the new Guru, he would call him back from Goindwal.

The village of Goindwal was earlier called 'Gobindwal' after the landlord of the area—Gobinda. According to Sikh tradition, Gobinda once approached Guru Angad Dev at Khadur and asked him to help him get his rightful property back, which had been taken over by someone. Angad Dev sent his favourite disciple, Amar Das to solve the problem. Amar Das found out that Gobinda was the rightful owner of the property and interceded on his behalf, getting him back what was his. To show his love for Amar Das, Gobinda constructed a house for him on his property, which is where Amar Das started to live.

In sending Amar Das to Goindwal, the Guru was following a tradition started by Nanak. Nanak too when he appointed Angad Dev as his successor, asked him to move to Khadur as opposed to Kartarpur Sahib where Nanak was settled. This was to avoid the ire of his sons. Angad Dev too had two sons, Datu and Dasu, and he was sure that they would oppose the appointment of Amar Das as Guru. When Amar Das appointed Ram Das as his successor over his sons, he too asked Ram Das to move to Ramdaspur.

When Amar Das was formally appointed, the earlier Guru, Angad Dev's eldest son, Datu, refused to accept their 'family servant'[77] as the next Guru, as was feared. After the death of Guru Angad Dev, Amar Das moved to Goindwal where he established his seat, while Datu sat on his father's seat at Khadur. However, the majority of the followers of Guru Angad Dev preferred to visit Amar Das at Goindwal, hence gradually the influence of the seat at Khadur became weak. One day, in fury, Datu went to Goindwal where he found Amar Das seated. He kicked the Guru off his place and sat there. Amar Das did not return this act of violence with violence and left for a place called Basarke. Datu was under the impression that once at Goindwal he would be in command of the Sikhs but that was not to be. The people there refused to accept him as the Guru and soon Datu had to leave Goindwal for Khadur. After much pleading, the devotees of Amar Das were able to persuade him to come back to Goindwal and be their Guru once again.

The era of Amar Das as the Guru of the Sikh community played an important role in defining the Sikh community as a separate religious community. P. S. Grewal writes the following:

> The need for providing Sikhism as an organised religion, with features of identification led Amar Das to evolve various symbols, customs and institutions, many of which were quite similar to the Hindu ones. Thus Amar Das built a pilgrimage centre at Goindwal. Here a holy well or a *baoli* with 84 steps were constructed and it was declared that 'whoever would reverently repeat the Japji on every step should escape the pangs of rebirth'. Thus while pilgrimage to Banaras and Haridwar and bathing in the Ganga for purification had been decried by Nanak, pilgrimage to Goindwal and bathing in the 'holy' water there was advocated as a means to salvation! Another departure from

---

[77] Singh, *The History of Sikh Gurus*, page 42

earlier Sikh doctrine was the new initiation ceremony introduced by Amar Das. The Guru's agents were given the right to initiate new members into the fold via the *charnamrit* ceremony, i.e. by making the convert drink the 'toe wash' of the religious agent, a typical Brahminical practice.[78]

Emperor Akbar is also said to have visited Guru Amar Das at Goindwal, after hearing of the fame of the Guru.[79] The Guru had a protocol that all his visitors had to follow. The tradition was that whosoever came to visit the Guru would have to have food at the langar of the Guru and only then would he or she be allowed to meet the Guru. When Emperor Akbar was told about the tradition he too agreed to have food from the langar of the Guru before meeting him. Impressed by the humility of the Emperor, the Guru joined the Emperor at the langar and they had food together.

The Emperor was so impressed by the institutions of the Guru that he offered to construct a number of langars for the Guru. Guru Amar Das politely turned down the offer saying that the langar should be run on the money of the humble Sikhs. Therefore Akbar allotted a huge tract of land to the daughter of Amar Das, Bibi Bhani, the wife of Guru Ram Das[80] instead. The Emperor also exempted the Sikhs from paying pilgrimage tax, which was compulsory for the Hindus. This too played an important role in establishing the Sikh community as a distinct religious group.

---

[78]Grewal, Nanak's Doctrine, pages 22–23

[79]Singh, *The History of Sikh Gurus*, page 45

[80]Ibid., page 46

22
An End and the Beginning

Nanak habitually woke up before dawn. The stars of the night still shone in the skies, hanging on for just a little while longer to catch sight of this old man preparing for his daily routine. Nanak lived in a simple hut that was built of wood and hay, both of which were found in abundance there. He was still in his night clothes, a white dhoti, bare-chested and no head cover. His long white hair flowed to his shoulders, while his beard too was unruly at this time of the day.

Singing his poetry, Nanak walked slowly towards the Ravi that flowed close to his hut. He had been doing this for the past seventeen years. He would bathe in the Ravi while singing songs. He walked with his eyes on the ground, while his shoulders were slouched. It was as if age had made this man even more humble.

While singing, he felt a teardrop on his cheek. He had not realised when it had fallen. Only after a few tears had been shed did Nanak realise that he was crying for his friend Mardana, who had passed away several years ago in Baghdad. If only death could have waited a little while longer, Nanak would have buried his friend with his own hands at Kartarpur, his final abode. Here he would have visited his friend's grave everyday and talked to him, but that last moment of closure was not given to him. It was after the death of his friend that Nanak gave up his ambition to travel the world and decided to settle down.

Nanak was finally living with his family. This should have been happy times and they were, but Nanak felt the absence of his best friend and lifelong companion. Nothing was the same without him. Today while picking up his clothes and the *lota* that he used for his bath, Nanak had unconsciously started singing a song that he had sung often with Mardana. It was because of this that he was crying.

He placed his clothes on the bank of the river and walked into the water. Far away in the horizon he could see the light blue dawn, the day was waking up from its slumber. He held both his hands in front of his chest and took a dip in the water.

During his wanderings around the world, Nanak had no fixed routine. He did not know where he would go next. At the start of his journey he had arbitrarily turned east and continued walking till he thought that he should now turn south. This is how he had travelled the four directions of the world. Often during their journeys, Mardana would ask when they would go back home. It was not that Mardana wanted to return but he just wanted to know their plan. Nanak usually had answers to all the questions that Mardana or others put to him but he had no answer for that. He simply shrugged his shoulders saying that they would return when it was God's will.

Meanwhile, back in Punjab where Nanak had left his wife and two sons, his family had become used to a life without the figurehead. Often they would hear stories of the holy man traversing new heights in religious matters. His wife, Sulakhni, was a simple woman who did not understand spiritual concepts. She often heard these concepts without commenting on them. Even though she never made any bitter remarks about her husband leaving her and his two sons, everyone who saw her could tell that she was sad. She spent days without talking to anyone, just focusing on her chores as the bride of the house and a mother of two sons. Bebe Nanki was particularly sympathetic towards Sulakhni. She would often spend hours with her trying to tell her that this was a sacrifice she had to make for the larger good of the world. She would say that God would reward her eventually for her patience. Sulakhni was close to her sister-in-law and found comfort in her words but she could never express with utter frankness what was in her heart. This was because she knew that Bebe Nanki was after all Nanak's sister and her devotion towards her brother was unquestionable.

The truth was that Sulakhni did not even know what it was in her heart that she was so eager to hide from the rest of the world. It was a pain that continuously ate away at her existence. This she was aware of but on the other hand she loved her husband too much to feel any resentment towards him. Every day while praying to Durga Mata she would pray for the safety and success of her husband's mission, a mission that she had a hard time understanding. Whenever someone came to her with news of her husband and the amazing things he was doing in the far away regions of the world, she would pray that more and more people come to know of Nanak and his spiritual mission. This she did knowing well enough that it would take Nanak further away from her.

Seeing Sulakhni's misery, Bebe Nanki decided to look after her eldest son, Sri Chand. She knew that raising two sons in the absence of a father would have been a difficult task for a single woman. Bebe Nanki did not have a child of her own, which made the decision to temporarily adopt Sri Chand easier. Looking into the deep eyes of this young child, Bebe Nanki used to feel that she was staring at her brother whom she too loved like a mother; such was the physical resemblance between father and son. In Sri Chand's presence, Bebe Nanki felt that she was in the presence of her brother.

With only Sri Lachman to hold onto, Sulakhni devoted herself completely to her younger child. Whereas Sri Chand followed the spiritual pursuits of his father, encouraged by Bebe Nanki, Sulakhni made sure that the younger son was kept away from such matters. She took him to the temple and he took part in Hindu rituals on the occasion of religious festivals, but that was all that religion mattered in the lives of mother and son. At an early age the young mother directed her son's attention towards worldly matters. While his elder brother discussed metaphysical concepts with dervish, fakirs, sadhus and jogis, Sri Lachman sat in the company of accountants, businessmen, traders and government officials.

When Mardana passed away unexpectedly in Baghdad on the way back from the Hajj, Nanak decided that it was time to go back to Punjab. He took up the offer to till the land that one of his devotees was willing to present to him and finally after almost three decades of travel, decided to settle down. He sent for his family from Talwindi and started living at this small village called Kartarpur.

Sulakhni finally started living with Nanak once again, along with their two sons. She served Nanak tirelessly, something that she had dreamed of doing for years. Even though her dreams had come true, she pretended that life had always been like this. When Nanak went for his morning dip in the river, she prepared his breakfast. Then while he was away in the fields working on the land, she busied herself with chores. In the evening, when Nanak would return from the fields, she would prepare to entertain all his devotees who would come to listen to the songs of their spiritual master. While everyone listened to the songs, she, along with a few other women of the community, prepared for the langar which concluded the evening. She did not object when Nanak told her that Muslims and even untouchables would be welcome to the langar. She was aware of her husband's radical views but she had not known that someday they would be implemented in her own house. The idea repulsed her initially and for the first few days she could not eat after looking at the sight of Hindus, Muslims and untouchables sitting under one roof. But over the years she had become accustomed to the sight.

Behind the veil of his wife's utter devotion to him, Nanak could sense the resentment that had accumulated over the years that he had been away. He could listen to the complaints that those silent eyes made to him. He knew that he had wronged his wife and children and he wanted to apologise to them but it was too late, he thought. He did not know how to broach the topic, especially when everything looked perfect on the surface. Every day he looked at the devotion of his family towards him and every day the guilt of abandoning them grew. The fact that they never expressed their resentment caused Nanak even greater pain. Had they said something, he would have offered them his excuses but they accepted him unconditionally.

Till the time that Nanak had been away from his family, he felt that he was satisfied with the way he had spent his life. When his best friend passed away, Nanak believed that his time was near as well but the years passed and life seemed to continue even without Mardana. Nanak now wondered if he had done the right thing in abandoning his family at the time that they needed him the most for his spiritual pilgrimage. Now that he was in their company, he felt selfish, since he was an old man and needed someone to look after him. Nanak often longed for his old life, of travel without a destination. To relive some moments of the life that had now ended, he travelled to nearby places with some of his devotees or his sons. One of his favourite travel companions after Mardana was a young man known as Bhai Lehna. Bhai Lehna would often visit Nanak at Kartarpur Sahib from Khadur where he lived. Often these two would spend hours locked in a room talking to each other, while the rest of the community waited for their spiritual master to present himself to them. In his company, Nanak lost track of time, whereas Lehna too adored the company of his spiritual master. In Nanak he had found everything that he was looking for.

Born into an orthodox family, Lehna was religious to begin with but as he grew older his interest in religious questions exceeded that of his family members. He travelled to Hindu temples on pilgrimages to far away regions. It was on one such pilgrimage that he met Nanak and his life changed forever. Instead of going to the temple of Durga where he was headed, he decided to come to Kartarpur Sahib along with Nanak and spent several days with the spiritual master.

Guru Nanak, on the other hand, was also impressed by the curiosity and passion of this young man. He had thought that when he came back his sons would express an interest in the spiritual journey that Nanak had taken but he was disappointed with their attitude towards his cause. Both of them were adult men when Nanak returned and had started living the life that they had chosen for themselves. Lachman Das had become a businessman and was not at all interested in the spiritual and intellectual pursuits of his father. Sri Chand, on the other hand, took an active interest in spiritual matters but his dispensation was to the extreme. After a few conversations with him Nanak could tell that he was highly inspired by the yogis and would soon take to the path of the yogis, becoming an ascetic.

Out of his two sons the choices of his elder son bothered him more than those made by his younger one. In his journey Nanak had severely criticised the extreme practices of the ascetics and now in his very home his son was on his way to becoming one. Nanak tried arguing with him and convincing him that he needed to be moderate in his religious practices but the words that had moved the world to tears and made thousands of people the followers of Guru Nanak failed to move his son. His mind was made up. Nanak blamed himself for the extremes of his son's behaviour. He thought that by rebelling against Nanak's own teachings his son was punishing him for abandoning him at such a young age.

It had now been seventeen years that Nanak had been leading a sedentary life. Hundreds of devotees from neighbouring villages and beyond came to visit him every day to listen to his sermons. Nanak tried meeting all of them in person but that had become impossible in recent years. When Nanak set up his base at one place and started his kirtan session every evening, his popularity spread far and wide. In the initial years there had only been a handful of followers but this number had swelled into hundreds in subsequent years. In the initial years the community could gather at his house but eventually a new hall was constructed which could host the huge gathering. This place was reserved for the evening prayers and was referred to as a Gurdwara by Nanak, where the Ultimate Guru resided.

Initially, Nanak's devotees posed all sorts of difficult questions to him. Some even dared to call him a liar to his face while others argued until they were convinced. But as the community grew bigger so did the stature of Nanak as someone who could never be challenged. The questions grew less and sceptical conversations faded away. Now what remained between Nanak and almost all of his devotees was a relationship between a spiritual master and his followers. Nanak felt that people were now starting to follow him blindly and this depressed him.

It was in this situation that Nanak met Lehna for the first time. Lehna showed respect to the older spiritual master but was not afraid to challenge his religious beliefs. He was not one to give up on his beliefs easily and argued rigorously. This debate between Nanak and Lehna continued for months. Lehna would present points in favour of Hindu deities and Nanak would put them aside one by one through his counterarguments.

If there was one person besides Mardana who understood the poetry of Nanak as Nanak himself did, then it was Bhai Lehna. After their initial arguments Lehna became a devoted disciple of Guru Nanak and both of them started to discuss Nanak's poetry. Lehna would ask Nanak questions about where and why he had composed particular verses. Lehna also learned from Nanak the correct *raag* in which they were meant to be sung, for the raag in which a particular poem was sung also had a great influence on the impact those words would have on the listeners.

As much as Lehna wanted Nanak to live forever he was aware of the mortality of his Guru, which is why he wanted to spend all his time with his Guru. Lehna was also aware of the fact that if he wanted to preserve the message of Guru Nanak, it was important that his words were recorded. He knew that the songs Nanak had composed would be preserved for generations to come through singers and dervish, like the words of other poets had been preserved. But for Lehna, Nanak was no ordinary poet. He was also a spiritual reformer and it was essential that along with his poetry his religious message also travelled through generations. It is for this reason that Lehna decided to collect the poetry of Nanak in written form.

This was a bold decision as till that point Punjabi was still largely an oral language. Nobody considered it worthy enough to be written, hence it had no script. Lehna could have used Shahmukhi, the script used for Arabic and Persian, but he felt that Nanak's words should be preserved in a new script as his message was different from all the other spiritual reformers before him. In this way, Lehna laid the foundation for the Gurumukhi script, the script of the Guru, in which Punjabi is now written the world over, except for the land where Nanak actually lived and died.

After his bath, Nanak returned home to find that all his family members were up and preparing for the day. His wife had prepared his breakfast, while his sons had already eaten and were now getting dressed for business. Sulakhni, as she always did, remained silent and busied herself with other activities around the house.

Nanak could sense some tension in the house. He could tell that all the family members of the house had been engaged in a passionate conversation before he had entered and now all of them had gone quiet. The silence in the room was too strong to be casual. This was a forced silence. Nanak longed to be a part of the family conversation but his long absence had estranged him from his family. In the past his various attempts at conversation had failed and he noticed that it was only when he was not around that the two sons and their mother became garrulous.

Sri Chand and his mother were particularly close. Nanak could tell by looking at their expressions that they were discussing something serious and that too about him. There were a few stress lines on the forehead of his eldest son, while his wife looked embarrassed. Nanak did not know how to ask them what they were talking about but before he could think of a strategy to broach the topic, his son Sri Chand said, 'Bapuji, I need to talk to you about something important.'

'All my time is for you, my son. What is it that brings so much frustration on your face?' said Nanak.

Sri Chand ignored the polite reply of his father and continued speaking, 'I am not happy with how much time you spend with Lehna. He says that he is your devotee but he is still a practising Hindu. He still worships Durga in his house. People have told me. He doesn't understand your message like your own blood does. And now I have heard that you are about to appoint him as your spiritual successor. How can that be? That has no precedent in history. By the laws of spirituality your spiritual prowess has been passed onto me, your eldest son, not to someone who is not even related to you. How can you do this to us? Your own family? You left us when we needed you and now this.'

Surprised by his own audacity, Sri Chand became silent. Sulakhni continued pretending to be busy with her household chores. Lachman was also quiet and wore an expression which showed that he knew that there was no point to this conversation. He was a businessman and his job had hardened him. He had seen the ugly side of the world and nothing surprised him anymore.

After a poignant silence Sri Chand asked his father, 'Have you made up your mind, Bapuji? Are you going to make Lehna your successor? What will the world say? I will become a laughing stock.'

'You should listen to your blood,' said Sulakhni. 'Who will take care of us? Don't you want your family to be happy?'

Nanak listened to his son and wife with patience. He was not expecting such a reaction from his own family. He too was disappointed in them as they were in him. Maybe, he had expected too much of them. He had thought that they would understand his decision but this outburst made it clear that he was alone even in his family. 'Sri Chand, listen to me. You will always be my son and no matter what anyone says, that can never change. My God knows that I love you more than anything else in the world and can do anything for you but what you ask me to do, that I cannot do. That is not my decision. These decisions are written in our destinies. It was your destiny to be born into my household but it is not in your destiny to be my spiritual descendant. That has to be Bhai Lehna.'

Saying this, Nanak walked out of the house to his fields, where he worked every day after breakfast. He was not going there to work today but to spend some time away from his family. Nanak did not have his breakfast that morning. His family's reaction had put him in mental agony.

Nanak walked in the fields all day, inspecting the wheat that he had grown. He passed his hands gently over them as if caressing them. He watched the birds fly over his head and observed the path of the sun. He walked around the river, allowing his thoughts to flow with the currents of the Ravi. In the evening he returned to the gurdwara he had constructed, where as usual, the audience was starting to gather. Bhai Lehna was there as well, waiting for his Guru and so was Baba Budha, another loyal disciple of Nanak.

'What is it, Guruji? You look tense today?' said Bhai Lehna, as soon as he saw the forlorn face of Nanak.

'I have something on my mind, Bhai Lehna. I am worried about what will become of my movement after my death. I know that my sons don't think like me and soon my message would be lost forever,' said Nanak.

'We are your children, Guruji,' said Lehna. 'We will keep your message alive. We will not let this movement die.'

For the first time in the day a smile appeared on Nanak's face. He took Lehna's hand and said, 'Lehna you are my true son. You are my flesh and my blood. You are a part of my body, my *angad* (of one's body). I am sure that you are the best person to continue my mission after my

death. Nobody understands my message better than you. You are my
spiritual successor.'

Saying this, he gestured towards Baba Budha to come forward and
apply saffron paste on Bhai Lehna's forehead. Nanak then put five copper
coins and a coconut at Lehna's feet and bowed to him. Bhai Lehna tried
stopping Nanak but he was persistent. Facing the crowd Nanak then
said, 'Hear this, my devotees. I have appointed Bhai Lehna, who is from
now on to be known as Guru Angad, as my successor. He is your second
Guru. I have appointed him as the Guru and if you have ever accepted
me as your Guru you should now accept him as your Guru.'

ੴ

Sitting on a charpoy, the policemen who were having tea looked at us
suspiciously. Trying not to provoke them, I parked the car near the main
gate instead of taking it inside the gurdwara, even though the gate was
open. An old man walking with his wife walked straight into the gateway
that I was reluctant to enter. I was sure he was a Muslim and belonged
to a neighbouring village. I was surprised that he was allowed to enter
without any trouble. This was not like any other gurdwara, it turned out.
This was Kartarpur Sahib, the final resting abode of Guru Nanak and
here, Muslims were allowed to enter.

This gurdwara is located about an hour away from the city of Narowal.
This is the border area; hence the roads are in a bad condition. To get
to this shrine, we had to get off the main road and drive on a mud track
towards the Ravi, which still flows next to the shrine.

'Do you know, when I came here for the first time, I had to walk
from the main road to the gurdwara,' said Iqbal Qaiser, while we were
driving on the track. This was a road of about three kilometres. There
were rice paddies around us, partially flooded. This year too the monsoon
had arrived earlier than expected, flooding the agricultural fields. In the
case of rice paddies, flooding was good as rice requires a lot of water to
grow.

It seemed as if Iqbal Qaiser knew the policemen. One of them had
recognised him and greeted him quite respectfully, something that is

unusual of Pakistani policemen. He stood up on seeing him and laughed along with him. Sitting in the car, I could see that he was gesturing to Iqbal Qaiser to take the car inside the gurdwara.

We drove into the gurdwara. The main shrine was protected by a newly constructed wall. We parked our car next to what appeared to be an airplane missile preserved in a glass case. On a marble plaque next to it, it was written that this missile was dropped here by the Indian forces in 1971 but due to the miracle of Guru Nanak, it did not blow up.

This was rather strange as I had imagined Sikh heritage would prepare the ground for the two hostile countries to come together but in this case it was being used to further antagonise the two countries. This had its legacy in the Khalistan movement of the 1980s when Sikhs in India fought against the Congress-led Indian government to carve out a separate state for the Sikhs. They were supported by the Pakistani government in this struggle. The Sikh diaspora residing in England, Canada and USA were sympathetic towards the cause. In those times, they established a relationship with the Pakistani government, a relationship that continues to survive, even though the movement has faded away. It is due to the pressure of these wealthy and powerful Sikhs that the government initially renovated the Sikh gurdwaras.

Next to the showcase with the missile, there was a well, covered with marble. A plaque next to it read that this was the well that was used by Guru Nanak to water his fields. I looked deep into the fields to imagine a peasant-like Nanak tolling away in the humid monsoons. In front of me was some haphazardly grown sugarcane. A peasant, wearing muddy clothes, worked in the fields. Looking at Nanak toiling under the sun, who could have said that he was the Nanak of history, who had inspired millions of people? Some scholars have argued that the beauty of Nanak's message is that through his own example, he glorified peasantry. His message was that work, no matter what it is, should be treated as a sacred activity and hence an act of worship. We took our shoes off, covered our heads with skullcaps that were placed next to the entrance and walked into the shrine. The main structure was in the middle of a courtyard, while around it there were rooms meant to be used to house pilgrims.

There was a grave next to the main shrine. It was out in the open with artificial flowers covering it all over. There was no tombstone identifying its occupier; however, there was a couplet etched on it.

The Muslim family that had crossed us at the entrance was standing in front of the grave offering prayers. After a little while, the man bowed towards the feet of the grave, while the woman touched it with her hand and passed it over her head, blessing herself with the auspicious touch of the holy person buried within. The family left soon after.

'Iqbal Sahib, I find it really odd that no grave marks the spot where Mardana was buried. According to one story, he passed away in Baghdad but there is another story which says that Mardana returned to Punjab with Nanak and died here in Kartarpur. It was, however, his last wish that no shrine be constructed over his grave. Let's discard the first story for a little while and assume that Mardana came back. Is it possible that the story about Mardana not wanting a shrine was added later on to explain the origin of this grave and is it possible that this is the grave of Bhai Mardana next to the samadhi of his Guru?'

ੴ

When Nanak passed away a controversy erupted. His followers started to argue about the rites that they should perform over his body. The Hindus argued that since he was born into a Hindu household they should cremate him, whereas the Muslims argued that since he had challenged the doctrines of Hinduism he was a Muslim and should be buried as a Muslim. Isn't it interesting to note that in this argument Nanak's followers lost the point of Nanak's teachings? If something like this happens several years after one's death, that is a separate matter, but this was happening right after his death. While this argument was brewing, it turned into a fight, and the group decided to postpone the decision till the next day.

The next day when the followers of Guru Nanak gathered, they found that his body had disappeared, and there were flowers in its place. It was decided that the flowers be divided into two parts. One of which was cremated and then a samadhi was constructed on top, while the other was buried like a Muslim. The Sikhs say that even in death Guru Nanak had performed a miracle.

ੴ

A young boy who must have been in his late teens or early twenties approached me and said, 'No photography.' I couldn't tell if he was a Muslim or Sikh boy. My guess was that he was probably a government official deputed here and most probably a Muslim.

'It's alright,' said Iqbal Qaiser, jumping into the conversation. 'My name is Iqbal Qaiser and I already have all the photos of this place. Everyone knows me here. Who is the Granthi here nowadays?'

'Inderjit,' said the boy in a meek voice, not sure what to make of these two strange men in front of him refusing to stop taking photographs.

'Where is he?'

'He is there in the camps.'

'Go tell him Iqbal Qaiser is here.'

The boy ran off with a worried expression on his face. Perhaps he thought he might have offended two very important people and now he was in trouble.

'Go ahead, photograph all you want,' said Iqbal Qaiser.

I too was surprised. I had never seen Iqbal Qaiser so confident and defiant. His manner of talking usually comes across as very meek and sombre, a sign of his humility, but today he was authoritative.

I tried opening the glass door that led into the main shrine, where the samadhi of Nanak was situated but it was locked. If the samadhi and the grave are both considered to be the final resting place of Nanak then why is the grave discriminated against? This too should be within the main shrine. The main building was constructed around the samadhi, whereas the grave was on one side of the building. Iqbal Qaiser told me that the original building was destroyed in a flood several years ago and this new one was built later. Perhaps when this was constructed the Muslim and Sikh communities had drifted further apart. The grave of Nanak became a casualty of the growing Muslim-Sikh antagonism.

'Sir, Inderjit Sahib is calling you to his room,' said the boy after he returned in a little while. We were escorted to Inderjit's shed, which had been constructed recently with the help of the Sikh Diaspora. The boy asked us to wait for a little while as Inderjit was getting dressed. It was a Sunday morning and we had arrived unexpectedly.

We took off our shoes at the entrance and entered his room. It was a spacious place with a double bed on one side and a sofa set on the other. Geo, the most popular news channel of the country was playing on the television, covering the floods in Sindh and lower Punjab. Inderjit appeared from another room, which I assumed to be the bathroom.

'*Sat Sri Akal ji Shri Maharaj* Iqbal Qaiser Singh Sahib,' he said. He gestured to touch Iqbal Qaiser's knees in a teasing manner, while Iqbal Qaiser patted him on the back. After brief introductions, Iqbal Qaiser told me to ask Inderjit the questions that I wanted to for my research, while he busied himself watching the news.

Inderjit told me that his family belonged to a village in Faisalabad district. They weren't Sikhs but Nanak Panthi Hindus. However his garb was that of a baptized Sikh, the Khalsa of Guru Gobind Singh, perhaps reflective of the larger change in trend since the past few years as the Sikh community in post-Khalistan days exerts its separate identity. At the time of Partition when the rest of the Sikhs from their village migrated to India, his grandfather too was on his way but they were stopped near the border by the Muslims of their village. They assured him that if he came back and lived with them they would provide him with security. Overwhelmed by the love that was offered to him, his grandfather moved back to his ancestral village and lived a peaceful life till the war of 1965.

In 1965, his family moved to Nankana. I asked Inderjit if that was because of the blowback of the war but he said he didn't know. I asked him if their land like that of Boota Singh was taken away from them but it seemed as if he didn't want to talk about it. I didn't need him to tell me that something horrible happened with their family during the India-Pakistan war of 1965. Theirs would not be an isolated case. Instances of violence against Sikhs and Hindus were reported from all over the country during the three wars that were fought between India and Pakistan. But I am surprised that Inderjit refused to talk about that era, whereas he was candid about so many other things. Is it because he was now a government official and lived under its protection?

The Pakistani establishment is paranoid that talking about minority issues would present a bad image of Pakistan and hence they are particularly wary about the minorities talking about their woes to journalists and writers. Inderjit lives under the blessings of the Pakistani establishment which regularly monitors the activities of Sikhs in Pakistan. Perhaps he doesn't want to offend his protectors.

Somewhere towards the east, across the river is the India-Pakistan border, the symbol of hostility between these two countries. I ask Iqbal Qaiser and Inderjit to show me the border. We walked out of his room and headed towards the Ravi. In front of us was the meandering river, flowing peacefully on the plains of Punjab. Defying man-made boundaries, the river sometimes crosses into India while at other points it comes back to Pakistan.

The river was a beautiful sight, its brown water refurbished by the early monsoon. Otherwise, the river is parched throughout the year. At certain points the river had broken its banks and flooded the fresh green fields that surrounded it, most of which were rice fields. The river must have been much stronger about five hundred years ago when Nanak lived. Standing here I could imagine Nanak walking into the river and performing *ashnan*. Had Radcliffe made a minor error on the map of Punjab in front of him by only a few centimetres, the shrine of Kartarpur Sahib would have ended up in India and today hundreds of devotees would have been taking a dip in this holy water. The Ravi would have been a holy river, like it was at the time of the Vedas.

'Do you know the locals have a myth about the Ravi and the shrine of Nanak?' asked Inderjit. 'They say that the river floods every twenty odd years and comes right up to the shrine. This is the river paying tribute to the shrine of Nanak.'

'By locals you mean local Muslims?' I asked.

'Yes.'

'Do the locals still come to the shrine?'

'Yes. There is a grave of Nanak next to his samadhi. They come here regularly and offer their *fateha* (first verse of the Quran, used as a prayer) just like they would at any Muslim shrine. The locals regard Nanak as a saint,' elaborated Inderjit.

'Do you know when I came here the first time, this had not become a shrine it is today?' added Iqbal Qaiser. 'This used to be a centre for smugglers because of its proximity to the border. Drug addicts too had established a place for themselves. Other locals though still came to the grave of Nanak. Here they would present their offerings and also clean the shrine as a service. This tradition continued since it was prevalent even before Partition.'

'So these people must have been those whose ancestors were devotees of Nanak before Partition. Perhaps some of them even met with Nanak when he lived here,' I said.

'We established this gurdwara in 2001,' said Inderjit. 'This is when we renovated the structure. We also prepared our first langar here at that time. Even today, rich Muslim families of the neighbouring villages provide us with monetary support to cook langar. This is their offering to the shrine. For them this is a sacred space. The wood that we require for cooking langar is provided to us by the Rangers.'

'Do the Muslim devotees also eat langar?' I asked.

'Well not at the beginning. They were hesitant to eat food cooked by Sikhs. They had all sorts of absurd ideas about how we cooked our food. They would come to us and ask us the most absurd questions. But over the years as the myths dispersed they started eating langar here. Today, more Muslims eat food here compared to Sikhs.'

This was a fascinating revelation for me. The shrine of Nanak as it was meant to be, continued to be sacred for Muslims as well as Hindus and Sikhs.

I tried catching a glimpse of the border but it was obscured by the thick foliage of trees. Somewhere behind those trees was the Indian border, behind which was a thick fence. Behind that fence, looking in our direction through powerful binoculars, were Indian pilgrims, who gather there to perform darshan of the shrine of Guru Nanak. Hundreds of people gather there every day.

'How amazing would it be for them if they were allowed to enter Pakistan from here, visit the shrine of Nanak and then return?' I said.

'Discussions on those lines are going on nowadays. There are talks to declare this region a peace corridor and under that arrangement Indian pilgrims will be allowed to enter Pakistan without a visa to visit the shrine of Guru Nanak. The Pakistani government has given its approval to the proposal; however the Indian government is not ready to implement the deal. They say that this peace corridor would be used by terrorists,' said Iqbal Qaiser.

Iqbal Qaiser and Inderjit engaged in discussions about agriculture while I made notes about my visit to this place, sitting next to them. After a little while, I overheard Inderjit telling Iqbal Qaiser about a giant snake that they had recently seen in the neighbouring fields. 'It was bigger than two humans combined,' he said. It turns out that this place has a lot of snakes. 'We find them regularly in our fields. We then place them next to the shrine. After paying their respects they return. All they want to do is to catch a sight of the shrine.'

On the way back to the car, Inderjit showed us the renovations that were taking place at the shrine. Right now there was only the shrine and a few rooms which were reserved for the caretakers. Soon there would be a langar hall as well as a pool. 'Iqbal Sahib, I don't understand our Sikh community,' said Inderjit while showing us his plans for the renovations. 'A lot of Sikhs from England and Canada have complained that the architecture of the shrine is not, strictly speaking, Sikh. They say that it has a lot of features of Muslim architecture.'

He pointed out the arches of the shrine, which were plain. This was a feature of Muslim architecture. Sikh arches were usually three-cusped. But at the end of the day these were only vague distinctions as architectural influences crept from one tradition to another. I remember that in my ancestral house in Sargodha, the arches were three-cusped, hence Sikh, even though we were a Muslim family.

This comment on Sikh architecture took me back to the lecture of Iqbal Qaiser at LUMS, where I first met him. The lecture was titled *Sikh Architecture in Lahore*. In that lecture, Iqbal Qaiser pointed out that like the Sikh religion, which picks up from both Hinduism and Islam, Sikh architecture draws inspiration from both Hindu and Muslim architecture. He pointed to the domes of Sikh shrines, which were initially part of the Muslim buildings, but when the Sikhs picked it up they interpreted it in their own manner, making them smaller and adding other features to it. Now such domes are also used in Muslim buildings in Pakistan. One can find similar Islamic architectural influences on Sikh arches. Within Sikh shrines there are usually elaborate graphic depictions of Sikh Gurus and also sometimes Hindu deities (in older buildings). These influences crept in from the Hindu tradition.

In such a complex relationship within architectural and religious traditions, how can one make distinctions between Muslim, Hindu or Sikh influences? Islam carried forward a lot of pre-Islamic Arabian religious practices. Hinduism was immensely influenced by Buddhism in the first century CE. Nanak was aware of these fluid boundaries. That's what he preached and that's what he wanted his sect to be. Instead of which, Sikhism, a distinct religion with its own exclusive boundaries, emerged out of Nanak's philosophy. Had Nanak supervised the construction of his own shrine, would he have allowed Muslim influences in the building, which the Sikh Diaspora now complained against?

As Iqbal Qaiser and I drove away, I caught a glimpse of Nanak's shrine in the rearview mirror. As the car slowly moved further away, the building appeared to grow smaller, and then after a little while, it disappeared completely.

We were now on our own path; the image of the shrine of Nanak was only a memory.

Bibliography

Bhattacharya, Sabyasachi. *Approaches to History: Essays in Indian Historiography*. New Delhi: Indian Council of Historical Research in Association with Primus, 2011. Print.

Cunningham, Joseph Davey, and H. L. O. Garrett. *A History of the Sikhs, from the Origin of the Nation to the Battles of the Sutlej*. New Delhi: S. Chand, 1966. Print.

Dhillon, Harish. *The First Sikh Spiritual Master: Timeless Wisdom from the Life and Teachings of Guru Nanak*. Woodstock, VT: SkyLight Paths Pub., 2006. Print.

Gandhi, Surjit Singh. *History of the Sikh Gurus: A Comprehensive Study*. Delhi: Gur Das Kapur, 1978. Print.

Grewal, J. S. *History, Literature, and Identity: Four Centuries of Sikh Tradition*. New Delhi: Oxford UP, 2011. Print.

Grewal, P. S. 'Nanak's Doctrine and the Feudalisation of the Sikh Gurudom.' *Social Scientist* 11.5 (1983): 16–32. *JSTOR*. Web. 20 Aug. 2014. <http://www.jstor.org/stable/10.2307/3517100?ref=no-x-route:699f2def62feec6c81235b0a59d51197>.

Kohli, Mohindar Pal. *Guru Tegh Bahadur: Testimony of Conscience*. New Delhi: Sahitya Akademi, 1992. Print.

Qaiser, Iqbal. *Historical Sikh Shrines in Pakistan*. Lahore: Punjabi History Board, 1998. Print.

Singh, Khushwant, trans. *Hymns of the Gurus*. New Delhi: Viking, 2003. Print.

Singh, Nikky-Guninder Kaur. *Sikhism: An Introduction*. London: I. B. Tauris, 2011. Print.

Singh, Prithi Pal. *The History of Sikh Gurus*. New Delhi: Lotus, 2006. Print.

Singh, Trilochan. *Guru Nanak: Founder of Sikhism; a Biography*. Delhi: Gurdwara Parbandhak Committee, 1969. Print.

Syan, Hardip Singh. *Sikh Militancy in the Seventeenth Century: Religious Violence in Mughal and Early Modern India*. London: I. B. Tauris, 2013. Print.

'Chapter X.' *Life of Guru Nanak: Chapter X*. N.p., n.d. Web. 15 Dec. 2013. <http://www.sacred-texts.com/skh/tsr1/tsr113.htm>.

Sri Guru Granth Sahib Raags Index—Author: Baba Sheikh Farid—SearchGurbani. com. N.p., n.d. Web. 12 Feb. 2014. <http://searchgurbani.com/guru_granth_sahib/author/Baba%20Sheikh%20Farid>.

Chronology

1469 – Guru Nanak is born

1487/88 – Guru Nanak is married to Mata Sulakhni

1497 – Guru Nanak experiences his spiritual awakening at Sultanpur Lodhi

1519 – Babur invades North India and captures the city of Saidpur

1521/22 – Guru Nanak settles at Kartarpur

1539 – Guru Nanak passes away and Guru Angad is appointed as the next Guru

1545 – Guru Ram Das marries Bibi Bhani, the daughter of Guru Amar Das

1552 – Guru Angad passes away and Guru Amar Das is appointed as the next Guru

1574 – Guru Amar Das passes away and Guru Ram Das is appointed as the next Guru

1577 – The construction of Amrit Sar begins on the orders of Guru Ram Das

1581 – Guru Ram Das passes away and Guru Arjan is appointed as his successor

1605 – Prince Salim becomes Emperor Jahangir

1606 – Prince Khusro rebels against Emperor Jahangir

1606 – The rebellion is defeated and Guru Arjan is assassinated on the orders of the Emperor as an accomplice to the rebellion.

1606 – Guru Hargobind is appointed as the next Sikh Guru

1617–1619 – Guru Hargobind is jailed at the Gwalior Fort by Emperor Jahangir

1644 – Guru Hargobind passes away and Guru Har Rai is appointed as the next Guru

1657 – A battle of succession begins between Emperor Shahjahan's sons

1658 – Dara Shikoh is captured by Aurangzeb and the latter is proclaimed Emperor

1660 – Ram Rai, the eldest son of Guru Har Rai, appears in the Mughal court to clarify the position of his father during the civil war between the Mughal princes

1661 – Guru Har Rai passes away and Guru Harkrishan is appointed as the next Guru

1664 – Guru Harkrishan reaches Delhi to appear in the court of Emperor Aurangzeb

1664 – Guru Harkrishan passes away and Guru Tegh Bahadur is appointed as the next Guru

1675 – Guru Tegh Bahadur is asked to appear in front of the Mughal Emperor Aurangzeb and is assassinated

1675 – Guru Gobind Singh is appointed as the next Guru

1705 – All the sons of Guru Gobind Singh are assassinated by the Mughal forces

1707 – Emperor Aurangzeb dies

1708 – Guru Granth Sahib is declared to be the living Guru for eternity by Guru Gobind Singh

1708 – Guru Gobind Singh is assassinated by a Pathan horse trader

The Gurus of Sikhism

1. Guru Nanak (1469–1539)

Guru Nanak, the first Guru, is believed to be the founder of Sikhism. Born at Talwandi (now known as Nankana Sahib in Pakistan) on October 20, 1469, he regarded Hindus and Muslims as equals and referred to himself as neither Hindu nor Muslim. He is believed to have made four great journeys that spanned for almost three decades. During his travels he visited many Hindu and Muslim pilgrimages including Banaras, Hardwar, Mecca and Baghdad, challenging their rituals, dogma, and the caste system. After his travels he settled at Kartarpur Sahib where he tilled land for seventeen years and preached his message through his songs and poetry. He is considered one of the greatest Punjabi poets following in the same literary tradition of Baba Farid of Pakpattan. He instituted the concept of *Kirtan* and *Langar* which became an integral part of Sikhism.

2. Guru Angad (1504–1552, Guru from 1539 to 1552)

Originally called Lehna he was given the title of Guru Angad by Guru Nanak when he appointed him as his successor bypassing his progeny. Guru Angad became a disciple of Guru Nanak after he had settled at Kartarpur Sahib. After his appointment as the Guru he moved to Khadur on the instructions of Guru Nanak to avoid conflict with Sri Chand, Guru Nanak's eldest son. Guru Angad played a crucial role in preserving Nanak's poetry by inventing the Gurmukhi script, and committing his words in the written form. Following his Guru's tradition he too composed verses and appointed not his son but his disciple as the next Guru.

3. Guru Amar Das (1479–1574, Guru from 1552 to 1574)

After being appointed as the next Guru, Guru Amar Das was asked to move from Khadur to Goindwal by Guru Angad Dev to avoid conflict with Guru Angad Dev's son, who wanted the seat of Gurudom for himself. Guru Amar Das played an important role in establishing the Sikhs as a distinct religious community, separate from Hindus and Muslims, by introducing various symbols, customs and institutions. He had cordial relationship with Emperor Akbar who is believed to have allotted a vast tract of land to his daughter, where later the city of Ramdaspur (Amritsar) was established. Therefore it was under him that the feudalisation of the Gurudom began.

4. Guru Ram Das (1534–1581, Guru from 1574 to 1581)

Born in 1534 Guru Ram Das became the first Sodhi Guru. Following him the institution of Gurudom remained within the Sodhi family till Guru Gobind Singh. Guru Ram Das is known for starting the construction of the Harminder Sahib, which during the time of his son became the most important pilgrimage for Sikhs. Guru Ram Das is also believed to have appointed his *Masand* or deputies in different regions which were responsible for spreading the Guru's message into farflung regions and also collect offerings from his devotees. This system was finally abolished by Guru Gobind Singh because of the corruption that had seeped into it. Guru Ram Das also encouraged trade which meant that the revenue of the seat of the Guru began to increase under him. Before passing away he bypassed his elder son Prithi Chand in the favour of his younger son, Arjan Dev, to be appointed as the next Guru, thus beginning a conflict that was to last for several generations after him.

5. Guru Arjan Dev (1563–1606, Guru from 1581 to 1606)

Regarded as the first martryr of Sikhism, Guru Arjan was assassinated by Emperor Jahangir in the year 1606 for his alleged support to Khusro, the eldest son of Jahangir, who had rebelled against his father. The Sikhs believe that he was assassinated due to the connivance of one Chandu Shah who wanted to marry his daughter to Guru Arjan's son, but was refused by the Guru. The assassination of Guru Arjan marks the beginning of a long conflict between Mughal authorities and Sikh Gurus. Guru Arjan is responsible for the completion of the Harminder Sahib and Amrit Sar, the pool of nectar. He also began the compilation of Guru Granth Sahib, collecting the poetry of all former Gurus and other saints of Hindu and Muslim origin which aligned with the philosophy of the Gurus. A prolific writer himself he has the greatest number of hymns in the Guru Granth Sahib followed by Guru Nanak. Guru Arjan is also responsible for introducing the *daswandh*, a system through which his followers were expected to contribute 10% of their earning to the cause of the Guru.

6. Guru Hargobind (1595–1644, Guru from 1606 to 1644)

Known as the 'soldier-saint' Guru Har Gobind began the process of militarisation of the Sikh community following the assassination of his father. He became the first Guru to wear two swords on his person, one of which represented temporal power while the other spiritual power. He was also the first Guru to not have composed any single hymn. In the beginning of his office he remained in conflict with Emperor Jahangir, who also incarcerated him in Gwalior, but later on they established a cordial relationship with the Guru helping the Emperor in a couple of his military expeditions.

7. Guru Har Rai (1630–1661, Guru from 1644 to 1661)

During the civil war between Aurangzeb and his elder brother Darah Shikoh, Guru Har Rai supported the former. It is asserted that once when Darah Shikoh fell sick and no one was able to provide him respite, he recovered through a medicine that was sent to him by Guru Har Rai. After his recovery Dara Shikoh became his devotee and their relationship continued till his death. Following in the tradition of his father he too kept a military force which he promised to Dara Shikoh against his brother. Once Dara Shikoh was captured and killed Guru Har Rai was ordered by Emperor Aurangzeb to present himself to Delhi and clarify his position during the civil war. The Guru is believed to have sent his elder son, Ram Rai, who in order to appease the Emperor misquoted a poem by Guru Nanak. The Guru disowned him hence giving birth to a new sect which was to cause trouble for the next Gurus. At his deathbed the Guru was disillusioned by the Mughal authorities and ordered his son, the next Guru, to stay away from Mughal politics.

8. Guru Harkrishan (1656–1664, Guru from 1661 to 1664)

Appointed as the Guru at the age of 6, after the insolence of his elder brother Ram Rai, the child Guru found himself in a difficult situation when he was summoned to Delhi by the Emperor Aurangzeb for pretending to be the heir to his father on the complaints of Ram Rai. At his deathbed his father had ordered him to stay away from the Mughal court, however a direct order from the Emperor could also not be rejected. Travelling to Delhi with his retinue the Guru stalled his meeting with the Emperor and instead chose to serve the people of the city who were suffering from cholera and then chicken-pox. The Guru too fell sick to chicken-pox and passed away before he could appear in the Mughal court thus keeping his promise to his father.

9. Guru Tegh Bahadur (1621–1675, Guru from 16644 to 1675)

Guru Tegh Bahadur was appointed as the next Guru when the Sikh community was in a precarious position. The community was divided due to the claims of various descendants of the previous Gurus. In order to take control of the situation the Guru travelled immensely forging relationship with his community and also forming new political alliances. Guru Tegh Bahadur was the second Sikh Guru to be assassinated by a Mughal Emperor. It is believed that he stood up for the right of oppressed Hindu Brahmins from Kashmir against the mighty Aurangzeb, for which he had to lose his life. Guru Tegh Bahadur was also a poet like the former Gurus and many of his hymns are included in the Guru Granth Sahib.

10. Guru Gobind Singh (1666–1708, Guru from 1675 to 1708)

Before heading to Delhi Guru Tegh Bahadur appointed his son Guru Gobind Singh as his heir and the next Guru. Thus at a young age he became the head of the Sikh community. Known as a warrior and a poet the Guru worked tirelessly to protect the Sikh community from being extinguished by the Mughal Empire. He founded the Khalsa (The Pure Ones) in 1699, giving the Sikh community its distinct attire and identity. He saw the death of all of his sons during his lifetime at the hands of the Mughal authorities. He completed the composition of the Guru Granth Sahib and before his death appointed it as the next Guru for eternity.

11. Guru Granth Sahib (Guru from 1708 to eternity)

Believed to be a living Guru, the Guru Granth Sahib contains the poetry of several Sikh Gurus including Guru Nanak, Guru Angad Dev, Guru Amar Das, Guru Ram Das and Guru Arjan. The Granth also contains poetry of several non-Sikh saints including Baba Farid, Bhai Mardana and Bhagat Kabir. Treated as a living Guru the Granth is provided with a special room in all Sikh Gurdwaras and is present at every Sikh ceremony.

Acknowledgements

This book would have never seen the light of the day without the help and support of the following people—my wife Anam Zakaria, who patiently listens to all my ideas and bears with my moments of insanity, vulnerability, anxiety and paranoia. I don't feel comfortable about my writing before I pass it through her. Thank you for being a part of my life and enduring me.

Kanishka Gupta—my agent. Kanishkha signed me for my first book about ten minutes after I sent him my proposal. This is our third book together and our relationship has only strengthened since then. He is a gem of a person who I have the privilege of calling my friend.

My father—Khalid Manzoor. He told me once that writing is the greatest thing a person could ever do. Thank you for telling me that when I was in doubt.

My mother—Nyla Khalid, for living her dreams through me.

Neelofar Zakaria—my mother-in-law. Like a rock she has stood beside me facing every obstacle head on and supporting her children no matter what.

Karthik Venkatesh—my editor. This is my second book with him and we have over the years established a relationship that goes beyond our professional lives. He is the best editor I could have asked for, empathetic, curious, meticulous, and receptive.

My sincere thanks to Ms. Mala Dayal for allowing us to use translations from Khushwant Singh's *Hymns of the Gurus*. Attempts were also made to contact the owners of other copyrighted material. My apologies for the omissions. I will correct it in future editions if brought to my notice.

My sisters, Nida and Sana, and my brothers-in-law, Umer and Shoaib, who take immense pride in me. My uncle and aunt Javed Manzoor and Lubna Manzoor, who have never missed a single event of mine. My friends Usman, Ammar, AQ, Hashmi, Bash, Khurram and Ammad, who have always loved and supported me even when we could not agree upon certain things. My professors Furrukh Khan, Sadaf Ahmad and Marta Bolognani, who continue to promote my work years after I stopped being their student, and finally Iqbal Qasier, my Guru, without whom none of this would have been possible.